When Valuations Misfire

Corporate Tales of Deception

When Valuations Misfire

Corporate Tales of Deception

Dr Shailendra Singh Rathore

NU VOICE
PRESS

First published by NU VOICE PRESS 2025
An imprint of Hubhawks Pvt. Ltd
www.nuvoicepress.com

This is a work of fiction. Space and time have been rearranged to suit the convenience of the book. Except for public figures, hotels, and institution names, any resemblance to persons living or dead or the real events are purely coincidental. The opinions expressed in the book are those of the characters, and should not be confused with that of the Author.

ISBN: 978-81-993684-2-2

Cover by: Amit Singh Rajendra Singh Chauhan, Gondia, Maharashtra

Editing Assistance by: Aishwarya & Riya Singh Rathore

Typeset by: Pooja Sharma

Published by Nu Voice Press

Limits of Liability/Disclaimer of Warranty

This book is a work of narrative non-fiction. It draws upon publicly available sources, including news reports, regulatory filings, parliamentary debates, court records, company disclosures, and academic research. The narrative is as accurate as the sources are. Certain passages are dramatised for readability, using reconstructed dialogue and descriptive scenes, but these are intended solely as illustrative storytelling devices.

All allegations, controversies, and disputes discussed herein are attributed to their original sources. The companies, individuals, and institutions named have, in many cases, denied or contested such allegations. Legal, regulatory, and political proceedings referenced in the text remain subject to further adjudication, appeal, or revision.

The book does not make independent factual findings, nor does it assert guilt, liability, or wrongdoing. Any opinions expressed are intended to foster discussion and learning in the fields of finance, valuation, and business history.

Readers are encouraged to consult primary documents, official filings, and authoritative reports for a comprehensive understanding of each case. Nothing in this book should be construed as legal, investment, or professional advice.

Dedicated to the wonderful woman who taught me the value of being savvy about life, love, and dreams.

Prologue

The Theatre of Corporate Deception & Valuation Failures

Author's Study Room, Gondia, Maharashtra, India

September 2025

When I sat in my study, ready to begin a textbook on corporate valuation failures, I felt an uncanny silence. The spreadsheets on my desk were no longer mere numbers; they seemed alive, and started whispering. Slowly, the whispers turned into stories. Behind the cold arithmetic lay ambition, blackmail, betrayal, perjury, lies, lust, deceit, deception, greed, and seduction—a narrative so gripping that it could rival fiction. Out of those whispers, this book began to take shape.

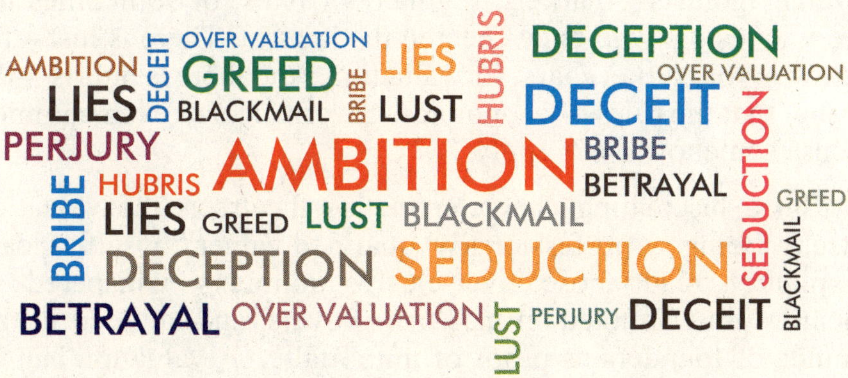

The world of startups is often painted in bright, Instagram-worthy colours: bean bags and brainstorming sessions, midnight pizzas, and slogans about "changing the world." Founders are romanticised as visionaries—modern gladiators who step into the arena of innovation armed with nothing but ambition and caffeine. But beneath the glossy veneer lies another story—a darker one.

This is the story of misfires.

Misfires are not small or quiet, but spectacular—like fireworks that dazzle the night sky for a moment before crashing into darkness. The kind of failures that newspapers splash across their front pages, that investors whisper about at private dinners, and that founders carry as scars long after the world forgets their names.

Writing about startup failures is not an exercise in balancing the books. It is a study of ambition that turned into arrogance, of dreams swollen by greed, of boardroom dramas that could rival the best courtroom thrillers, and of litigations that stripped away the last pretences of friendship. Every startup that collapses leaves behind more than debt—it leaves behind betrayal, broken trust, and the tragic poetry of what could have been.

In many ways, these stories read like fiction. There are protagonists—young, charismatic, sometimes reckless. There are antagonists—markets, regulators, rivals, or sometimes the very investors who once cheered the loudest. There is lust—for growth, for market share, for valuation. And there is hubris—the belief that the rules of economics, governance, or even common sense somehow don't apply.

But a fascinating character in this theatre is the valuation itself. Being a professionally qualified valuer myself, I can explicitly read those ever-elusive numbers whispered in boardrooms, flaunted on magazine covers, and tattooed in the minds of founders as proof of immortality. A valuation can be a crown or a curse. It can seduce investors, inspire employees, and even blind the most visionary leaders. And when the bubble bursts, it can bring down empires faster than any competitor.

Consider this: a single number that brings together ambition, greed, drama, and collapse. Is it any wonder that startup failures read like Shakespearean tragedies?

In this novel, we will walk into those tragedies with vivid foreshadowing vignettes that would tease the reader, not with the cold detachment of analysts, but with the pulse of dramatists. You will hear the excitement in the voices of founders as they ring the stock exchange bells. You will feel the electric optimism of employees who believe they're building history. You will see the cracks forming silently—in governance lapses, in unrealistic projections, in the intoxication of unchecked ambition. And finally, you will stand in the ruins: empty offices, worthless stock options, lawsuits stacked like epitaphs.

*

Glimpses of What Awaits

The stage is wide, and the characters unforgettable.

In Bangalore, a celebrated edtech titan fills entire stadiums with cheering parents and students, as if education had become a rock concert. Yet behind the LED lights and motivational speeches, its empire of debt grows faster than its students.

In Mumbai, an ambitious fintech giant rings the stock exchange bell with trembling pride. Cameras flash, investors clap, the ticker explodes. But within days, the IPO hailed as India's future begins to unravel, and the market's applause turns into mockery.

In the sun-drenched Bahamas, a crypto wunderkind builds a financial empire, complete with penthouse views and promises of a decentralized utopia. Politicians listen; investors swoon. But one morning, the empire vanishes—like sandcastles at high tide.

In New York, a messianic founder convinces the world that office spaces are not rentals but a movement, a way of life. Billion-dollar checks flow in. Employees chant slogans like disciples. Yet soon, the visionary is ousted, the empire crumbles, and "community" is revealed as nothing more than a lease agreement dressed in spiritual robes.

And these are just the headliners. Behind them lie dozens of quieter implosions: startups that flew too close to the sun, that mistook hype for substance, that built castles on projections instead of foundations. Each story is unique. Each failure was spectacular.

*

The Curtain Rises

This book is built on a real corporate background, but it is not a manual for judgment, nor a guide to fortune-making. The companies, founders, and investors who walk through these pages tell their stories after the fire has burned. What you read is an interpretation, not an indictment, only the echoes of choices made and prices paid.

It is not our intention to hurt anybody—if it so happens, it is purely unintentional. This is simply a chronicle of corporate misfires—some tragic, some absurd, all very real. In corporate valuations, as in life, the line between genius and ruin is only visible in hindsight. Please read it as a fictionalised dramatisation of the situations, while still retaining the essence of facts that reveal the timeless truth: success and failure are never far apart. One pitch can make you a unicorn. One quarter can turn you into a cautionary tale.

So sit back. The curtains are rising. The spotlight is on. Welcome to the theatre of startup failures—where ambition soars, greed devours, and empires vanish in the blink of an eye.

***

How to Read this Book?
Glossary of Terms

Written for a general audience, this book keeps things simple, avoiding heavy corporate jargon and using plain language. It's written for curious readers who may not have a background in finance but still want to understand how corporate valuations rise, fall, and sometimes misfire. How do corporates play the game of deception? And who gets hit when it happens.

Along the way, you'll come across a few financial terms. Don't let them scare you— they're easier to grasp than they sound. In fact, once you see the examples and stories, you'll realise that learning these terms is far from rocket science. Think of it as picking up a new set of everyday words, the kind that help you read markets the way you already read headlines.

*

Glossary in Simple Terms

- **Asset:** Something valuable a company owns, like a house, land, or a golden goose that lays eggs.
- **Balance Sheet:** A snapshot of what a company owns and owes, like checking your cupboard and debt list on the same day.
- **Book Value:** What the company is worth on paper. Often different from what the market thinks.
- **Brand Value:** Imagine two identical cups of coffee. Same beans, same taste. One cup has no name, while the other carries the green siren of Starbucks. Most people would happily pay more for the branded cup, even though the coffee is identical. That "extra money"

people are willing to spend because of the name, the trust, or the emotional connection—that is brand value. It's like invisible gold dust sprinkled on a product.

- **Cash Burn:** When a startup spends money faster than it earns, it's like a car leaking fuel on a long journey.
- **Cash Flow:** The actual movement of money in and out. Think of it as water flowing through pipes, not just numbers on paper.
- **DCF (Discounted Cash Flow):** A way of valuing a company by guessing tomorrow's money and bringing it back to today. DCF is like time-travelling of money. It's like plucking fruits from a tree that will grow for years. DCF asks:

  "If I gather all those future fruits, what's their value in my basket today?" As such, waiting incurs costs (inflation, risk, and missed opportunities).
- **Discount Rate:** The "risk lens" we use to shrink future money to today's value. Like saying: "₹100 tomorrow is only worth ₹90 today."
- **Dutch Auction:** A Dutch Auction is like a shopkeeper who keeps lowering the price tag until the first customer jumps in to buy. A few companies (like Google in 2004) have used Dutch auctions to let the market decide a fair price for their IPO.

  In a regular auction, prices go up until the highest bidder wins. In a Dutch Auction, prices come down until someone says "yes." This is the essence of a Dutch Auction.
- **Earnings Before Interest, Taxes, Depreciation, and Amortisation (EBITDA):** A fancy profit number before loans, taxes, and accounting tricks. Think of it as the "engine's raw power" before expenses.

- **EBITDA Multiple:** Think of a shop in your neighbourhood. The shop makes money after paying for rent, staff, and daily costs, but before paying taxes or loans. That money is like the shop's EBITDA—a measure of operating profit.

  Now imagine someone wants to buy this shop. How much should they pay? Instead of guessing, buyers often say: "I'll pay X times the shop's yearly EBITDA."

  That "X" is the EBITDA multiple.

  In short, the EBITDA multiple is a quick way to value a business—it tells you how many years of operating profit the buyer is willing to pay for today.

- **EBITDA Margin:** The EBITDA margin is a profitability ratio that indicates how much of a company's revenue is converted into operating profit before accounting for interest, taxes, depreciation, and amortisation.

  Perplexed? Think of revenue as all the money coming in.

  The EBITDA margin indicates how much of that money the business retains as core profit (before the "extras" such as loan payments, taxes, and accounting write-offs).

  For example, if a real estate company earns $100 million in revenue and has an EBITDA of $65 million,

  The EBITDA Margin = x 100 = x 100 = 65

  This means the company keeps 65 cents out of every dollar of revenue as operating profit.

- **Equity:** The authentic ownership slice. What's left for the owners after debts are paid?

- **Forecasting:** Predicting the future of sales and profits. Like guessing the weather—sometimes right, often wrong.

- **Free Cash Flow (FCF):** The spare cash a company has after paying its bills and investments, similar to the pocket money left over after shopping.
- **Hubris:** Hubris is like flying a kite so high that you forget you're still holding the string. The wind feels like it belongs to you, the sky feels within your control—until the string snaps, and the kite crashes down. In simple words, hubris means too much pride or arrogance, when success makes someone blind to reality.
- **Intrinsic Value:** The real worth of a business, not the mood swings of the stock market.
- **Liabilities:** What the company owes, like unpaid credit card bills.
- **Market Cap:** The stock market's price tag for a company. Share price × number of shares.
- **Multiple:** A quick shortcut for valuation. Like saying, "This house is worth 10× the rent it earns."
- **Net Present Value (NPV):** Summarising all future cash flows and adjusting them to their present-day value. If the sum is positive, the project is worth doing.
- **Overvaluation:** When the hype exceeds reality.
- **Undervaluation:** When the treasure chest is priced like an old box.
- **Risk Premium:** The extra reward investors want for taking bigger risks instead of playing it safe. Like saying: "If a bank deposit pays 5%, I need at least 10% to risk money on a startup."
- **Terminal Value:** The big lump of value at the end of a DCF forecast. Like the "happily ever after" of a company's story.

- **Valuation:** The art (and guesswork) of putting a price tag on a company.
- **Weighted Average Cost of Capital (WACC):** The average cost of satisfying both lenders and shareholders. Like the blended interest rate, a company pays for using other people's money.

*

Armed with this simple wisdom, let's step into the world of finance and fantasy—a stage where dreams clash with numbers, greed wrestles with ambition, deceit shakes hands with desire, and truth hides behind balance sheets.

Each corporate tale carries a different flavour, a different setting, a different taste. The taste of Kingfisher's champagne-soaked flights, where glamour masked a financial nosedive. The sterile labs of Theranos, where a drop of blood promised miracles that never existed. The basement of a gamer in Ohio, clicking "buy" on GameStop while billionaires panicked in glass towers. The humid streets of Hyderabad, where Satyam's Raju jogged in the morning sun, carrying the weight of a billion-dollar lie.

Different cities, different accents, different boardrooms—Mumbai, Houston, Palo Alto, New York, Seoul, Tokyo, Wolfsburg. But the thread is the same… Corporate deception… Greed disguised as vision… Confidence twisted into arrogance… Glamour wrapped in hubris.

And human weakness—the oldest story of all—hiding in balance sheets, board minutes, and whispered deals.

This book is not just about the corporations that failed.

It is about men and women who fell to temptation, to ego, to the illusion that rules were meant for others.

Join a banquet of hubris.

***

Table of Contents

Chapter 1

The Kingfisher Airlines: A Brand Oversold to Banks

Earlier: Goa (2003); Later: London (Since March 2016)

Over-Valuation of Brand ☑ Startup Failure ✗ Cash Burn ☑ Over Expansion ☑ Litigation ☑ Glamour ☑ Alleged Political Connections ☑

> Kingfisher Airlines (2005–2012) was more than just an airline; it was a lifestyle statement, sold on the flamboyant charisma of its promoter, Vijay Mallya. Banks lined up to lend, not against robust financials, but against the glitter of the Kingfisher brand, valuing it at nearly ₹4,000 crore at its peak.
>
> But behind the glossy image of luxury flights and glamorous calendars, the business bled cash. By 2012, the airline collapsed under ₹9,000 crore of unpaid debt, exposing how lenders had mistaken brand aura for sustainable value. The saga became a textbook case of how the overvaluation of intangibles can turn into a catastrophic misjudgement.

The Candolim Beach, Goa

The Shoot Begins, India, November 2002

The morning sun was still soft when the crew began to gather on the beach. The Arabian Sea stretched out in front, restless yet inviting, its waves breaking against the sand like a slow drumbeat. Fishing boats, painted in bold reds, yellows, and greens, lay scattered along the shore. It wasn't just another day in Goa; it was the day a new symbol of aspiration was about to be born—the first Kingfisher Calendar shoot.

Katrina Kaif was poised against the Arabian Sea, the Kingfisher logo discreetly in the background, the waves catching the light like liquid gold. She was just nineteen, shy and cautious, having just arrived from London. "Am I standing right?" she asked Kasbekar.

He gave her a reassuring nod, adjusting her posture with a quick hand gesture. Behind her youthful uncertainty, the lens caught something rare—potential. She wasn't the Bollywood star the world would come to know—yet.

Diana Hayden, Miss World 1997, moved with the calm elegance of someone who had been under countless spotlights. When Katrina struggled, she stepped in with gentle advice: "Tilt your chin… let the sun kiss your cheek." She was both mentor and muse, carrying herself like royalty amidst the chaos of a beach shoot.

The beach was still quiet, only the sound of waves folding into the sand. On a makeshift set framed by palm trees and bright umbrellas, Atul Kasbekar adjusted his lens, scanning the horizon. His eyes scanned the beach, searching for the perfect spot where light and water would meet to create the illusion of eternal summer. Around him, the models—some already stars, others on the cusp of fame—waited, adjusting sarongs and brushing windswept hair from their faces.

"Light's perfect," he said, squinting. "We've got about an hour before it gets too harsh. Let's make it magic."

Ujjwala Raut, tall and effortless, stepped onto the sand in a flowing white wrap. "Atul," she teased, "if I burn my skin in this Goan sun, it's on you." She was India's most successful international supermodel, having walked for Yves Saint Laurent, Gucci, Hugo Boss, and Victoria's Secret.

Kasbekar grinned, "Don't worry, Ujjwala. The light loves you. Just pretend the sea is your runway." He adjusted the aperture when she walked barefoot on the sand.

The local fishermen paused to stare at the glossy figure, as though an apparition had descended on their beach.

She laughed, tossing her hair back, then struck a pose against the rising tide. The camera clicked—sharp, rhythmic, like a heartbeat.

Nearby, Sheetal Mallar adjusted her *Sarang*, watching. "You photographers," she said, "always chasing the sun like it's a lover."

Men are men. Kasbekar swallowed hard. He was a man before being a photographer. Averting his gaze at the internationally recognised supermodel, he chuckled: "And you models—always knowing how to break its heart." Another click… another frame frozen.

Nina Manuel, ever the mischief-maker, called out, "Hey Atul, is this a photoshoot or a philosophy class? Because I didn't bring my notebook." The crew burst out laughing, the tension easing.

Kasbekar lowered the camera. "Alright, Nina, you're next. Let's see some attitude."

She strutted across the sand with mock seriousness, hand on hip. The shutter fired rapidly, catching her playfulness, her bold stare, her laughter caught mid-gesture.

From behind the monitors, Vijay Mallya arrived, sunglasses gleaming, a silk shirt half open to the breeze. He raised a glass of chilled Kingfisher beer and surveyed the scene like a director on his private stage. "Beautiful," he said. "This isn't a calendar. This is a lifestyle."

Yana Gupta laughed loudly, kicking water at the assistants, "Careful, Vijay, or you might fall in love before the camera does!" A Czech-born model, her energy was infectious, loosening up the entire crew. Yana was one of the original bold faces of the Kingfisher era, representing the fusion of Western glamour with Indian showbiz dreams.

The crew worked in rhythm: stylists adjusting, assistants holding reflectors, the models posing, and Kasbekar calling out directions in short bursts. “Shoulders back, eyes to the horizon. Perfect. Hold it. Click. Click. Click.”

The hours rolled by. The crew battled the shifting light, the sea breeze, and curious onlookers who tried to sneak closer for a glimpse. But in those stolen moments—models draped across driftwood, leaning against palm groves, wading into foamy waters—Kasbekar captured images that would set a new benchmark for glamour in India.

As dusk fell, the sky exploded into hues of orange and purple. The final shots were taken in near-silhouette—the models walking hand in hand into the ocean, their figures dissolving into the horizon. It was more than just photography. It was theatre, it was desire, it was spectacle.

Amid the roaring waves and on that beach in Goa, the first Kingfisher Calendar came alive—not just in photographs, but in the glittering illusion it promised… an illusion that would go on to define the next decade of Mallya’s empire—shiny on the surface, fragile beneath.

And when the Kingfisher Calendar 2003 was finally released, it wasn’t just pages of beautiful women on a beach—it was a statement. Vijay Mallya had declared to India that his brand was no longer just a beer; it was a lifestyle of indulgence, luxury, and excess.

Unlike ordinary calendars meant for kitchens or office walls, this one was destined for boardrooms, penthouses, and ministerial desks. Only a few thousand copies would ever be printed, each carefully couriered to CEOs, politicians, film stars, and socialites. Owning one was like holding a passport to

Mallya's world—a world of yachts, beaches, fine wine, and no boundaries.

Looking back, that first shoot on a Goan beach was not just the birth of a calendar. It was the prologue of a saga—a saga of ambition, glamour, and, eventually, downfall. It wasn't just a photoshoot; it was the birth of a cultural symbol. For Mallya, the Goa shoot was not about dates and months. It was about branding Kingfisher as more than beer. It was about selling aspiration—a promise of "The King of Good Times."

Long before Kingfisher Airlines took to the skies, Vijay Mallya was already busy selling a dream.

*

A Royal Take-off

The Skies of India, 2005

India's skies were buzzing with air travellers. Budget carriers were expanding, middle-class families were discovering air travel, and aviation was becoming the new playground for ambitious entrepreneurs.

Into this landscape swooped Vijay Mallya, the flamboyant liquor baron, often called the "King of Good Times." Known for his yachts, Formula 1 team, racehorses, and lavish parties, Mallya wanted an airline that matched his persona—glamorous, extravagant, and larger than life.

Thus, Kingfisher Airlines was born, promising luxury at 35,000 feet.

From the very first flight, Kingfisher broke the mould. Red-uniformed air hostesses, gourmet meals, in-flight entertainment, and even a personal valet to escort passengers at airports—it wasn't just flying, it was an experience. The ads declared: "Fly the Good Times."

Investors, dazzled by the aura of Mallya and the buzz of India's growing aviation market, poured in. The airline's valuation soared, even though profits were nowhere in sight. The DCF method was misused.

*

The Poisoned Chalice

Deccan Airlines, 2007

Kingfisher had one problem from the start—it was bleeding cash. The luxurious model came with crushing costs: premium aircraft, high fuel consumption, and lavish service expenses.

But instead of fixing the fundamentals, Mallya doubled down. In 2007, Kingfisher acquired Air Deccan, a struggling low-cost carrier, to expand aggressively. On paper, this made Kingfisher rich in market share. In reality, it was like mixing champagne with tap water—neither a luxury nor a budget option, just chaos.

The merger looked like a masterstroke. Kingfisher's red glamour would now fly side by side with Deccan's no-frills blue. To the world, Mallya boasted of "synergy," of a grand vision that would dominate Indian skies.

But behind the marketing gloss, the cracks were already showing. Air Deccan was bleeding losses, its balance sheets gasping for oxygen. The acquisition was less a marriage and more a poisoned chalice—a desperate attempt to buy market share at the cost of financial sanity.

And yet, bankers and investors were charmed by the performance. The "King of Good Times" played his role perfectly. Deccan was rebranded as Kingfisher Red, but the red ink on the accounts grew darker. Instead of saving Kingfisher, the acquisition shackled it with debt, inefficiency, and conflicting business models.

Deccan was not the ladder to the skies; it was the anchor that dragged Kingfisher into the abyss. Still, the markets valued

Kingfisher as if it were destined to be "India's Emirates." Banks showered it with loans. Analysts wrote glowing reports.

It was this reckless expansion masked as vision that set the stage for the brand valuation deception years later... the valuation not based on real cash flows, but on charisma, brand appeal, and blind optimism. When reality soured, Mallya turned to glossy reports and inflated numbers to keep the illusion alive.

*

The Boardroom Battles

Kingfisher House, Vile Parle (East), Mumbai

The polished mahogany table gleamed under the fluorescent lights as Kingfisher's directors gathered, their leather-bound files stacked like weapons of defence. Vijay Mallya swept into the room, draped in his trademark flamboyance—gold cufflinks, silk tie, and the aura of a man who believed the world bent to his charm.

Mallya sat at the head of the table, a glass of vintage wine by his side. His swagger filled the room, even as the walls seemed to be closing in on the empire he had built. Around him sat his loyal executives, each weighed down by the airline's spiralling debt.

But behind the bravado, unease simmered. A. Raghunathan, the CFO, shuffled papers nervously, his eyes darting to balance sheets that screamed in red ink. "Chairman," he began cautiously, "our operating costs are outpacing revenues. Jet fuel prices are soaring, and our load factors remain unchanged. We need to reconsider this expansion into international routes."

Mallya waved his hand dismissively, as if brushing away a fly. "Gentlemen, Kingfisher is not just an airline—it is a statement. We cannot appear small. We will fly to London and to New York. We will show the world what Indian luxury feels like."

"Sir," Raghunathan began, his pen tapping against the balance sheet, "our liabilities now exceed ₹7,000 crores. Lenders are circling, and we have less than two months of runway cash left. Without urgent restructuring, we—"

Mallya waved him off with a flamboyant flick of his hand. "Raghu, numbers are numbers. You worry too much. Kingfisher is a brand, a lifestyle, a dream. Do you think India will let the King of Good Times fall?

"Sir, lenders have already frozen some accounts," Raghunathan persisted, his voice rising slightly. "If we don't pay staff salaries this month, the fallout—"

"Enough!" Mallya's voice thundered. He leaned back, a smirk tugging at the corner of his lips. "Do you want to run this airline, or shall I? I built this brand. The world loves it. One bad quarter, one stubborn banker, and you're ready to write the obituary?"

Raghunathan lowered his gaze, his shoulders heavy. He knew the numbers didn't lie. But he also knew Mallya would never listen. The King of Good Times was too high on his own myth to hear the whispers of collapse.

A silence hung heavy. Some directors exchanged glances—this wasn't strategy, it was ego flying the plane.

One board member dared to interject: "But, sir, the debt burden is already unsustainable. Unless we restructure—"

Mallya's voice boomed across the room, cutting him off. "Banks will line up to fund us. They need us as much as passengers do. Do not mistake temporary turbulence for failure. We are building a legacy!"

The room fell quiet again. Pens tapped nervously. Chairs creaked. No one wanted to be the man who openly questioned the flamboyant billionaire in his own kingdom. And so, hesitation won. The sound of champagne being sprinkled drowned out risk warnings.

Unknowingly, this boardroom—meant for sober corporate decision-making—had turned into a theatre where one man's charisma overruled collective reason.

And so, the boardroom adjourned, not with a decision, but with denial.

The stage was set for the empire's spectacular crash.

*

The Downward Spiral

2010

By 2010, cracks were visible. The airline was drowning in mountains of debt. Employees often went unpaid for months. Operational losses kept piling up.

Yet the illusion continued. Mallya's flamboyance reassured many. He was still spotted at horse races, F1 paddocks, and high-society parties. The contrast was striking: on the ground, Kingfisher staff protested unpaid wages; in the air, their boss partied with champagne.

For Mallya, it was time to make a call.

*

The Boardroom of Brand Valuers

Somewhere in the Heart of a Financial District, London

In a sleek boardroom of glass walls and a polished oak table, the Kingfisher files lay open. The consultants assembled—suits crisp, voices precise—as if conducting a ritual. It was here that Mallya's call had been received.

Slides flickered across the screen: revenue projections, brand-recall surveys, industry benchmarks. But one fact loomed over all—Kingfisher's cash flows were bleeding red, year after year.

"DCF won't work," Alex Fraser, the lead valuer, declared flatly.

"Then we must find another way to justify the case," countered Jessica Roback, tapping the whiteboard. She had been with the team for years, her voice carrying the authority of persistence.

The boardroom air buzzed with arguments between the two. Many whispered they were lovers outside the office, though nothing was ever confirmed. The ambiguity only heightened the tension when they sat across from each other in meetings.

The Relief-from-Royalty Method surfaced next. If Kingfisher licensed its name, what royalty could it command?

Alex shook his head. "That assumes someone would pay for the brand. With debts piling up, who would license it now? The Excess-Earnings Method is closer to reality. Kingfisher's value lies in the extra profits it once generated."

Jessica frowned. "You're missing the point. Investors will demand benchmarks. Without comparables, our valuation looks like theory. We need evidence—something rooted in the market."

Alex sighed. "But what brand compares? In India, none match Kingfisher's flamboyance—or its troubles."

Jessica leaned back, measured. "Perhaps the answer lies in a blend… the Relief from Royalty method for glamour and the Economic Use method for figures. That way, we capture both the shine and the cracks."

The Chairman nodded. "Yes. Kingfisher is both an asset and a cautionary tale. Value it as such. Assign equal weightage to both the methods."

Alex rolled his sleeves. "Let us verify the projections supplied by the company."

"We are running against time." The Chairman had a tone of finality. "Use the projections provided by the company itself."

Jessica frowned. "What if they are inflated?"

"I take the responsibility." The Chairman dismissed the meeting.

*

The corporate machinery began to whir. Drafts circulated. The brand's value was based on projected earnings and savings from hypothetical royalty payments. Assumptions were polished, discount rates debated, and percentages assigned. Weaknesses of the business were carefully muffled beneath the shimmering language of "brand strength."

At last, a number emerged—₹4,000 crore. Not born of profits, but conjured from clever equations—a valuation that would march into India like gospel, dazzling bankers and silencing doubters.

"Don't forget the caveats and disclaimers," the legal advisor called out amid the frenzy. "Valuation must be framed as opinion, not fact."

Indeed, under Section 45 of the Indian Evidence Act, 1872, valuation was considered mere opinion, not evidence. The revised Bhartiya Sakshya Sanhita, 2023, retained the same under Section 39. Courts reserved the right to accept—or reject—the report.

Yet no one stopped to ask: *Was Kingfisher truly worth billions, or merely the price of illusion?*

*

Brand Value: An Illusion Sold as Collateral

The Boardroom of a Leading Public-Sector Bank

Nariman Point, Mumbai, 2011

The mahogany-panelled boardroom was unusually tense that evening. Files lay open on the desk; the top sheet stamped in red: "Kingfisher Airlines—Loan Restructuring."

The CFO's numbers were bleak; the airline was bleeding cash every day. Aircraft were grounded. Fuel bills are unpaid. Yet, the man in question—Vijay Mallya—still commanded an aura that bent the air around him.

One director cleared his throat. "Gentlemen, we must not forget—the Kingfisher brand itself has been valued at ₹4,000 crore by Brand Finance. This is no ordinary airline. This is a lifestyle empire."

Another banker shifted uneasily. "Brand value?" he muttered under his breath. "Can brand value pay salaries? Can it fuel planes?"

Yet the room fell silent as a glossy dossier, filled with red and gold Kingfisher logos, was passed around like a talisman. The numbers on the page glittered, but behind them lay nothing but smoke.

One younger officer dared to voice what others only whispered: "Sir, we cannot mortgage a man's lifestyle."

But the Chairman leaned back, steepling his fingers, his eyes betraying both doubt and pressure. Calls had already come from corridors of power. Mallya was not just a borrower; he was the man politicians toasted and bankers feared to cross.

The bankers shifted uneasily, their pens tapping like drumbeats of doubt.

The glass doors of SBI's corporate office slid open with a hiss, and in swept Vijay Mallya, flanked by a retinue of sharply dressed executives. The air seemed to shift—his Italian suit gleamed under the lobby lights, the fragrance of expensive cologne trailing behind. Assistants scurried ahead, announcing his arrival, while the bank's officials rose stiffly from their seats.

Outside the windows of the boardroom, the growl of imported cars still echoed, a reminder of the empire he carried with him.

Pleasantries were exchanged, concerns expressed.

Mallya adjusted his cufflinks, flashed his trademark smile, and declared in a voice brimming with confidence, "Shall we begin?"

Like a magician pulling a rabbit out of a hat, Mallya slid a glossy report across the table. Brand Finance Inc., London, was stamped in bold across the cover. Inside, in charts and glowing prose, the Kingfisher brand was valued at a staggering ₹4,000 crore.

Every banker worth his salt was familiar with Brand Finance, the London-based valuation powerhouse, located just steps away from St. Paul's Cathedral. To utter its name in boardrooms was to summon authority, credibility, and a touch of mystique.

"Gentlemen," Mallya declared, his voice dripping with charisma, "you are not lending to a failing airline. You are investing in a brand—a brand worth more than your balance sheets can imagine. Kingfisher is India's lifestyle statement, not just an airline."

The bankers leaned forward, hypnotised by the glitter of the brand valuation report with ₹4,000 crore in high gloss. Diagrams of global rankings across the pages, bar graphs comparing Kingfisher with international giants, valuation formulas dressed in financial jargon - it looked scientific, irrefutable, divine.

"₹4,000 crore," the number danced before the bankers like a mirage in the desert. A figure too prominent to ignore, too tempting to challenge.

One mid-level executive hesitated, whispering: "But sir... this is intangible. A brand cannot fly an aircraft."

Mallya shot back with a smile: "Neither can goodwill, but it moves markets. Neither can reputation, but it drives profits. Gentlemen, the Kingfisher brand is collateral enough."

The room fell silent. Pens stopped tapping. The ₹4,000 crore gospel of Brand Finance had done its work. Signatures followed. More credit lines were extended—not against factories or cash flows, but against a mirage. The ₹4,000 crore "brand value" became the invisible collateral. And with that, the banks tied themselves to a phantom asset, dressed in glossy numbers.

The room exhaled, the deal was sealed. Outside, the city lights glittered, but inside the boardroom, history had just been written in invisible ink.

*

Brand Value: A Gospel of Deception

Somewhere in the Mediterranean Sea, 2011

The champagne flutes clinked softly against the polished teak deck of Vijay Mallya's yacht, a floating palace of excess moored in the Sea. Velvet sofas, gold-plated fixtures, and a dining table that gleamed under crystal chandeliers—every corner whispered luxury. The man at the centre of it all reclined with the smug smile of someone who had once again bent the system to his will.

He was celebrating—not a business turnaround, not an airline revival—but the triumph of illusion. He had manipulated the bankers again.

In 2010, Grant Thornton declared the Kingfisher Airlines brand to be worth a staggering ₹3,406 crore, a number so audacious it drowned out reason. Bankers, however, quietly estimated it at a fraction—barely ₹160 crore—but Mallya knew which story to sell, and he sold it well.

And when Brand Finance was roped in, another glossy valuation appeared, crafted with the elegance of financial scripture. Selective truths, selective numbers—each deployed like a magician's trick to dazzle the gullible.

Yet in all the glitter, no one asked the one question that mattered: *"How much was paid for this gospel of deception?"*

The fees to the valuers—whether to Grant Thornton or Brand Finance—would remain shrouded in secrecy, wrapped in confidentiality clauses and hidden in the smoke of corporate boardrooms. A number that would never be disclosed, a cost never debated.

And so, the grand irony played out. The exorbitant valuation fees in millions of dollars were mere pebbles compared to the mountains of billions that the banks would lose.

On the yacht, the music rose, the waves shimmered, and Mallya raised his glass. The illusion had worked again.

*

The Flight Descends

By 2012, the airline was grounded. Licenses were revoked. Airports refused to service its planes due to unpaid dues—Kingfisher's market capitalisation, once in the thousands of crores, evaporated to nearly zero.

Investors, banks, and employees were left stranded.

The collapse of Kingfisher Airlines was not just a corporate story—it became a national scandal. Mallya's empire crumbled under scrutiny. Banks chased him for unpaid loans exceeding ₹9,000 crore.

Kingfisher Airlines had become a symbol—not of glamour, but of reckless ambition and valuation without fundamentals.

*

The Absconding King

Indira Gandhi International Airport, New Delhi

March 2, 2016

With a guarded demeanour, Mallya boarded Jet Airways Flight 9W122 from Delhi to London around 11:30 p.m. under the cover of night. The "King of Good Times" slipped out before the banks and investigators could tighten their grip. By the time morning broke over India, Mallya was already in the UK, beyond the immediate reach of Indian authorities.

A billionaire playboy turned into a fugitive businessman. The man once hailed as "India's Richard Branson" was now branded an absconder.

In April 2017, He was arrested in London on India's extradition request but released on bail the same day.

*

The Ordeal of Trials

The Westminster Magistrates' Court, London (2017-2018)

The court was a far cry from the sunlit runways of Kingfisher Airlines or the lavish parties on Mallya's yacht in Goa. The oak-panelled hall carried none of the glamour—only the heavy silence of justice.

On April 18, 2017, Vijay Mallya walked into the courtroom for the first time after being arrested in response to India's extradition request. The man once hailed as the "King of Good Times" now stood as a defendant in exile, wearing a subdued suit instead of flamboyant silk.

The prosecution laid out its case: more than ₹9,000 crore in unpaid loans, misrepresentations to banks, a trail of unpaid employees, and abandoned investors. India demanded his return.

Mallya's lawyers countered fiercely: "He is not a fraudster, my Lord. He is a businessman whose airline failed because of high fuel costs and excessive taxes. To treat him as a criminal is unjust."

For months, the hearings dragged on. Cameras clicked as Mallya entered court, still smiling for the press, as though trying to keep alive the aura of his past. Outside, angry ex-employees gathered with placards, reminding the world of unpaid salaries.

Then came the decisive moment. On December 10, 2018, Chief Magistrate Emma Arbuthnot ruled against him. Her words struck with finality: "This court finds a clear case of misrepresentation to banks. Extradition is justified."

The gavel echoed like the last boarding call for a flight that would never take off.

Yet, Mallya did not board the plane back to India. He appealed to the Royal Courts of Justice, dragging the fight through 2019 and 2020.

*

Royal Courts of Justice

The Strand, London (2019-2020)

The chill of a grey London morning seeped into the marble arches of the Royal Courts of Justice, that towering neo-Gothic cathedral of law standing along The Strand. Inside, under the vaulted ceiling, the hallways echoed with hurried footsteps, hushed whispers, and the clicking of pens from international reporters waiting for a glimpse of the man who had once been called the "King of Good Times."

When Vijay Mallya entered, dressed in a tailored suit with his silver mane flowing, the air seemed to shift. For a moment, he looked less like a man on trial and more like a celebrity making a grand entrance. Yet behind the defiance in his eyes lay a shadow of unease. He was not here as a tycoon, not as the flamboyant sponsor of Formula One or the host of glamorous yacht parties—but as a fugitive fighting against time and justice.

The courtroom itself felt like a theatre of reckoning. The oak-panelled walls rose high, stern portraits of judges past glaring down from centuries of justice. The judge's bench, elevated and commanding, became the stage where Mallya's fate would be dissected.

The prosecution's voice rang out first, sharp and relentless: "My Lords, here stands a man who owes Indian banks over ₹9,000 crores. He fled under the cover of night, leaving a trail of debt, broken employees, and collapsed dreams. This is not mere mismanagement—it is deception."

Mallya's lawyers countered in polished tones, speaking of political persecution, unfair treatment, and a vendetta disguised as justice. They painted him as a scapegoat, not a villain.

But outside, reality was harsher. Protestors had gathered beyond the iron gates, their placards raised high: "Bring Back Our Money!" and "No More Escape for the Rich!" Their chants filtered faintly through the stained-glass windows, a reminder that public anger was also on trial.

As arguments twined to twist and turn, the judge listened, expression carved in stone. Mallya shifted occasionally, sipping water, straightening his tie, whispering with his counsel. He looked, in flashes, like the man who once promised India a new era of aviation luxury, but the illusion cracked each time the debt figure was mentioned: ₹9,000 crores.

Hours passed, but the weight of judgment hung heavy, suspended in silence.

Finally, the gavel struck on April 20, 2020, echoing like thunder through the chamber.

His appeal was dismissed—another blow.

This was not the end, only another step in a long legal maze. But in that instant, the grandeur of the High Court could not hide the reality: Mallya's empire of excess had collapsed into a desperate struggle for survival.

Outside, the London sky was still grey, as if even the weather refused to give him a break.

*

The Plea of Asylum

Post Conviction

Mallya sought asylum in the UK. His extradition stalled, entangled in what the British government later described as "confidential legal matters."

And so, the saga continued. The man who once raised champagne toasts at the Monaco Grand Prix now sat in quiet courtrooms, watching lawyers argue over his fate. The King of Good Times had become the fugitive of bad debts, his destiny no longer in his own hands but in the cold deliberations of British judges.

*

The Parliament Echo in the Meantime

Lok Sabha, Winter Session, India

December 2016

Vijay Mallya had left India on March 2, 2016. Opposition was armed with fresh revelations about how the CBI lookout notice was diluted before his escape.

Mallikarjun Kharge, then Congress leader, raised the papers in his hand: "How did Mallya flee India with ₹9,000 crore in unpaid loans? Who allowed him to board that flight to London on March 2, 2016? Why was the CBI lookout notice downgraded—from 'detain if seen' to 'inform if seen'? This is no accident. This is collusion!"

Opposition benches explode in protest.

Arun Jaitley, the finance minister, stood firmly: "Let the House remember: Mallya's defaults began during the UPA years. Banks continued to lend to him between 2004 and 2009, when your government was in power. Who pressured the banks then? Who protected him then?"

Kharge jabbed a finger, “Don’t mislead the nation! When Mallya fled, you were in charge. He met you, Mr Jaitley, in Parliament, just days before he escaped. Did you or did you not know?”

Shouts of “Shame!” rose from the Opposition benches. BJP MPs countered with chants of “Sit down! Sit down!” The Speaker struggled to restore order.

Speaker Sumitra Mahajan banged the gavel: “Order! This House will come to order!”

The uproar continued. Papers flew across the aisle. Cameras captured the fury.

Arun Jaitley cut through the noise in a firm voice: “I met him casually in the corridors of Parliament. He said he was going abroad to settle matters. I told him to speak with his bankers, nothing more. Any other claim is baseless!”

The uproar deepened. Opposition MPs waved documents, demanding an independent probe.

Kharge shouted above the din: “Then why was he allowed to leave? Who turned the lookout notice into a free pass? The nation demands the truth!”

*

London, 2017…

Outside Westminster Magistrates’ Court, Mallya was facing reporters during his extradition hearings. He smirked in front of flashing cameras: “I did not flee. I left India with the full knowledge of the government and authorities. Ask them how I left.”

Back in Delhi, news channels flashed the clip. Parliament echoed again with the same unanswered cry.

Chorus of MPs: “Who let Mallya flee?”

However, India is a country where such episodes are soon forgotten.

*

Why No IPO?

Thankfully for investors, no IPO was ever launched by Kingfisher Airlines. When it started in 2005, it was a fully-owned subsidiary of United Breweries Holdings Limited (UBHL), the flagship of Vijay Mallya's UB Group.

There was talk in 2005-2006 about a possible IPO to raise funds, and merchant bankers were even consulted. But it never materialised. Instead, Kingfisher relied heavily on bank loans and debt for its expansion, including the costly acquisition of Air Deccan in 2007. By the time it desperately needed equity capital around 2009-2010, the financials were so bad that an IPO was impossible.

God saved the investors.

*

Who Paid the Price?

Since March 2016

In the Kingfisher Airlines saga, the people who truly paid the price were not just Mallya or his flashy empire, but a wide circle of unsuspecting victims. Over 3,000 staff went unpaid for months, struggling with rent, school fees, and daily survival.

A consortium of 17 Indian banks, led by SBI, saw loans worth over ₹9,000 crores turn sour. With a lending to the tune of 1600 crores, SBI was the biggest loser. All bankers scrambled for recovery, even auctioning off Mallya's properties, luxury cars, and even the iconic Kingfisher House in Mumbai, often at a fraction of their loan value.

The Shareholders in United Breweries Holdings and other group companies saw their shares plummet as the contagion of Kingfisher's debt spread across Mallya's empire.

While not villains, Raghunathan and other executives were left tarnished by association. Some faced questioning by regulators, others saw their careers eclipsed by the shadow of the scandal.

Vijay Mallya was no king—only a cheap court jester draped in Armani, juggling borrowed millions until the lights went out. A cowardly general who abandoned his soldiers on the line of fire to face the bullets on the battlefield, sipping champagne in London while thousands of workers in India went hungry. A hollow monarch of deceit, crowned not with honour, but with debt.

An absconder!

*

The Hunt for the King's Treasure

When Kingfisher Airlines went down, it didn't just ground airplanes—it pulled India's banking system into one of its most embarrassing corporate scandals. Over ₹9,000 crore in unpaid loans had vanished into thin air, leaving behind nothing but unpaid staff, angry investors, and a trail of luxury.

The banks, once charmed by Mallya's charisma and the sparkle of the Kingfisher brand, were now chasing shadows. In boardrooms across Mumbai and Delhi, the question echoed: How do you recover money from a man who spent it all on yachts, palaces, and parties?

The hunt began.

His luxury villas in Goa, his Maseratis and Ferraris, even his private jet, were seized. Shares in United Breweries and other companies were attached. Even the Kingfisher beer trademark, once the crown jewel of his empire, was put on the block.

Auctions were held. Some assets fetched reasonable prices; others barely stirred interest.

Meanwhile, Mallya was spotted in the grandstands of Formula One races in Europe, sipping champagne while banks in India filed lawsuits. By 2016, he had fled to London, calling himself an "entrepreneur in exile," while Indian authorities called him a "wilful defaulter."

The Enforcement Directorate pursued his global assets, and slowly, money trickled back. Villas were sold, shares liquidated. By 2022, banks had managed to claw back nearly ₹7,000 crore—a remarkable recovery, though still less than the original debt once compounded by years of interest.

But the damage was already done. Kingfisher Airlines had become a ghost. Its flamboyant branding lived on only in the pages of calendars and the foggy memory of its parties. Investors learned a bitter lesson: glamour doesn't pay loans.

Mallya, once the "King of Good Times," had become a fugitive of bad debts. His empire of excess was stripped piece by piece, leaving behind a cautionary tale for corporate India: when valuation becomes fantasy, recovery becomes a treasure hunt in ruins.

*

Closing Thought

The Kingfisher saga is one of India's starkest valuation misfires. Overvaluation by Glamour—the brand and lifestyle appeal masked the absence of profitability. Banks and investors funded a dream without testing its financial runway. Cash Burn and negative cash flows were overlooked in the chase for market share.

Kingfisher Airlines promised passengers the "good times." For investors, employees, and lenders, it delivered the opposite—a hangover that lasted years.

It was not just an airline that crashed. It was a valuation that never learned to land. Banks valued Kingfisher like royalty. But without profits, it was only a paper crown. Kingfisher showed India that style can take you sky-high, but only substance keeps you flying.

*

Years Later

In Parliament, the finance minister's voice cut through the winter air of December 2024: "Banks have recovered ₹14,131 crore linked to Vijay Mallya. More than double the dues."

The statement causes a ripple of disbelief. How could banks claim more than what was owed, and yet Mallya remains branded an "economic offender"?

On social media, the rebuttal of Mallya arrived swiftly, sharp as a dagger: "If the banks have recovered more than I owe, why am I still hunted? I am entitled to relief."

*

The Royal Courts of Justice

London, 2025

The fog curls around the gothic fortress of law where history whispers through stone arches. Inside, under cold chandeliers, a silver-haired figure sits at the defendant's bench. Once the flamboyant "King of Good Times," Vijay Mallya now looks less like a tycoon and more like a man cornered by time.

Across the seas, in India, the legacy of his empire lies scattered. Strangers now own the Goa villa that once hosted starlets and parties under neon lights. The Sky Mansion in Bengaluru, a glass palace in the clouds, stands empty—its helipad gathering dust, its infinity pool reflecting only silence.

But relief does not come. Instead, in April 2025, the London High Court slams down its gavel—his appeal against bankruptcy is rejected. The tycoon who once flew models across continents for his calendar shoots now fights to keep his name afloat in the records of law.

Meanwhile, in Bengaluru, his lawyers move the Karnataka High Court, arguing that the banks have recovered "multiple times over." The once-defiant voice of Mallya has turned into a plea, echoing down corridors of justice: not for more yachts, not for more parties—but for relief.

And yet, outside those courts, in the collective memory of India, his story remains a cautionary legend. A man who promised the Good Times, but left only unpaid bills, empty runways, and a question that still lingers in the air:

When banks recover more than they lost, can a fallen king ever truly reclaim his crown?

*

Captain G.R. Gopinath and Mallya were accused of committing fraud in the 2007 merger of his company, Air Deccan, with Kingfisher Airlines. The Serious Fraud Investigation Office, SFIO, alleged that corporate ethics were compromised in the merger and that Gopinath received improper "windfall gains" from the deal. However, the Karnataka High Court quashed the SFIO case against Gopinath and Mallya in April 2024, citing jurisdictional issues.

***

Chapter 2

India: A Real Estate Bubble in the Making?

44 West 4th Street, New York, Stern School of Business & India

Market Hype ☑ Over Pricing ☑ Academic Sermons ☑ Startup Failure ✗

At NYU, Professor Aswath Damodaran warns that India, despite its powerful growth story, is now the world's most expensive equity market, with prices racing ahead of fundamentals.

Although Damodaran hasn't spoken directly about a real estate bubble in India, the author has taken the liberty, with some theatrics, of explaining how his approach can help assess the potential for one. The author has never met him, but has read many of his books. Had Aswath Damodaran chosen to speak of India's real estate hype, his words might have sounded familiar: "Prices are climbing faster than incomes, expectations are detached from fundamentals, and everyone believes the rise will never end."

From India's luxury launches, unsold inventories, struggling homebuyers, and restless developers, the narrative contrasts glittering ambition with fragile reality.

Forgiveness is solicited!

NYC Stern School of Business

September 2025

September is a moment of transition in New York. The Leonard N. Stern School of Business rises just off Washington Square Park, its glass-and-stone façade reflecting the restless pulse of Manhattan. Inside, lecture halls hum with fresh beginnings: new notebooks, eager faces, the crisp smell of coffee. Outside, Washington Square itself is alive with late-summer light—students sprawled on lawns, jazz musicians under the arch, the fountain sparkling before autumn claims the city.

The trees in Washington Square remain mostly green, but hints of gold creep into the edges of leaves. In the gardens and planters around NYU, chrysanthemums—the classic fall flower—burst with yellows, purples, and deep reds.

*

The War Room of Damodaran

September 2025

Armed with a laptop, chalk, and a duster, Professor Damodaran was prepared for the series of lectures scheduled today.

In the corner of his chamber, amid polished mahogany shelves lined with leather-bound reports and trophies of past victories, stood a neat row of bestselling books authored by him, ranging from *Damodaran on Valuation* (2006) to *The Little Book of Valuation* (2024)—that were like quiet sentinels in the chamber, otherwise littered with spreadsheets and buzzing with ambition.

To visitors, they were more than books; they were a subtle declaration that behind every bold gamble and boardroom manoeuvre lay the discipline of valuation, the cold clarity of discounted cash flows, and the wisdom of the man Wall Street reverently called the "Dean of Valuation."

The bell rang.

*

Damodaran's Classroom

Henry Kaufman Management Centre

The Camellias' Numbers, September 2025

The lecture hall buzzed with anticipation of hearing Damodaran. Students shuffled laptops open, and the projector hummed. At the podium, Professor Aswath Damodaran adjusted his glasses. The man was calm, almost understated. But the room knew his reputation: the Dean of Valuation, the man who could strip a billion-dollar empire with a bare spreadsheet.

Professor Aswath Damodaran was a man equally feared and admired by his students. Today's lecture was not about the intricacies of a valuation model or the fine lines of a discounted cash flow. It was about a time when markets lost their minds.

On the slide: DLF's The Camellias, Gurugram—the crown jewel of Indian luxury real estate.

Damodaran clicked his remote. "Here's what the market is saying," he intoned.

Slide #1 **DLF's The Camellias, Gurugram, India**

The Crown Jewel of Indian Luxury Real Estate

Key Statistics

- In December 2024, an ultra-luxury penthouse of 16,290 sq ft sold for approximately ₹190 crore, translating to an eye-watering ₹1.18-1.82 lakh per sq ft on super/carpet area.
- Standard 4-BHK units (~7,400 sq ft) start at around ₹30 crore, increasing to ₹55 crore for premium 5-BHK units (~9,000 sq ft).
- Early 2025 average base selling prices are now ₹65,000–₹85,000 per sq ft, depending on floor levels, with rentals starting from ₹10.5 lakh per month unfurnished, rising to ~₹14 lakh furnished.

Only a few knew he was only narrating his thoughts aloud, which he had shared in an interview with NDTV only a few days ago.

Another slide flashed on screen:

Slide #2 **DLF's The Camellias, Gurugram, India**

The Crown Jewel of Indian Luxury Real Estate

The heaven for Startup founders and global executives:

- Zomato co-founder Deepinder Goyal finalised the paperwork in March 2025 for a 10,813 sq ft flat, which was initially purchased for approximately ₹52.3 crore. Similar units in the same tower are now valued at ₹140 crore+ in resale markets.
- A recent deal in August 2025 saw British businessman Sukhpal Ahluwalia buy an 11,416 sq. ft apartment for ₹100 crore, underlining international demand.

On screen, Damodaran clicked on a high-resolution aerial shot of The Camellias, Gurugram. "Look closely," he said, voice calm but insistent, "these aren't just luxury towers. They're status statements—signed by names most will never forget."

A quick montage of names and portraits flashes behind him. Each name carries weight; each purchase defines a social postcode:

Slide #3 **DLF's The Camellias, Gurugram, India**

The Crown Jewel of Indian Luxury Real Estate

Occupants Behind the Façade:

- Deepinder Goyal (Zomato)
- Rishi Parti (Info-X Software Technology)
- Smiti Agarwal (Wesbok Lifestyle/spouse of Hemant Agarwal)

- Deep Kalra (MakeMyTrip)
- Sameer Manchanda (Den Networks)
- Ashish & Sanya Gurnani of Assago Group
- Peyush Bansal (Lenskart)
- Members of the Dhanuka family (Dhanuka Agritech)
- Aman Gupta (boAt), Varun & Ghazal Alagh (Mamaearth)
- Ashneer Grover (former BharatPe/TV personality).

Damodaran's voice returned as the names faded: "What these names tell us isn't just who can pay. It's who believes—and how much. When value is determined less by utility or cash flow, and more by prestige, the price becomes a mirror: showing not what a property generates, but what people imagine it represents."

The screen zoomed out to reveal the skyline. Glistening glass. Private golf views. Concierge services. Fiction crafted in marble and ascent.

"And when the dream gets bigger than the foundation underneath," Damodaran added, "that's where risk lives."

He paused the lecture. A hush. "Do those numbers reflect cash flows?" Damodaran asked. "Or are they simply proof of belief, confidence, and speculation?"

The slide advanced:

Slide #4, #5, #6 **DLF's The Camellias, Gurugram, India**

The Crown Jewel of Indian Luxury Real Estate

- Champagne toasts in marbled lobbies.
- Flooded service roads outside.
- A young tech founder marvels at the price-per-square-foot charts.

Damodaran leaned close. “The Camellias isn’t just an address—it’s a monument to excess. When prices are rising solely because of proximity, luxury, status, not utility, you aren’t buying value. You’re buying hope. And hope isn’t the same as cash flow.”

A hand rose in the lecture hall. A student asked: “Professor, are you saying that real estate in India is in a bubble?”

Damodaran smiled faintly. “I avoid the word. ‘Bubble’ kills the conversation. Instead, I ask: are you paying a price that future cash flows can never justify?”

Chrysanthemums nodded in affirmation outside the classroom windows.

Yellow flowers… He smiled at them. “Overvaluation should be addressed carefully with valuation analysis, not dismissed as bubble talk.”

“Are bubbles often a sign of distress?” Another question was shot from across the benches.

“Bubbles aren’t inherently destructive. Many a time, a bubble can be a sign of progress.” Damodaran reflected his words in a Forbes piece. “Bubbles often arise around disruptive change. They are wildfires. They burn too hot, too fast. But after the fire, the soil is richer, and the real seeds of innovation grow.”

A murmur swept the room. Some students looked shaken; others, exhilarated.

He continued. “They allow markets and industries to experiment and evolve—valuable even if some excesses occur. While corrections may follow, bubbles can lead to innovation.”

“Professor, you say that bubbles are not inherently destructive. The dot.com bubble made the market lose trillions of dollars.”

“Ah, the dot-com bubble,” Damodaran’s voice had a faint curl of irony. “A generation that believed revenues could wait, that eyeballs were enough.”

Graphs appeared like ghosts of the past—the late '90s arc, the dramatic fall of 2000.

The students chuckled nervously.

He turned to the class. "It rose faster than any before it, and collapsed just as spectacularly. Between 1995 and 2000, markets believed the Internet would rewrite every rule. And they were right—just not in the way they thought."

Students scribbled feverishly. He continued.

"Companies with no revenues, no profits—sometimes not even a clear business plan—were trading at billions of dollars in market cap. Pets.com, Webvan, eToys… all vanished. Trillions of dollars of investor wealth evaporated. It was destruction on a massive scale."

He paused, letting the silence sink in.

"But here is the paradox: the bubble was both foolish and necessary. It was irrational, but it paved the way for the digital revolution you are all living in today."

The chalk struck the board again, and this time he wrote just three names: Amazon. eBay. Google.

"These companies emerged from the rubble. The bubble-funded infrastructure—fibre optic cables, data centres, early platforms—that outlived the crash. The capital wasted on failed dot-coms was, in some strange way, an investment in the foundation of the Internet economy. Without that madness, there is no Facebook, no YouTube, no cloud computing, no digital marketplaces."

He paced slowly, chalk in hand, scrawling numbers across the board with an elegance born of repetition.

The silence in the hall thickened as he spoke of fortunes made and vaporised, of valuations spun from dreams rather than cash flows.

"The bubble burst, yes," he said, turning to face them fully. "But every bubble leaves something behind. Railroads, electricity, the internet—bubbles finance revolutions."

The students leaned forward.

"That crash," he continued, softer now, "paved the way for the companies you use every single day. Amazon survived. Google was born in the ashes. What looked like destruction was actually creation, just very expensively financed."

The room erupted into quiet scribbles, laptops clattering, eyes bright with the realisation that finance is not just about numbers, but about the stories those numbers fail to tell.

The lunch bell rang.

He closed his notebook with a soft thud. "Remember this: the dot-com bubble wasn't just about greed—it was about imagination. Markets mispriced the timing, not the idea. The Internet did change the world. But only after the hype died, and the survivors proved their worth."

Students rose, buzzing with debate, carrying not just notes on valuation but a cautionary tale etched into their minds. Outside, the streets of New York pulsed with technology—Wi-Fi hotspots, flashing billboards, Nasdaq tickers. The very world that the bubble had promised was now taking shape.

And in that moment, it was clear: sometimes it takes a burst bubble to build a new world.

*

Post Lunch Session

"Is it a bubble or boom in the context of India?" the same student returned to the original question.

Damodaran folded his arms. "It doesn't yet fit the classic 'bubble-and-bust' profile yet. India's real estate market is more nuanced—characterised by strong asset demand, fragmented supply, and slow-moving corrections rather than volatile crashes."

He ran another slide:

Slide #5 **DLF's The Camellias, Gurugram, India**

The Crown Jewel of Indian Luxury Real Estate

Key Indicators from Recent Data:

1. **Price Surge, Especially in Luxury Segments:** Prices have jumped significantly. In Q2 2025, Delhi-NCR saw a 49% increase in price per square foot (from ~₹5,800 to ₹8,650). Bengaluru and Hyderabad rose by approximately 32%; Mumbai rose by 25%.
2. **Decline in Sales and Changing Demand:** Home sales in top cities dropped approximately 20–28% year-over-year.
3. **Supply-Demand Mismatch in the Luxury Segment:** Unsold luxury inventory (₹1.5 Cr+) grew by 24% in Q1 2025.

A branch of Chrysanthemums was trying to poke its way into the classroom windows, as if it wanted to look at the slides.

Damodaran ran another slide:

Slide #6 **DLF's The Camellias, Gurugram, India**

The Crown Jewel of Indian Luxury Real Estate

₹190 crore @ ₹1.8 lakh/sq. ft

The screen cut to black.

The numbers: *₹190 crore @ ₹1.8 lakh/sq ft* lingered.

He faced the lecture hall. His voice was calm but edged with warning.

"India," he began, his voice measured but firm, "is the most expensive market in the world today. Thirty-one times earnings. Three times revenues. Twenty times EBITDA. Beautiful story. Dangerous price."

The words fell like stones in a still pond. Everybody present in the audience knew that even in the US, the real estate market was 14-16 times EBITDA multiple.

Some students typed furiously. Others glanced at one another. A few Indian faces tightened, as if he had just questioned not numbers, but faith.

*

Gurgaon

A Typical Night

From afar, Gurugram looks like the future of Indian real estate—bold, aspirational, unstoppable. Up close, it feels like a mirage, shimmering in the heat, beautiful but fragile.

Floodlights glared over half-finished towers. Workers in yellow helmets hammered steel into concrete skeletons. Inside a plush sales office, a scale model glows—glass towers, fountains, manicured parks.

A sales manager whispered to an NRI buyer: "Half sold before launch. Price will only rise."

The NRI smiled, signing papers with a flourish. Behind him, the manager hid the notification on his phone: "Unsold luxury inventory: +24% this quarter."

The construction noise outside felt louder.

*

Back to NYU Stern

Damodaran moved to the next slide: a graph of India's real estate prices soaring.

"We love stories," he said. "And India's story is magnificent. But remember, every story has a catch beneath its shine. If you pay for the dream, be ready to live with the nightmare."

Students were listening intently to the Global Valuation Guru.

"Growth. Energy. Demographics. Technology. But stories are not valuable. Value is cash flows, risk, and time. Even the most credible story, if overpaid for, becomes a bad investment."

His tone was almost regretful, like a teacher cautioning children running too fast toward a cliff.

"What's the acid test?" asked a curious student.

"Ask the only question that matters," Damodaran cautioned. "Will the cash flows ever justify the price you pay?"

*

Mumbai, Early Morning

The sun was rising over the Arabian Sea, gilding Mumbai's skyline. Cranes dotted the horizon like giant steel insects.

In a cramped apartment, a young couple sat with a bank officer.

Price: ₹1.5 crore.

Monthly EMI: suffocating.

The husband clenched his jaw, doing the math in silence. The wife looked around at peeling paint, their toddler tugging at her *sari*. For a moment, hope flickered. Then the officer slid the numbers across. The hope dies quietly. They leave without a word.

Meanwhile, in a nearby luxury tower, champagne glasses clinked at a launch party—Bollywood music boomed. Models in gowns posed beside mock-up kitchens.

The billboard outside screamed: "Live the Dream. Own Tomorrow."

*

NYU, Rising Tension

Bubble or a Boom?

"Which parameters to watch next, Professor?" asked a female student. "How do we decide whether it is a bubble or a boom?"

"Sales-to-launch ratios," The Professor replied. "A slowdown in sales but continued launches could signal trouble. Among other indicators demonstrated by PE inflows, also look for loan defaults and inventory clearances, particularly in luxury projects."

Some students scribbled furiously on their notebooks.

A spectacled student raised his hand. "Professor, India has never experienced a full-scale housing crash, despite past slowdowns. Did it?"

"You are right," Damodaran affirmed. "India's real estate market has historically avoided major crashes, often rebounding quickly after downturns. Even if something goes wrong, black money will keep things afloat for the time being.

"Too early to comment," Damodaran raised an appreciative look towards the student. "The Rapid price inflation, especially in high-end segments, is decoupling from wage growth and affordability.

"Exports → Earnings → Real Estate."

He turned to the class.

"When the U.S. raises tariffs on Indian exports—textiles, steel, IT services—profits don't just shrink on paper. They shrink in households, in salaries, in confidence."

The previous slides flashed again: Gurugram Skyline: the Camellias, the Aralias, Cyber City's glowing towers.

"Think about it," Damodaran said, pacing. "The same executives who buy ₹50-crore penthouses in Gurugram are the ones whose bonuses ride on export flows. Tariffs tighten their wallets, and suddenly those glossy towers begin to look less like assets, more like anchors."

The screen flickered again: U.S. tariff graphs in red, Indian real estate sales dipping in tandem.

He lowered his voice: "Real estate doesn't exist in a vacuum. It breathes the same air as trade policy. Tariffs in Washington ripple into unsold apartments in Gurgaon."

The students leaned forward, seeing the invisible thread: a customs duty in D.C. echoing as empty lobbies in India.

Damodaran ended with a chalked phrase on the board: "Trade wars build walls—but sometimes, they collapse towers."

Silence. Outside, autumn flowers sway, indifferent to the fragile balance between policy and property.

His words were echoing in the classroom when he left. *"When the music slows, and it always does, will you still want to hold the ticket?"*

*

Delhi, Afternoon

Marble floors, champagne glasses, a glowing scale model of futuristic towers.

A young executive couple sipped cappuccino as a salesman unfurled the dream: infinity pools, concierge services, golf-course views. The price is staggering, but the salesman smiles, "Sir, you don't buy a home here—you buy a future." The couple hesitates.

The salesman pressed on, "You are buying a legacy for your children."

They signed. Pulled by the promise of tomorrow.

Applause, a ceremonial bell.

*

Gurugram

Developers were toasting under chandeliers. Charts show sales slipping, inventory swelling.

"Then we launch bigger, louder," the chairman insisted. "Gurugram is India's Manhattan. Prestige will always sell."

A junior analyst studied the numbers—luxury stock up 24% in a year—and stayed silent.

*

The Mirage of Gurugram

The drive into Gurugram feels like entering another country. Wide expressways slice through gleaming glass towers, luxury malls glitter with international brands, and giant billboards shout: "Live Above the Rest—Starting ₹5 Crore Onwards."

But step outside the gated compounds, and the illusion begins to falter. Migrant workers, who built the towers brick by brick, huddle on unfinished sites, their wages delayed.

In a high-rise society in Sector 24, a woman gets stranded in elevators during a blackout, and WhatsApp groups buzz with complaints.

A sudden downpour leaves entire streets submerged. Monsoon rain drowns the arterial roads of Gurugram. BMWs stall, scooters float, residents wade barefoot.

The glittering towers loom above, untouched, almost mocking.

Somewhere in the world, Damodaran was saying, "Optimism, unchecked, is the fuel of bubbles. In every story, there comes a point.

*

The Boardroom

Gurugram

On the 20th floor. A real estate tycoon, balding, heavyset, restless, flipped through charts.

"Sales down twenty per cent," an executive muttered.

The tycoon slams the table. "Then we launch bigger. Louder. A new tower every quarter. People don't buy homes—they buy prestige. We sell the dream!"

The room echoes with forced applause, but one junior analyst stares at the graph—red lines sliding downward, unsold units piling higher. He says nothing.

*

In a tea shop, a builder sipped *chai*, pointing at half-finished towers rising like ghosts. "Authorities inflate base prices. Developers inflate hope. Buyers chase illusions. But empty towers don't lie."

*

NYU, Crescendo

Across the continent, Damodaran was teaching, "Stories sell. Growth. Legacy. Prestige. But the story is not value. Value is cash flows, risks, and time."

The professor showed another slide: past bubbles. Tulip mania. Dot-com crash. Subprime mortgages.

"Do you notice a pattern?" he asked softly. "Optimism always outpaces reality. And optimism, unchecked, is the fuel of bubbles."

He paused, almost whispering: "India is not immune."

*

A Construction Site

Gurugram

Migrant workers hammered steel under floodlights. They sleep on damp mats, unpaid.

One whispered, "They sell flats for crores. We can't afford a room here."

Across town, migrant workers slept on concrete slabs, still sweating from the day's labour on another luxury tower.

One of them whispered, "Who will live in these palaces?"

Nobody answers.

*

Split Screen

In New York, the voice of Damodaran echoes in the classroom. "The dream is often built on the backs of those who cannot share it. That dissonance… eventually shows up in value."

He gathers his notes, stepping into the winter night, snowflakes swirling under the lampposts.

In India, cranes rise higher, neon billboards promise "Luxury Redefined," and developers toast record bookings.

Over both worlds, his words echo like a warning bell across oceans: "Even the best story, if bought at the wrong price, becomes a tragedy."

The screen faded to black.

*

Gurugram's skyline glows, selling tomorrow with every flicker of its neon lights. The numbers tell the hidden story: Surging unsold luxury inventory indicates supply is outpacing real demand. Development authorities have inflated base rates. Yet the robust demand remains from NRI investors and wealthy buyers; property retains long-term value appeal. Demand for prestige keeps the machine whirring.

But Damodaran's voice lingers, steady, relentless: *"Even the best story, if bought at the wrong price, becomes a tragedy."*

***

Chapter 3
The Adani Group: Allegations Under Suspension

Stock Crash ☑ Startup Failure ✗ International Scandal ☑

The Adani Group, India's infrastructure powerhouse with businesses spanning ports, power, and renewables, came under intense scrutiny in 2023 after a report by U.S. short-seller Hindenburg Research alleged stock manipulation and accounting irregularities. The fallout erased over $100 billion in market value within weeks, shaking investor confidence and sparking global headlines. The Adani Group, however, strongly denied the charges and was later stabilised by deleveraging and restructuring.

The Tycoon on the Prowl

Somewhere Over the Atlantic Ocean

Early January 2023

The jetliner's engines roared softly, a muted thunder cloaked in luxury. Gautam Adani reclined in a leather seat, the world map glowing on the digital console before him. Outside, clouds folded like sheets of silk, but inside the cabin was a war room in velvet disguise.

Aides hovered around him with dossiers—port acquisitions, energy contracts, coal corridors, and green energy bids. Adani's eyes flickered over the documents, sharp, calculating. According to critics, India's Prime Minister had opened doors in capitals across the globe; Adani's task was to walk through them.

Numbers shifted on the screen. Charts appeared. Aides scribbled as though they were in a command centre, not in the belly of a flying palace. The jet's interiors gleamed: polished walnut, chrome finishes, a bar stocked with single malts. But the real intoxication in the room was power—the kind measured in megawatts, terminals, and capital flows.

Below, nations stretched out like chessboards—ports, power plants, airports—each a square to be occupied.

He closed his eyes, and vivid scenes began to roll.

*

Red carpets rolled out in Washington, Tokyo, Canberra, and Tel Aviv. Prime Minister Modi descended from the aircraft, greeted by honour guards and world leaders. Cameras captured the moment of India's rising global profile.

But behind the spectacle, speculation brewed. Opposition leaders in India alleged: "Prime Minister goes first, Adani follows." Rahul Gandhi sharpened the line further, describing Adani as a "shadow businessman." Both the government and the Adani Group categorically denied such claims. Diplomats dismissed the chatter as a conspiracy, yet timelines often appeared closely aligned.

*

The aircraft lurched in turbulence. Adani smirked. We were never on the same stage, yet always in the same script—one wielding political legitimacy, the other corporate capital.

Unaware that a storm was brewing in New York, he slept.

*

631 West 207th Street, New York

Hindenburg HQ, Early January 2023

The blinds were half drawn against the Manhattan sun. Screens glowed with filings, spreadsheets, and news clippings.

"Another shell company?" one analyst asked, circling a name in red.

"Not just one," replied another, pushing a stack of annual reports across the table. "It's a maze. Subsidiaries feeding into subsidiaries, like Russian dolls."

Nathan Anderson leaned back, eyes fixed on the tangle of lines. Complexity isn't protection—it's camouflage, he told his team.

The researchers prepared their report. In their view, the empire contained troubling inconsistencies. They decided to publish—knowing the consequences could ripple across global markets.

*

The Morning After the Storm

January 24, 2023, Ahmedabad

The January air in Ahmedabad carried a quiet tension. At dawn, the Sabarmati glistened under a fragile mist, the chill biting enough to make even the city's early joggers draw their shawls tighter. But by afternoon, the sun blazed mercilessly, the mercury swinging wildly—just like the fortunes being debated in corporate boardrooms.

Inside Adani House, where the glass façade caught both the pale winter light and the dry heat of Gujarat's sun, Gautam Adani sat surrounded by advisors. The city outside moved with its usual hum—rickshaws honking, vendors calling—but inside, silence pressed heavily. Rumours, reports, whispers of storm clouds from overseas markets filled the air thicker than the winter smog.

On the mahogany table of Gautam Adani lay copies of the Hindenburg report, which accused the group of "the largest con in corporate history."

Television screens blared:

"Adani Group Wiped Out by $100 Billion Market Loss"

"India's Growth Star Under Global Scrutiny"

Gautam Adani, unshaken, listened more than speaking. Around him, his closest advisors shuffled papers, phones buzzing with alerts.

A senior executive finally broke the silence. "This report is everywhere. International channels, social media, and even the parliament floor. If we stay quiet, thc market will punish us. If we speak too much, we give it legitimacy."

Another voice added, sharper:

"Investors are calling nonstop. They want reassurance. They want to know if our debt is safe, if our numbers are intact."

Adani raised his hand, calm but firm.

"This is not the first storm we have faced. The empire is built on fundamentals—ports, power, infrastructure—real assets, not paper. But perception matters. We must answer swiftly."

The CFO leaned forward. "Then we release a detailed rebuttal. Line by line, number by number. We show the world this report is agenda-driven."

Nods circled the table. The decision crystallised: not retreat, but counterattack. The corporate machine would draft a 400-page response, a dossier intended to convince regulators, investors, and the watching world that one outsider's report would not undermine the Adani Group.

But the day was not yet over.

*

Gautam Adani's attention shifted to the screen. Group's stock charts bled red, market capitalisation eroding by billions within hours.

A senior director broke the silence: "Our immediate challenge is preventing a liquidity crunch. If leverage ratios start flashing alarm and collateral cover weakens, lenders will tighten the screws."

Another board member added, "Promoter pledges are already under scrutiny. We must pre-empt margin calls—either by infusing fresh equity or accelerating debt repayment."

The CFO spoke with precision, "We can deploy cash reserves to retire short-term obligations. That will buy us credibility. A partial buyback or stabilising action in the FPO could signal confidence."

An external advisor leaned forward: "Foreign investors are jittery. If FIIs exit in bulk, volatility will worsen. But if we can get LIC and domestic mutual funds to hold, it will create a floor for the stock."

Gautam Adani, composed but visibly calculating, finally addressed the room: "Perception drives valuation. Fundamentals remain intact—our EBITDA is strong, and assets are operational. Let's communicate that debt is serviceable, that our balance sheet is resilient. We must project cash flow stability, highlight deleveraging, and assure the market we're not over-leveraged."

Every eye turned to the scrolling ticker. The strategy was clear: manage liquidity, anchor institutional support, and reinforce confidence in fundamentals—the only levers available to stabilise a storm-hit stock.

As the meeting closed, Adani's words lingered in the room: *"Others cannot write our story. We will write it ourselves."*

*

The Fightback

The Adani Group denounced the report as baseless, asserting that it was a targeted attack on both the company and India's growth story. Still, markets responded brutally: shares of Adani

Enterprises, Adani Ports, and Adani Green Energy plummeted. The market capitalisation plunged by nearly $140.1 billion by February 27, 2023. This resulted in an approximate $82.9 billion (₹7 lakh crore) loss in investor wealth and stock drops of up to 50% across various Adani companies.

Over the following weeks, the group maintained its stance of furious defence. Statements were issued, balance sheets dissected, and press conferences called. A $2.5 billion share sale was dramatically pulled as investor confidence wavered.

Adani himself appeared on television: "This is not just about Adani. This is an attack on India's growth story. We will emerge stronger."

Advisors urged deleveraging, pledging more collateral, and wooing back foreign investors. Allies in the political establishment offered public solidarity, though questions lingered behind closed doors.

*

The Human Side of the Empire

Beyond trading screens, the storm reached the docks of Mundra and the streets of Ahmedabad. Dock workers whispered about their jobs. Small investors debated whether Adani was a visionary under siege or a manipulator unmasked.

*

New York

November 2024

U.S. media reported that a federal grand jury in the Eastern District of New York had unsealed a five-count indictment naming Gautam Adani, his nephew Sagar Adani, and several executives.

The filing alleged bribery, securities fraud, and obstruction.

The Group responded that "no one from the group has been served with a summons" and emphasised that the enforceability of such charges outside U.S. jurisdiction remained uncertain. The U.S. Securities and Exchange Commission also filed parallel civil proceedings.

The cases are ongoing, with no final judicial outcome.

*

Years Later

Summons still unserved, Adani Group survived the cyclone and emerged stronger.

In January 2025, Hindenburg Research announced it was winding down operations. Founder Nate Anderson described the decision as personal, citing the intensity of investigative work, and pledged to open-source the firm's methods.

*

Epilogue

By 2025, the dust had partly settled. The Adani Group survived—leaner, more cautious, and more transparent in its disclosures. To critics, Gautam Adani symbolised unchecked ambition; to supporters, he remained a nationalist entrepreneur unfairly targeted.

In the corridors of corporate history, the Adani saga remains a story of allegations under suspension.

Had he crossed the thin line between vision and overreach?

Only time will tell.

***

Chapter 4
Byju's: The Classroom that Collapsed

Bangalore (2013); Later Singapore (2020); London & Silicon Valley, (2021); Back to Bangalore (2023)

Governance Lapses ☑ Expansion Frenzy ☑ Fraud ✗

Byju's (founded 2011) rose from a Bangalore classroom to become India's most celebrated edtech unicorn, valued at $22 billion in 2022. Riding on aggressive marketing, stadium sponsorships, and pandemic-fuelled online learning, it scaled at breakneck speed. But mounting losses, questionable acquisitions, governance lapses, and investor exit eroded confidence. By 2023–24, Byju's had become a cautionary tale of how unchecked growth and overvaluation can undo even the brightest startups.

The Stadium as a Classroom

Indraprastha Estate, Indira Gandhi Stadium

New Delhi, 2013

The lights dimmed, and the stadium erupted in a roar. Not for a cricket match, not for a Bollywood concert, but for education. An extraordinary scene it was.

On the giant LED screens, formulas danced, numbers turned into animations, and a tall, charismatic man in a black t-shirt paced across the stage like a rock star. His name was Byju Raveendran, and at that moment, he wasn't just a teacher—he was a messiah. Thousands of parents and students sat spellbound, believing they were part of a revolution: learning made magical.

Byju raised his hand, and the crowd hushed. He was the founder of India's largest ed-tech company and the creator of India's most loved school learning app. Launched in 2015, BYJU'S offers highly personalised and effective learning programs for classes and aspirants of competitive exams like JEE, Civil Services, etc. With 50 million registered students and 3.5 million paid subscriptions, BYJU'S has become one of the most popular education platforms worldwide.

"Education in India," he declared, "has always been about fear. Fear of exams, fear of failure. We are here to change that." He spoke in fluent English with a South Indian accent, quick rhythm, passionate delivery—not polished, but authentic. "We are here to make learning an experience of love, joy, and confidence."

The crowd erupted. Cameras flashed. Students relate to him as a fellow traveller, not as an authority. He had cracked exams the hard way and showed them how to do the same. He was a charismatic, approachable, and almost "rockstar teacher" to them. High-voltage and restless as he was, students loved him when he treated math like a game. They felt they were part of a live show.

Investors nodded too. Somewhere in the VIP box, venture capitalists whispered to each other, This isn't a company. This is a movement. The man in a shirt half-tucked, sleeves rolled, sneakers, moving like a coach rather than a lecturer. He was a teacher-hero to his students. To investors, he was a visionary founder who could turn an Indian startup into a global unicorn.

But what looked like a revolution was also the beginning of a bubble—one inflated not by equations and explanations, but by ambition and unchecked growth.

*

Cubbon Road, M. Chinnaswamy Stadium

Bangaluru, India, 2019

The lights blaze inside the stadium. Tens of thousands of cricket fans roar as a new sponsor's name flashes across the giant scoreboard—"BYJU'S" emblazoned on Team India's jerseys. For a moment, it seems like nothing can go wrong. A startup born in the living rooms of middle-class parents has taken centre stage in the nation's most sacred sport. Years later, those same parents scroll through the news on their phones, reading about mounting losses, unpaid debts, and valuation cuts. The echo of the stadium roar now feels like a ghostly reminder of ambition that sprinted too far ahead of its numbers.

*

The Investors' Paradise

Singapore, 2020

In the glass towers of Singapore, venture capitalists poured champagne into crystal flutes. The pandemic had just begun, schools were closing, and online learning suddenly looked like the future.

"Byju's is the right place at the right time," one investor toasted. "If we don't double down now, we'll regret it."

And they did double down. Billions of dollars flowed into the company. Each funding round pushed the valuation higher: $5 billion, $10 billion, $16 billion, $22 billion. Byju's became India's most valuable startup—an edtech unicorn crowned emperor.

But behind the celebratory toasts, some cautious voices wondered: "Isn't this too much too fast? Can children really learn from screens alone? Are we confusing downloads with education?"

Those voices were drowned in the fizz of champagne.

*

The Story Inside Byju's HQ

IBC Knowledge Park

Bengaluru, Karnataka, India, 2021

Inside the headquarters, employees worked in a frenzy. Targets were everything. Sales teams dialled numbers endlessly, pushing subscriptions on anxious parents.

A junior sales executive whispered to her colleague, "I just convinced a family to take a ₹2 lakh loan for a two-year package. Their son is in class six. They looked scared but… I hit my target."

The colleague smirked. "Don't think. Just sell. That's the mantra."

Behind the motivational posters and neon-lit walls, pressure was mounting. Employees celebrated targets with claps and slogans, but at home, guilt brewed. Many felt they weren't selling education—they were selling debt disguised as dreams.

And yet, the revenue graphs soared. Investors remained blinded by numbers. The story was too good to question.

*

The Boardroom Unease

The boardroom gleamed with glass and chrome, a cathedral for numbers. On the wall-sized screen, slides flashed in quick succession: GMV curves, user acquisition costs, retention cohorts, and a freshly modelled DCF projection that claimed a billion-dollar upside within five years. Screens glowed with slides packed with numbers: soaring valuations, global acquisitions, and a pipeline of markets yet to conquer. Investors sat stiff in tailored suits; eyes fixed on the projections climbing higher like a fever chart.

At the far end of the long table sat a teacher—one of the company's early voices, invited almost ceremoniously. His appearance was more formal—crisp shirts, blazers, occasionally the startup-casual polo. The sneakers were replaced with polished shoes. His collar was a little crumpled; chalk dust still seemed to cling to his cuffs.

Byju was authentic, raw, unpolished on stage—magnetic precisely because of his accent, his natural metaphors, his natural teacher's body language. But in boardrooms, he became guarded, polished, ambitious—someone who had to translate that charisma into the language of business and valuation. Less kinetic, more controlled. Instead of bounding across a stage, he leaned into slides, metrics, and valuation narratives. The tension between these two personas—teacher versus CEO—was almost palpable in the boardroom.

As the CFO clicked through slides of "user stickiness" and "gross bookings," the teacher shifted uneasily. In his hands lay a thin folder of student feedback—notes scribbled in uneven handwriting, questions about concepts that remained unanswered despite hours on the app.

Investors leaned forward, nodding as the CFO spoke with precision: "Our burn rate is stabilising, and with the latest acquisition, we expect a revenue multiple expansion from 8x to nearly 12x. The terminal growth assumptions put us in line with global edtech comparables."

At the far end of the table, almost swallowed by its length, sat a teacher; his folder filled not with projections but student test papers marked with hesitation. *You need to inspire trust in investors in boardrooms rather than excitement in students,* he reminded himself. That meant numbers, expansion plans, and global aspirations. His stories need to shift from "how to crack math" to "how to crack markets."

When invited to speak, his words were halting yet sincere: "Sir… the children are struggling. The app moves too quickly. Many don't absorb the fundamentals." More measured and deliberate, he slowed his pace to fit investor expectations, balancing passion with gravitas. "We should consider slowing down the scale-up—perhaps revisit how learning outcomes align with our growth."

A silence followed, brittle and heavy. One investor adjusted his cufflinks and asked, almost dismissively: "But how does this affect EBITDA margins or our next funding round valuation? If we shift the growth trajectory, won't it jeopardise the unicorn premium we're defending?"

In that instant, the boardroom's imbalance was laid bare: pedagogy and valuation sat across the same table, but they were not equals.

The teacher lowered his gaze. His language of learning had no footnote in the valuation model. Around him, the glow of projections continued, indifferent to the quiet truth that no spreadsheet could capture.

*

The Expansion Frenzy

London & Silicon Valley, 2021

Byju wasn't just content with India. The world was its classroom.

In London, it acquired a coding platform. In the U.S., it bought a digital reading company. The shopping spree continued: acquisitions worth billions, paid for with investor money.

Board meetings turned into pep rallies. "We will be the Amazon of education," Byju declared. His voice brimmed with conviction. Slides showed growth curves climbing sky-high.

But one quiet board member leaned back and murmured, "Amazon sells goods. Education sells trust. If trust breaks, this house of cards won't stand."

Few listened.

*

Cracks in the Blackboard

India, 2022

Parents began to complain.

"The salesman forced us into a loan."

"My daughter has anxiety. These lessons are not helping."

"They promised a refund. It never came."

Social media buzzed with stories. Newspapers reported mounting losses. Employees shared stories of a toxic work culture. Slowly, the glittering glow began to fade.

And then came the regulatory questions. Auditors delayed signing the financials. The company pushed deadlines, avoided clarity, and built excuses. Each unanswered question added another crack to the blackboard.

*

The Fall

Bangalore, 2023

It didn't happen in one dramatic collapse, but in slow, painful unravelling. Investors walked away slowly. Employees quit in droves. Parents filed lawsuits. Regulators sharpened their knives.

The empire that once stood at $22 billion was now valued at less than $1 billion. Byju, the rock-star teacher, became a symbol—not of innovation, but of excess.

In a dimly lit office, once buzzing with energy, an employee whispered, "We thought we were changing the world. Turns out, we were selling dreams we couldn't deliver."

*

The Lesson

Byju's story isn't just about one founder or one company. It is a parable of ambition unchecked. A reminder that education is not a stage for rock stars, nor a commodity to be forced upon anxious parents. It is trust, fragile and sacred.

And when trust is broken, no valuation—whether $22 billion or $2 trillion—can save a company.

*

Years Later

The once-unstoppable unicorn that promised to "revolutionise learning" now lies in tatters. Byju's, once celebrated as India's most valuable startup, became a cautionary tale of hubris.

The gleaming billboards, stadium sponsorships, and celebrity endorsements have faded. The Bengaluru headquarters—once buzzing with investor visits and product launches—felt like a ghost town of missed deadlines and unpaid salaries. The same corridors that once echoed with motivational speeches now carry only the whispers of legal notices and debt collectors.

Investors, who once poured billions into Byju's with blind faith, now write it off as a lesson in excess. At every startup board meeting, the word "Byju-fication" lingers like a warning of reckless expansion.

Parents and students, once dazzled by glitzy promises, learned to be wary. Trust, once broken, does not easily return.

And Byju Raveendran—once hailed as the poster boy of Indian edtech—now stands in the shadows, his empire dismantled, his reputation shredded in headlines. For him, the fall is not just financial; it is personal, the collapse of a dream built too fast, too large, too blind.

Byju's became what no teacher wants to be remembered as—a failed lesson.

***

Chapter 5

The Tesla Puzzle: When Valuation Misfires Upward

Earlier: Palo Alto; Later: 1 Tesla Road, Austin, Texas (Since 2021)

Over-Valuation ☑ Fraud ✗ Charismatic Leadership ☑

Defiance of Fundamentals ☑

Tesla represents the most dramatic valuation puzzle of our age. At its peak, Tesla was worth more than the next nine automakers combined, despite producing a fraction of their cars. The valuation seemed to run not on fundamentals, but on Elon's vision, charisma, and the market's appetite for disruption. Its market cap defied every ratio, every precedent, every sober analyst's warning. It thrived on dreams as much as deliveries, on Elon Musk's personality as much as production lines.

While many valuations collapse due to fraud or overreach, Tesla shows how it can soar to dangerous heights, creating constant pressure in the boardroom. This contrast reflects the core idea that valuations are stories in disguise—sometimes heroic, sometimes reckless.

Tesla is the riddle at the heart of modern capitalism—the valuation that misfires upwards and soars to heights that mathematics cannot easily explain.

NASA Headquarters

300 Hidden Figures Way SW, Washington, D.C.

When people hear the word "NASA," they often picture Houston, the voice crackling through the radio: "Houston, we've had a problem." Yet, the actual headquarters of NASA is far from Texas, in the political heart of Washington, D.C., where policies are shaped and strategies are signed off. Houston, by contrast, is where dreams are tested—the Johnson Space Centre, home to astronauts, mission control, and the beating pulse of spaceflight.

The room was packed with tension. Screens flickered across the walls of NASA's Mission Control, maps of orbit lines glowing in red and blue. Astronauts were stranded aboard the International Space Station after a systems failure; their return module had been compromised.

At the long steel table sat the nation's most powerful minds—NASA administrators, Air Force generals, engineers, and White House liaisons. Every minute of silence carried the weight of lives hanging in orbit.

The 14th Administrator of NASA, Bill Nelson, jaw clenched, broke the silence: "We don't have time for bureaucracy. Our backup modules aren't ready. Boeing's Starliner is grounded."

Silence followed.

Bill's background as a lawyer, politician, and longtime public servant commanded a lot of respect and credibility with astronauts and NASA insiders. Astronauts saw him as someone who "gets it" from personal experience. "We need a solution now, or we risk losing them," he was thinking aloud, perhaps.

A voice at the far end of the table, calm yet commanding, cut through the panic. "Elon Musk is on his way."

Heads turned. A murmur swept the room. For some, relief; for others, resentment. Musk had always been the wild card—half saviour, half disruptor.

Moments later, the doors flew open. Elon strode in wearing a black jacket over a plain T-shirt, his hair slightly dishevelled, eyes blazing with restless intensity. He didn't sit. He walked to the head of the table, scanning the anxious faces.

"Dragon can do it," he said without preamble. "SpaceX has a capsule ready. We launch in forty-eight hours. We bring them home."

The words hung in the air like a thunderclap. NASA officials blinked in disbelief. Rescues were the stuff of movies, not corporate pitches.

A NASA veteran slammed a fist on the table. "This isn't your boardroom, Musk! Lives are at stake. Do you even understand the political storm this creates? Do you understand what happens if we fail?"

Elon leaned forward, voice low but cutting: "I understand exactly. Failure means death. Success means survival. Politics doesn't matter in orbit—oxygen does. Trust me, or write the obituaries yourselves."

The room went silent. Screens hummed. Somewhere outside, a storm rumbled across the skies.

Bill had handled emergencies like a Soyuz coolant leak before in 2022. But this was huge. "Safety of U.S. astronauts is a matter of national security. We cannot authorise a private company to launch astronauts into orbit without FAA, DoD, and White House coordination."

Elon smiled knowingly. Bill knew firsthand the dangers of space programs. In January 1986, he himself had flown aboard the Space Shuttle Columbia (STS-61-C) as a payload specialist.

He folded his arms. "History doesn't wait on permission slips, Bill."

"Many a time it does," Bill said with an old-school politician's charm. "The President wouldn't sign the launch order directly, but the White House would be briefed, and the final greenlight for an emergency rescue would be politically cleared at that level."

Elon hit the bull's eye. "Do you have Plan B?"

Bill exhaled resignedly. NASA's deepening partnership with SpaceX during his tenure since 2021 had given him an opportunity to know the potential of Elon from close quarters. "Alright, Elon. Let me pull some strings."

Within hours, the crisis briefing had escalated from Houston to the Oval Office. The President listened, stone-faced, as NASA officials explained the only viable option: let Elon Musk's SpaceX launch a rescue mission. With a nod, the President gave tacit approval, knowing this decision would carry history's weight.

And so, the expedition began—not with cars Tesla is known for, but with rockets, lives, and a gamble that would intertwine Tesla's fate with the stars.

*

The Rescue Operation

Kennedy Space Centre, Cape Canaveral, Florida

March 14, 2025, 7:03 p.m. ET (2303 GMT)

Within hours, SpaceX teams were at launchpads, the Falcon engines roaring to life under floodlights.

The launchpad shook with raw power as SpaceX's Falcon 9 roared to life, its engines splitting the night with fire and thunder. Rising steadily into the sky, the rocket carried not just a spacecraft, but the hopes of a tense world watching. This was no ordinary mission—it was a rescue, a race against time to bring the stranded astronauts home.

The flames of ignition had lit up the Florida sky, and the world held its breath. Hours later, when the capsule pierced Earth's atmosphere and splashed down in the Atlantic, a cheer erupted at NASA headquarters. The mission was successful—every astronaut was brought back safely.

The face of Elon Musk was flashing on every TV screen in the world. The world watched history replay in real time. A private company, once mocked as reckless, had become the saviour of stranded astronauts. As the capsule returned safely to Earth, the headlines shifted overnight: Musk, the Maverick, the Rescuer.

He was regarded as the next President of the United States.

*

Shareholders Versus Starships

The boardroom was silent. A crisis had unfolded far beyond quarterly reports and stock charts. On the screens before them, live footage played: Astronauts rescued orbit, their return capsule crippled, communication uncertain. The world held its breath.

Then, against all odds, a new voice entered the chaos. Elon Musk leaned forward, his black T-shirt stark against the glow of monitors, eyes burning with the kind of certainty only he could summon.

"SpaceX did it," he declared. "A rocket—our rocket—brought them home."

The Tesla boardroom clapped, but the celebration was cut short with unease. Musk often divided his attention between Austin (Tesla), Hawthorne (SpaceX), Boca Chica (Neuralink), The Boring Company (Texas), and even X (Twitter). This multitasking fuelled investor anxiety, because each distraction raises the risk that Tesla's leadership might drift. Board members have at times unsuccessfully tried to push him to clarify how he divides time between ventures.

Elon's space ambitions often collide with Tesla's more earthbound concerns. For the board, every rocket launch brought global prestige but also the lingering question: Is Tesla the main mission, or just another stepping stone in Musk's larger cosmic puzzle?

But the reverse was true. When cash flows at Tesla looked shaky, his grand visions of Mars and rockets made shareholders wonder if he was chasing galaxies instead of grounding Tesla's fundamentals.

But no director dared to say that in the boardroom.

They all had learned the hard way that Elon thrives on confrontation, not for the sake of argument, but because friction fuels innovation in his world. Subordinates squirm under the intensity; some crumble, some resign. Silence in his meetings is better than facing a thunderclap.

*

Flashback

The Tesla Headquarters

The headquarters gleamed like a spaceship grounded on Earth. The glass walls caught the late-afternoon sun, refracting it across polished chrome fixtures. To outsiders, the building appeared to be a temple of innovation. Inside, however, the boardroom felt like a war bunker.

Elon walked into boardrooms in black T-shirts, dark jeans, and a casual blazer thrown on almost as an afterthought. When the occasion demands gravitas—earnings calls, high-stakes investor meetings—he might switch to a slim-cut suit, but without the stiff formality of ties.

Never a man in disguise.

A man of his calibre didn't need to wrap himself in the conventional armour of Wall Street pinstripes or the sombre greys of Fortune 500 chiefs. His dress sense reflected his paradox: a disruptor seated at the polished mahogany table of corporate tradition.

The long oak table stretched like a battlefield. At one end sat Elon Musk, not slouched but leaning forward, restless, as if the chair itself could not contain his energy. His eyes darted across the table—not at the papers or slides, but at the faces. He wasn't scanning numbers; he was scanning resolve.

Around him, executives and board members shifted uneasily. For every triumph in space, there was turbulence on the ground. Cash flows bled, debts mounted, production missed targets. Investors cheered his daring in orbit, but frowned at the numbers on Earth.

The glow of Wall Street's love affair with Tesla hung in the air, but so did the weight of impossible expectations.

Zach Kirkhorn, the CFO, finally broke the silence. He flipped open a folder as if it were a shield. "Deliveries have grown by forty-three per cent," he said. "Revenue is soaring. But margins…"

The pause was dangerous. Elon's eyebrow rose.

"…margins are thinning. Raw material costs—lithium, nickel—are surging," the CFO continued. "Shanghai is producing, but Europe is bleeding cash."

"Margins?" Elon said, his voice like a scalpel, leaping three steps ahead of the conversation, sketching galaxies while others are still debating roadmaps. "Margins are for accountants. We're not building sandwiches—we're building the future." He switched into a visionary mode—eyes narrowing, voice steady, describing futures so outlandish they feel like prophecies.

The words sliced through the air. Zach shut his folder a little too quickly, heat rising in his neck.

Antonio Gracias leaned back, arms crossed, voice deliberate. "Elon, the valuation is surreal. Larger than the combined top five automakers. Wall Street calls us a miracle. But miracles don't last forever."

Elon's smile was thin. "Let me ask you, Antonio, when was the last time Ford launched a rocket?"

A ripple of nervous laughter rolled across the table, but Antonio didn't laugh. "Investors don't invest in rockets when they buy Tesla. They invest in cars. Cars with steering wheels. Cars with recalls."

The tension thickened. Someone coughed, too loud in the still air.

Robyn Denholm, chair of the board, straightened in her seat. "Elon, you know I believe in the mission. But there's an elephant in this room. The SEC hasn't forgotten your tweets. Governance matters. Investors worry about volatility, not just in the stock, but in the leadership."

The word leadership landed like a stone.

Elon leaned back now, folding his arms. "Structure doesn't invent. Chaos invents. Controlled chaos."

Murdoch didn't flinch. "And if the control slips?"

For a moment, Elon's eyes darkened, like storm clouds forming. Then he smirked. "Then we build something even better out of the wreckage."

He stood suddenly, pacing to the floor-to-ceiling window. Beyond the glass, California hills rolled into the horizon, bathed in golden light.

"You see cars," he said softly, but his voice carried. "I see energy nodes. A fleet of millions, connected, storing, sharing, breathing life into a planet suffocating in fossil fuel smoke. Tesla isn't a car company. Tesla is humanity's survival company." When he was not talking about Starlink satellites and interplanetary colonisation, he pivoted his conversations to batteries and production bottlenecks. Some board members find it inspiring, others frustrating.

The room was spellbound. Even the sceptics found themselves leaning forward, drawn in by the gravitational pull of his conviction.

Inside their minds, however, doubts gnawed. Was this genius, or delusion? Was the man a prophet, or a gambler betting the company's future on visions too vast to measure?

Ira Ehrenpreis, the investor, gathering courage, whispered: "Then we must invest accordingly. More factories. More debt. More risk."

The word risk cracked the spell. A murmur spread around the table, uneasy, like thunder before a storm.

Elon turned sharply, eyes blazing. "Risk? The greatest risk is standing still. The greatest risk is mediocrity while the world burns. We go all in, or we go extinct."

Silence. The kind that felt heavy, suffocating.

Murdoch's voice broke the tension. Calm, precise. "Very well. Expansion at all costs. Let's put it to a vote."

Hands rose—hesitant at first, then one after another, until the motion carried.

Elon returned to his seat, finally smiling, but it was the smile of a man who had already seen the future and refused to believe it could be otherwise.

"Good," he said, almost to himself. "Now… let's change the world."

Outside, a crimson Model 3 glided silently past the headquarters, its wheels whispering across the asphalt. To the casual driver, it was just a car. But to those inside the boardroom, it was the embodiment of a gamble larger than steel, larger than money, larger even than Tesla itself.

The survival of Tesla defied every axiom of valuation.

The puzzle remained unsolved: was it brilliance, or hubris, that drove this machine forward?

*

The Boardroom Confrontation Sparks

June 6, 2025, Tesla HQ (Early Morning)

Elon Musk burst in, tension radiating in his stride. He'd posted on X hours earlier, accusing Trump's tax-and-spending bill of being a "disgusting abomination" and claiming Trump owed his election win to Musk's support, even hinting at "Epstein file" secrets. In response, Trump threatened to cancel billions of dollars in government contracts for Tesla and SpaceX. Tesla stock plummeted over 14%, losing $150 billion—or even $380 billion in broader valuation—instantly. Investors were reeling.

Robyn Denholm cut to the chase: "Elon, after the tweets… political bombs, personal grenades. Trump is promising to revoke subsidies and contracts. This isn't theoretical—it's a financial earthquake."

Ira remained guarded. "The stock tanked 14% in a day. Wall Street sees this as self-inflicted chaos. We cannot afford to antagonise the city's most powerful offices."

Elon leaned in, his voice razor sharp: "I'm not here to be a sycophant. If politicians want to play politics, I'll play chess. Tesla doesn't—won't—kneel."

The board listened intently to a relentless commander in spirit, and an architect of futures who makes the present feel unbearably small. Elon was magnetic, blunt, unafraid, and unsettling.

James Murdoch, a wary and pragmatic director, pressed on: "Tesla depends on EV incentives, regulatory goodwill, and procurement contracts. You've just turned a spotlight on us as politically unstable."

Silence.

Then Kathleen Thompson, the HR chief, burst out, "We talk of culture, innovation—but what people remember now is scandal. Customers, employees—they're unsettled." Her job warranted her to focus on damage control.

Elon slammed a hand on the table: "Let him cut contracts. We'll find other buyers. International. Mars."

The boardroom bristled. Kimbal quietly added, "Inspiration is fine, but if we lose Washington, we don't reach Mars. We may not even get to produce the next car." Being Elon's brother, he was always torn between devotion and reality.

Elon's gaze lingered on the Tesla emblem on the wall. After a long pause: "Then we need a Plan B… One that doesn't rely on politics."

*

Years Later

That morning of June 6, 2025, would be remembered internally as the day Tesla's board divided between political idealism and existential survival. The Musk-Trump feud continued through June and beyond, a glitch in the driverless narrative.

Washington remained unpredictable—reports of denied contracts circulated, and Musk's DOGE role became a lightning rod in Washington.

Externally, Tesla faced protests—"Tesla Takedown" demonstrations and vandalism hit showrooms in the U.S. and Europe. Activists decried Musk's political entanglement, and headlines talked of domestic terrorism investigations.

Yet Tesla endured.

The company shifted focus toward global markets, AI robotics like Optimus, and deeper tech innovations—diversifying beyond the political heat.

Tesla cars glided silently down highways from California to Shanghai, its gigafactories rose like cathedrals of steel, and its stock chart looked less like a financial instrument than a roller coaster built by a dreamer. The gamble of that Palo Alto boardroom was now history, its consequences visible in every city street.

At first, Donald Trump basked in Elon Musk's glow. He praised him at rallies: "Elon, great guy, tremendous, building rockets, building cars, real winner—just like me." For a while, Musk allowed it, shrugging off the theatrics. Both men thrived on spectacle, and both understood the currency of attention.

The high point came when SpaceX's Crew Dragon ferried NASA astronauts back from orbit, splashing down safely as Trump's White House claimed credit. Cameras caught the moment, Trump grinning, basking in the achievement of Musk's rockets as if they were his own. For a brief time, the aura of Trump Tower and the mystique of Tesla seemed aligned.

But the bond cracked when Trump pulled out of the Paris Climate Agreement. Musk resigned from the White House advisory council in protest. Trump lashed back in his familiar style: "Elon's smart but overrated. Without subsidies, Tesla is NOTHING. Sad!"

From then on, the relationship soured. Trump mocked electric cars as impractical toys, while Musk doubled down on his vision of a post-carbon future. What had once looked like an alliance of disruptors became a duel of egos.

To investors, the feud became part of Tesla's mythos. Musk was no longer just battling Ford, Toyota, or Wall Street short-sellers—he was jousting with the former President of the United

States. And in the clash, Tesla's identity sharpened: not a car company, but a crusade.

Yet the puzzle remains unsolved. Has Tesla proved that vision could outpace politics, or merely another theatre where personalities collided? The world keeps moving forward silently, even as the argument behind it grows louder.

***

Chapter 6
Reliance: The ₹17,000 Crore Reckoning

H Block, 1st Floor, Dhirubhai Ambani Knowledge City, Navi Mumbai

Alleged Corporate Fraud ☑ Litigation ☑ Alleged Money Laundering ☑

The ₹17,000 crore alleged fraud involved a web of defaults, diversion of bank loans, and the use of bogus documents and fake guarantees to secure projects. Investigations by the Enforcement Directorate uncovered forged bank papers and money laundering across multiple Reliance Group entities. Once hailed as corporate powerhouses, these firms now stand as stark reminders of how financial engineering and deception can erode investor trust.

From Want to Wealth

Bhuleshwar, South Mumbai to Navi Mumbai

The boy who once ran barefoot through the dusty lanes of Bhuleshwar, clutching a schoolbag too heavy for his frail shoulders, knew the sting of poverty. Meals were modest, clothes were passed down, and every rupee was stretched thin in the Ambani household's early years. He often studied under a kerosene lamp, watching his father dream aloud of a fortune yet to be built.

The same boy—now Anil Ambani—lounged aboard a glittering yacht on the French Riviera, sunlight catching the diamond-studded watch on his wrist. Helicopters ferried guests to his soirées, champagne flowed like water, and the world bowed to the Ambani name. The hardships of his childhood seemed like a forgotten tale, replaced by limousines, skyscraper boardrooms, and red-carpet premieres where Anil appeared more like a movie star than an industrialist.

His thought drifted when his father, Dhirubhai Ambani, was not yet a tycoon but a restless trader, his eyes always on the horizon, his pockets never quite full.

In the crowded lanes of South Mumbai, he chased kites across rooftops, his laughter rising above the din of textile mills. The Ambani family lived in a cramped two-room chawl, where the smell of kerosene mixed with the aroma of his mother's cooking.

Anil shared a thin mattress with his elder brother, Mukesh, the two of them whispering at night about the strange world their father described: of ships carrying oil, of deals struck in foreign lands, of fortunes that could be made if only one dared enough.

Every evening, Anil would accompany his father to the Bhuleshwar market, known for its vibrant shops selling textiles, jewellery, and other goods. He used to watch him argue over a few rupees with the same fire that he later used in billion-dollar boardrooms. The boy absorbed it all—the hunger, the street-smartness, the belief that money was never scarce, only courage was.

"Was I happier in those days?"

No one in that chawl could have imagined that the boy running barefoot on hot tar would one day sit in glass towers, commanding empires worth billions. But perhaps, even then, Anil knew.

But opulence is a fragile armour. Behind the gloss of wealth and the sheen of power, shadows gathered: debts, disputes, and the haunting question—had the boy who knew hunger learned how to guard against excess?

*

Reliance Power HQ

Transition Scene, The Boardroom

The glass façade of the Reliance Group headquarters in Mumbai shimmered in the morning sun, a monument to ambition and resilience. For the city below, it was just another weekday. But inside, in the boardroom on the top floor, a different reality was unfolding.

At the head of the table, Anil Ambani sat with his familiar air of studied composure. His once jet-black hair was now thinning, the baldness at his crown betraying the passage of years. The sharp suits still fit him well, but the weight he had shed over the last decade left him looking leaner, almost fragile, in contrast to the booming voice of his elder brother, who still dominated India's corporate stage.

Behind the wire-rimmed spectacles, his eyes darted from screen to screen, scanning the numbers with the intensity of a man who had spent his life defending an empire built on borrowed confidence. Those who knew him well said he had always been meticulous, even perfectionist, a man who prized presentation as much as performance. But beneath that exterior, the years of financial strain and courtroom appearances had carved out an unmistakable weariness.

Surrounded by his senior executives, Anil was staring at the screen.

The numbers on the boardroom screens told a harsher story: unpaid loans, ballooning interest, and balance sheets under enormous strain.

Anil adjusted his spectacles and leaned forward, his voice clipped but steady.

"Gentlemen," he said, "the markets are restless. Banks are pressing. We must project control. We cannot let confidence slip further."

For a moment, the room fell silent. The words carried the weight of déjà vu.

Because the men in that room remembered. They remembered 2008, when the Reliance Power IPO—once the most hyped listing in India's history—had turned from triumph to fiasco in a matter of days. Retail investors had poured their savings, only to see shares collapse after listing. Dreams sold as destiny had dissolved into disappointment.

That failure had been written off as a harsh lesson of the market. But now, in 2025, the shadows of that IPO loomed again—not as a memory, but as a reminder. History, it seemed, had circled back with sharper teeth.

Whispers had already been swirling: loan diversions, fake guarantees, shell companies. Bankers grumbled in private about repayment delays, regulators tightened their gaze, and the financial press sharpened its headlines. The confidence Anil spoke of was already cracking.

And yet, in that boardroom, the empire still wore its armour: glass towers, familiar logos, and a leader determined to project composure. What no one in that room could foresee was how quickly that armour was about to be pierced.

Even as Anil Ambani reviewed strategies with his board, convoys of Enforcement Directorate officials were preparing their move. Across Mumbai and beyond, officers in plainclothes had sealed their envelopes, readied their warrants, and mapped out their targets.

Within hours, the Reliance Group headquarters—this very building with its glittering façade and anxious boardroom—would no longer be a fortress of corporate power. It would become the epicentre of a ₹17,000 crore reckoning.

*

The ED Raid

July 24, 2025

Mumbai was softly waking up with hawkers, vegetable trucks, milk vans, and the rising Sun.

The sound of sirens broke the city's silence. At exactly 7:30 a.m., teams of the Enforcement Directorate (ED) fanned out across the financial capital and beyond. In total, 35 locations linked to Anil Ambani's Reliance Group were raided simultaneously.

At Reliance Home Finance's headquarters, startled employees watched as officers entered with search warrants. File cabinets were unsealed, laptops carried away, and floors of glass offices transformed into evidence warehouses. Panic calls bounced between executives, but it was too late—the dragnet had been cast.

*

The Allegations

The case was staggering in size: ₹17,000 crore in loans across Reliance entities that had soured into non-performing assets.

Investigators traced a web of alleged fraud.

₹3,000 crore borrowed from Yes Bank between 2017 to 2019 was diverted to shell firms under the guise of legitimate contracts.

Fake bank guarantees worth ₹68.2 crore, allegedly forged with State Bank of India stamps, were submitted to the Solar Energy Corporation of India (SECI) through a Reliance-linked associate, Biswal Tradelink Pvt Ltd.

Complex money trails across dozens of accounts pointing to systematic laundering.

The evidence, the ED claimed, suggested a playbook of deception: borrow big, shuffle funds, mask losses, and keep the façade of solvency alive.

*

The Market Fallout

The Brothers' Shadow

Mumbai, 2025

Anil Ambani sat alone in his Nariman Point office, half-empty, files stacked with debt notices.

A television mounted on the wall streamed a business channel. The glow of multiple stock tickers reflected on his weary face. Numbers bled red across the screens: Reliance Power down 7%, Reliance Infra sliding another 5%. Six consecutive sessions of free fall. His empire, once spoken of in the same breath as his brother's, was collapsing in real time.

He clenched his fist on the mahogany desk. Nineteen per cent gone in a week. Decades of ambition erased in the click of a mouse.

A television mounted on the wall streamed a business channel. The anchor's voice carried salt to the wound: "Meanwhile, Reliance Industries under Mukesh Ambani has crossed yet another milestone—becoming Asia's most valuable company with its foray into green hydrogen and AI-powered telecom services…"

The words hit like hammer blows. Same bloodline. Same inheritance. Same starting point. Yet one brother now commanded boardrooms from New York to Riyadh, while the other sat cornered by raids, court summons, and evaporating market caps. Despite the company's claim of "acting in good faith" and blaming third parties, trust was broken. The market had reacted swiftly—shares nosedived.

Anil's eyes drifted to a framed photograph on the shelf: he and Mukesh, smiling together in the early days after the division. Two heirs of Dhirubhai, two dreamers with the same springboard.

A bitter smile flickered across his face.

"Two brothers, two destinies," he whispered. "One builds galaxies. The other… fights to keep the lights on."

After one of the most iconic corporate divisions in 2005 in Indian business history, both started from the same inheritance. The divergence wasn't just financial—it was personal, strategic, and symbolic. One built; the other borrowed. One consolidated; the other scattered.

Two heirs starting with comparable resources, yet their paths diverged radically.

Valuations misfire when vision doesn't match execution.

Outside, the Mumbai skyline pulsed with energy—Jio's billboards lit up the night. Inside, silence reigned, broken only by the endless tick… tick… tick… of falling stocks.

The raids sparked a financial aftershock. On Dalal Street, investors dumped Reliance stocks in a frenzy. Reliance Infrastructure and Reliance Power tumbled nearly 19% in just six sessions, their market caps evaporating with each trade.

Newsrooms seized the story, flashing red tickers that screamed: "₹17,000 CRORE LOAN FRAUD." Prime-time anchors thundered about the fall of a once-proud empire, their screens replaying footage of files being hauled from Reliance offices.

For retail investors who remembered the Reliance Power IPO crash of 2008, this was déjà vu—a new wound in the same scar tissue.

*

The Interrogation

August 5, 2025

The drama reached its peak. Anil Ambani, once the billionaire poster child of India's infrastructure dreams, walked into the Enforcement Directorate headquarters.

The glare of cameras was merciless. Reporters shouted questions as flashbulbs erupted: "Mr Ambani, did you launder funds?"

"What do you say about the fake guarantees?"

Inside, the mood was grim. Interrogators pressed Ambani on loan diversions, questioned his role in forged guarantees, and dissected the actions of his closest aides. Amitabh Jhunjhunwala and Sateesh Seth, senior Reliance executives, had already faced hours of questioning.

Meanwhile, arrests had begun. Executives linked to Biswal Tradelink Pvt Ltd—accused of submitting forged guarantees—were taken into custody. The noose was tightening.

*

The Aftermath

The raids and interrogations left the Reliance Group battered. Its market value shrank, investor confidence collapsed, and regulators closed in from every angle.

For Anil Ambani, the scandal was more than financial. It was personal—another shattering blow after the collapse of Reliance Communications, another chapter of loss after the IPO fiasco that had once promised so much.

The man who once stood on stage promising to light up India with power projects now sat across from investigators, defending himself against charges of forgery, fraud, and money laundering.

And as the ED deepened its probe, the question hanging over the Reliance Group was not about future growth or expansion.

It was simpler.

Sharper.

Would it survive the ₹17,000 crore reckoning?

*

Sometimes Later

Reliance Power—Skeletons in the Grid

Anil's Reliance ADA Group, once hailed as the future (telecom, power, infra, finance), unravelled under debt, over-leverage, and scandals. Today, his firms are shadows of their past selves, marred by the ₹17,000 crore fraud probe.

The Bangalore office towers of Reliance Power still glow beneath the city lights, a testament to ambition unquenched. The company once projected strength through power plants, solar farms, and expansion plans—now it hums with subpoenas and scrutiny.

Stock prices cratered—the company's shares tumbled nearly 19% over six trading sessions, signalling investor panic and reputational haemorrhage.

Reliance Power, while asserting operational independence, could not fully escape the contagion of suspicion attached to its parent group.

Long gone are the days of sweeping statements about energy dominance. Now, whispers filter through the corridors—about bail conditions, boardroom denials, and pending court summonses.

Power projects still run, but with a lower hum. The solar farms that once promised a green future now stand shadowed by scandal. Where investors saw growth, they now see skeletons in the grid. In the annals of corporate India, Reliance Power is a testament that, even in energy, the greatest short-circuits may come from within.

***

Chapter 7
The Deal That Never Was: How Google Escaped Oblivion

Santa Margarita Avenue, Menlo Park, California, USA (1999)

Under-Valuation ☑ Fraud ✗ Negative Cash Flow ☑ Lack of Vision ☑

In 1999, long before it became a tech giant, Larry Page and Sergey Brin tried to sell Google's search engine to Excite for just $1 million. Excite's CEO turned down the offer, dismissing it as "not worth it." The deal never happened, and Google went on to become one of the most valuable companies in the world, worth over $2.13 trillion two decades later. The failed sale remains one of Silicon Valley's most legendary under-valuations.

Shadows in the Lab, 1999

The fluorescent bulb in the small research lab flickered uncertainly, casting long shadows across the floor littered with wires and stacks of servers. The hum was constant, like a heartbeat threatening to stop at any moment. Empty Mountain Dew cans crowded the desk. Pizza boxes lay open, their grease stains seeping into important-looking printouts of algorithms.

Larry Page sat hunched over the desk, his hands buried in his hair, staring at the screen as if it were mocking him. Sergey Brin leaned back in his chair, arms folded, rocking slightly, the optimist trying to mask his exhaustion.

Larry broke the silence. "We can't keep this going. Every day, the servers crash. Every day we fix one problem, two more appear. We're engineers, Sergey. We didn't come here to babysit machines."

Sergey smirked faintly. "Babysit? These machines are like our children."

Larry's eyes flickered with frustration. Google was getting 3 million hits every day, but it didn't have a model for revenue generation. "Children? No. They're parasites. Eating our time, our sanity. We need a way out."

Sergey stopped rocking, his grin fading. "What are you saying?"

Larry took a deep breath, as though releasing words that had been stuck in his throat for weeks. "We sell. We sell Google before it buries us."

The silence was heavier than the humming servers. Sergey leaned forward, elbows on his knees, staring at his partner.

Sergey gave a surprised look. "Sell? To whom?"

Larry had done his homework. "Excite. They're growing. They have money. They can handle the traffic. And we…" he trailed off, eyes weary "…we can move on."

Sergey looked at the messy lab: the boxes, the blinking lights, the chaotic wires. For a moment, he saw not chaos but possibility. But he also saw Larry's tired eyes.

He nodded, reluctantly.

Sergey shrugged, "Alright. Let's talk to them."

*

The Boardroom

450 Broadway Street, Redwood City, California

The Excite office was a sprawling, warehouse-style campus of about 800,000 sq. ft. in the Pacific Shores area. Known for its playful dot-com culture, it had open spaces, casual vibes, and quirky features like a red slide, pink bikes, and Hopper balls for employees.

For the Google duo, it felt like another world. Glass panels gleamed. The carpet smelled of money and fresh polish. Everything was sleek, modern, and confident.

George Bell, CEO of Excite, sat at the head of the long mahogany table, a man exuding the calm arrogance of someone who believed he already owned the future. Around him, board members shuffled papers, whispering calculations of revenue streams, banner ads, and portal growth.

Larry and Sergey entered with nothing but conviction and exhaustion. No glossy deck, no rehearsed pitch. Just their faith in PageRank.

Larry spoke first, voice steady, though his nerves betrayed him in the tightening of his jaw. "We've built something different. Something better. A search algorithm that ranks results by relevance. Not just words, but meaning. We're offering it to Excite for one million dollars."

The words landed like a pebble in an ocean of scepticism.

George Bell tapped his pen against the table. His expression never changed.

Bell raised his eyebrow. "One million… for a search engine? We already have one. Everyone has a search engine."

Sergey leaned forward, his energy spilling into the room. "Not like this. Users are drowning in irrelevant results. Our algorithm cuts through noise. Think of it as the compass for the internet."

A board member muttered under his breath, just loud enough to be heard: "Search is a commodity. Not a business."

The CFO of Excite raised his head. "The revenue is zero…. cash flow negative. If we deploy the Discounted Cash Flow method of valuation, the outcome would be zero, too."

Larry swallowed hard. He lowered the offer. "Seven hundred and fifty thousand."

For a moment, the room was silent. Then, almost imperceptibly, a chuckle escaped from one corner of the table. Another board member scribbled something dismissively.

George Bell leaned back. "Even at that price, it doesn't make sense. Search won't make money. Portals will. Users want stickiness, not utility. I'm sorry."

The air left the room. Larry's shoulders slumped. Sergey clenched his fists beneath the table, his jaw tight, his words trapped.

The meeting ended with forced smiles, perfunctory handshakes, and an unspoken understanding that something extraordinary had just been tossed aside.

*

The Walk Back

Outside Excite's headquarters, the California sun mocked them with its brightness. Larry walked in silence, staring at the pavement. Sergey tried to lighten the moment.

Sergey smirked. "Well… at least they gave us free coffee."

Larry didn't laugh. "They don't get it. Nobody does."

Sergey stopped, placing a hand on Larry's shoulder. "Then maybe… It's not the time to sell. Maybe it's time to prove them wrong."

Larry looked at him, torn between despair and a flicker of defiance. "Or maybe we just made the biggest mistake of our lives."

*

The Irony of Excite

Back in Excite's boardroom, George Bell celebrated restraint.

“We dodged a bullet,” he cherished. “Search isn’t the future. Portals are. Content, ads, services—that’s where the money is.”

The board nodded, congratulating themselves for their prudence.

They had no idea that in rejecting Google, they had just made the most expensive mistake in Silicon Valley history.

*

The Rise of the Rejected

Google grew quietly. Users told other users. The search box, clean and bare, became an entry point to the world’s knowledge.

By 2000, Sequoia Capital and Kleiner Perkins had invested $25 million. By 2001, Google handled 100 million queries a day. By its IPO in 2004, it was valued at $23 billion.

Excite, meanwhile, floundered—its portal strategy crumbling, its relevance evaporating. By 2001, it had been absorbed into Ask Jeeves, a shadow of its former self.

*

In An Alternate Universe

Imagine if Excite had said yes. Google would have been buried inside a portal, reduced to a widget, its brilliance smothered. Larry and Sergey might have returned to Stanford, anonymous academics who once had an idea.

But fate, disguised as Excite’s arrogance, had other plans.

*

Years Later

As I write this page, Alphabet’s market capitalisation, based on the current stock price, stands at approximately $2.13 trillion. It has grown from an IPO valuation of just $23 billion in 2004 to one of the most valuable companies on the planet. From a near-miss sale for under a million to a modern-day behemoth worth over two trillion, Google's trajectory is the very embodiment of valuation's dramatic power: tiny beginnings, enormous outcomes.

*

When asked about the failed sale years later, Larry Page allowed himself a small, knowing smile. "They could have had us for less than a million. They passed. And here we are."

It wasn't arrogance. It was destiny speaking.

*

Closing Note

Google started getting over 100 million hits every day the very next year. But revenue did not start pouring in until "Adwords."

After the evolution of Adwords, Google wasn't just a search engine. It transformed into the world's biggest marketplace for attention. Every time someone searched "best running shoes" or "hotel in Jaipur," Google held a mini-auction behind the scenes. Companies placed bids for those magic words. The winner got the top spot.

And each time a user clicked, Google pocketed a few rupees.

It was a simple idea—pay-per-click. But simple ideas, scaled across billions of searches a day, create empires.

The story of Google's almost-sale is not merely about numbers. It is about vision colliding with short-sightedness, about timing and destiny, about how rejection can be the greatest gift of all. In Excite's dismissal lay Google's survival. In failure to value lies the foundation for ultimate value.

*

A company was started with only 112 servers, and now deploys countless servers for swift response. Though there is no reliable recent public record for exactly how many servers

Google has, the latest solid number is from 2016, when analysts at Gartner estimated Google had about 2.5 million servers.

No exact count available… but considering the growth in spending, energy use, and infrastructure, it's almost sure Google has well more than 2.5 million servers now—strategically deployed all across the globe… an astonishing number.

*

Excite experienced a dramatic fall from a top web portal to bankruptcy due to the dot-com bubble burst in 2001, after its merger with @Home failed to make it profitable. Following its demise, its portal and services were sold, eventually acquired by IAC Inc. The company's email service was shut down in 2021.

***

Chapter 8

WeWork—The Office that Pretended to Be Religion

115 West 18th Street, 4th Floor, New York, USA (2010 – 2019)

IPO Over-Valuation ☑ Startup Failure ☑ Investors Frenzy ☑ Cash Burn ☑ Flawed Business Model ☑

> Founded in 2010, WeWork reimagined office spaces as hip, flexible coworking hubs, fuelled by the charisma of founder Adam Neumann and billions from SoftBank. At its peak, it was valued at $47 billion, hailed as the future of work. But lavish spending, a flawed business model, and Neumann's eccentric leadership unravelled the dream. Its 2019 IPO collapsed spectacularly, erasing billions and turning WeWork into a symbol of startup overhype and failed valuations.

The Prophet of Real Estate

New York, 2011

The warehouse smelled of fresh paint and ambition. Two men, Adam Neumann and Miguel McKelvey, stood in what looked like nothing more than a refurbished floor with mismatched furniture.

"Imagine," Adam said, his arms wide like a preacher, "a world where work is not just work. It is community, it is purpose, it is… a movement."

Miguel laughed nervously. "But Adam, we're just renting out desks."

Adam's eyes flashed. "No, Miguel. We are not a real estate company. We are building the future of work. People will worship here. They won't just come for WiFi and coffee—they'll come for belonging."

That was Adam's genius—and his downfall. He could turn the mundane into magic, desks into destiny.

*

The Seduction of Investors

Silicon Valley, 2014

He strode into boardrooms barefoot, spoke of world peace between tequila shots, and pitched office rentals as if they were a path to saving humanity.

Adam Neumann, the six-foot-five Israeli with a messianic charm and a mane of untamed hair, could make billionaires believe in dreams that defied balance sheets. At the height of his empire, WeWork was valued at $47 billion—more than the Ford Motor Company.

But behind the swagger, private jets, and grandiose promises of "elevating the world's consciousness," lay a business bleeding cash. When the illusion shattered, Neumann's fall was as theatrical as his rise—from visionary cult-leader of a startup to cautionary tale of hubris in corporate history.

Inside a plush conference room, Adam paced barefoot, a mess of long hair and confidence. The world's top venture capitalists watched, spellbound.

"WeWork," Adam declared, "is not a company. It's a state of consciousness."

A partner whispered to another, "What the hell does that mean?"

The other replied, "I don't know. But I want in."

And they did. Money flowed like a flood—hundreds of millions, then billions.

*

The HQ of SoftBank Vision Fund

Tokyo Port City Takeshiba Office

Minato-ku, Tokyo, Japan

Masayoshi Son had set up a $100 billion Vision Fund to reshape the future by backing "once-in-a-lifetime" companies. The fund poured billions into ventures like OYO, Katerra, and Greensill, often at valuations untethered to fundamentals.

Masayoshi Son, a man who prided himself on taking big risks, looked at Adam and saw not a founder, but a prophet.

"I want you to be crazier," Masayoshi told him after a 12-minute meeting.

Adam grinned. "Don't worry. I already am."

Masayoshi laughed. "Should I buy you some good shoes?" Adam Neumann's habit of not wearing shoes had become one of his quirks in the corporate world. According to Neumann. it was about comfort and grounding.

Adam waved his hand dismissively. "Don't worry, Masayoshi. I love walking barefoot on broken glass. Let's focus on valuation."

Valuation soared: $10 billion, $20 billion, $47 billion.

But underneath the glamour, the numbers didn't add up. The leases were long-term. The rentals were short-term. The gap was a black hole waiting to swallow billions.

*

The Cult Inside

New York, 2016

WeWork wasn't just an office. It was a lifestyle.

Employees were told they weren't working a job—they were serving a mission. Free beer flowed in hallways, DJs played in lobbies, and "Summer Camp" retreats turned into bacchanalian festivals with fireworks and tequila.

Adam strutted on stage like a rock star. "We are not just here to make money. We are here to elevate the world's consciousness!"

Crowds cheered, employees cried, and investors clapped. In the shadows, some whispered: "But… aren't we just subletting real estate?"

The whispers were drowned in music and madness.

*

The Cracks Begin

2018–2019

It started with questions.

Why is Adam cashing out shares while the company bleeds money?

Why is he trademarking the word We and selling it back to his own company for $6 million?

Why are his family members on the payroll?

The boardrooms grew tense. Some executives left. Journalists sharpened their pens.

In hushed tones, analysts warned: "This isn't a business. It's a theatre. And when the curtain falls, it'll be brutal."

*

The IPO Disaster

The $47 Billion Mirage, New York, 2019

The glossy IPO prospectus was meant to be WeWork's coronation. Instead, it was its obituary.

Buried in the pages were wild claims, reckless spending, conflicts of interest, and a single word that repeated like a drumbeat: community.

Wall Street laughed. Analysts tore it apart. Headlines screamed: WeWork Isn't a Tech Company; It's Just a Landlord with Beer!

Investors fled. The $47 billion dream shrank overnight to $8 billion. Adam Neumann, once hailed as a prophet, was pushed out in disgrace. He walked away with a golden parachute while employees packed their desks in silence.

*

The Aftermath

A former employee sat at a café near Times Square, staring at her severance papers.

"We thought we were building the future," she whispered to a friend. "Turns out, we were just decorating offices."

The WeWork sign still glowed on skyscrapers, but the glow was hollow. The movement had collapsed under the weight of its illusions.

*

The Lesson

The WeWork story was more theatre than business, more Shakespearean tragedy than startup story. It is not just about one man's hubris—it's about the collective hypnosis of an entire ecosystem.

Investors wanted a messiah. Adam played the role. Employees wanted meaning. He gave them parties. The market wanted growth. He gave them illusions.

In the end, it was all a theatre of glass walls and free beer. When the music stopped, the only thing left was the rent.

*

Years Later

Adam Neumann, the charismatic founder of WeWork, walked away with his golden parachute, leaving behind disillusioned employees, evicted tenants, and investors counting their losses. His barefoot vision of community was unmasked as nothing more than a costly mirage. A clean slate, Neumann primarily resides in Miami, Florida, following his financial exit from WeWork. Forbes estimates his net worth at around $2.3 billion as of mid-2025.

He's now spearheading Flow, a residential real estate company he founded in 2022. Flow manages thousands of rental units across U.S. cities like Miami, Fort Lauderdale, Atlanta, and Nashville—plus properties in Riyadh, Saudi Arabia. The venture was valued at over $1 billion thanks to a hefty $350 million investment from Andreessen Horowitz.

*

The dream of "elevating the world's consciousness" ended not with thunder, but with a whimper. WeWork, once valued at $47 billion, now exists as a hollow shell of its former self.

The glass towers and chic co-working spaces—once buzzing with kombucha taps and neon slogans—feel eerily empty. The walls that once shouted "Hustle Harder" now stand as silent monuments to hubris.

In New York courtrooms and boardrooms, WeWork became a case study of unchecked ambition, where governance failed, and fantasy masqueraded as valuation. What was once a global movement is now a cautionary tale, taught in MBA classrooms as "How Not to Build a Unicorn."

The legacy of WeWork? Not the stylish offices or the hipster coffee corners, but a bitter reminder that hype is not business, and charisma is not cash flow. What was once a $47-billion unicorn is now a cautionary tale. A tale of how fast the skyscrapers of ambition can collapse when built on clouds.

"Valuations built on illusions eventually collapse under the weight of reality."

***

Chapter 9
Theranos—The Blood That Was Never There

Earlier: Burlingame, Menlo Park

Later: 1701, Page Mill Road, Palo Alto, USA (2004–2009)

Investors' Frenzy ☑ Fraud ☑ Technology Failure ☑ Litigation ☑

> Theranos (founded 2003), led by Elizabeth Holmes, promised to revolutionise healthcare with a device that could run hundreds of tests from just a few drops of blood. Backed by high-profile investors and valued at $9 billion, it became one of Silicon Valley's hottest startups. However, in 2015, investigations revealed that the technology had never worked. By 2018, Theranos had collapsed, and Holmes faced fraud charges—turning the company into one of the most infamous cases of deception in modern business history.

The Golden Child

Stanford, 2003

A nineteen-year-old Elizabeth Holmes walked through the corridors of Stanford like she already owned the future.

Tall, blonde, with a piercing stare, she spoke with an ambition that unsettled even her professors.

"I don't want to complete my degree," she told one of them. "I want to change the world."

The professor raised an eyebrow. "Change the world with what?"

"With a single drop of blood," Elizabeth said. "A revolution that will make lab testing obsolete."

And with that, she left Stanford to start her company.

*

The Secret Room

3rd February, 2005

The glass walls of Theranos's Palo Alto headquarters gleamed under the California sun, but behind one locked office door, another kind of secrecy lived.

At the back of Theranos headquarters, past doors that few dared enter, there was a room where the glass was always tinted, the lights always dimmed. It was here that Holmes would disappear for hours with Ramesh "Sunny" Balwani, her COO and secret lover.

Elizabeth Holmes, in her black turtleneck, ponytailed her hair, her piercing blue eyes fixed not on data but on the man across from her. Sunny Balwani—older, seasoned, and stern—wasn't just the company's COO. He was her confidant, her lover, and her emotional shield.

"Happy birthday, Eliza," Balwani said, "you turned 21 with such grace, glamour… and talent."

"Thank you, Sunny," she smiled mischievously. "You, too, have hidden talents, I must say."

"And what are those?" Sunny asked.

"How do I know! They are hidden."

Both burst out laughing.

She leaned into him, her breath warm against his cheek, letting the silence stretch like a taut string. For a fleeting second, he thought she had surrendered—then, with deliberate slowness, she pushed him away.

Balwani played his part well, lowering his eyes, letting the ache of rejection flicker across his face, the picture of a wounded lover.

She laughed—not the laugh of amusement, but the one that could slice the heart of any man worth his salt.

"Maybe later, Sunny," she whispered, her voice dripping with both promise and denial, the kind of line that could haunt a man for nights.

Few knew of the relationship; it was scrubbed from every investor deck, erased from every public narrative. In the boardroom, they spoke like colleagues; in private, they spoke like co-conspirators. Their bond was the company's most guarded secret, more hidden than the flaws in the Edison machine.

And yet, as the walls of deception grew higher, so did their reliance on each other—a dangerous intimacy that blurred the line between power and passion. In the empire of lies, even love was a liability.

In the boardroom, Balwani was the iron fist, quick to rage, terrifying employees into silence. In that secret room, he was something else—confidant, enabler, conspirator. Together they whispered strategies, smoothed over lies, and tightened their grip on the empire. It was as if the room itself held their shared secret, shielding their forbidden bond from the board and the world outside.

The duo was onto something sinister.

*

Flashback: The Cult of Vision

Palo Alto, 2004–2009

The office was small, but Elizabeth made it feel like a temple.

She wore her signature black turtlenecks, inspired by Steve Jobs. On her desk sat "The Art of War"—her chosen bible. In her mind, she wasn't just building a company; she was rewriting history.

She began lowering her voice to a deep, hypnotic baritone that made every statement sound like prophecy. "Imagine," she told her early employees, "a world where you don't need needles. Just one drop of blood, and you'll know everything about your health. We are saving lives."

Some believed her. Others were sceptical. But the sceptics didn't last long. Elizabeth demanded loyalty, absolute and unquestioned.

"This isn't just a company," she said, staring down her staff. "This is a mission. If you're here for money, leave. If you're here for destiny, stay."

*

The Seduction of Elizabeth Holmes

2010–2014

She moved like a shadow in the bright lights of Silicon Valley. Elizabeth Holmes, with her black turtleneck, deep contrived voice, and unwavering gaze, seemed untouchable. Investors weren't just listening to a pitch; they were being invited into a forbidden promise—the revolution of medicine in a single drop of blood.

Her presence was intoxicating. Senators, generals, billionaires—men and women accustomed to power—leaned in closer, caught in her spell. She didn't offer them evidence, only conviction, and conviction can be far more seductive than facts. Her words wrapped around them like silk, binding them to the Theranos vision.

Theranos grew, quietly at first, then like wildfire. Elizabeth courted powerful men—Henry Kissinger, George Shultz, James

Mattis—men who didn't understand science but understood influence. They sat on her board, lending her legitimacy.

Investors, seduced by her charisma, poured in hundreds of millions.

The valuation soared to $9 billion. Elizabeth was hailed as the next Steve Jobs. She appeared on magazine covers, her ice-blue eyes staring out like a messianic figure.

But inside the labs, engineers whispered the truth:

"The machines don't work."

"The results aren't reliable."

"The data is faked."

Anyone who questioned too loudly was fired or silenced with legal threats.

She was a siren in black.

*

Media Interlude (2014)

Wall Street Journal Headline: "This Woman Will Change Medicine Forever."

Fortune Cover: "The Next Steve Jobs?"

Investor Note: "Theranos has the potential to disrupt a $75B industry. Recommendation: Strong Buy."

*

The Cracks

2015

It began with a whisper in the newsroom.

John Carreyrou, a Wall Street Journal journalist, received a tip: "Theranos isn't what it seems. The machines don't work."

In a dimly lit café, he met a whistleblower—an anxious young lab worker.

"They're lying," the worker said, trembling. "The blood tests—they don't actually run on our machines. They run on modified Siemens machines in the back."

Carreyrou raised an eyebrow. "And the patients?"

"They don't know. Nobody knows. But people's lives are at risk."

*

The Fall

2015–2016

The Journal article hit like a bomb. Headline screamed: *"Hot Startup Theranos Has Struggled with Its Blood-Test Technology."*

Elizabeth walked into the Theranos auditorium the next morning, dressed in her turtleneck, voice deeper than ever.

"They don't understand us," she told her employees. "We are fighting for humanity. The haters can scream, but we will win."

But the walls were closing in. Regulators investigated. Walgreens ended its partnership. Patients sued. The media turned hostile.

Inside the labs, employees cheered quietly. "Finally, the truth is out."

*

The Courtroom (2018–2022)

U.S. District Court, Northern District of California, San Jose, California

The Heart of Silicon Valley

A modern federal courthouse with glass façades, steel lines, and pale stone, designed to appear transparent and open—a sharp contrast to the secrecy of Theranos. The courtroom was designed in a classic federal style: high ceilings, wooden benches, the American flag on one side, and the judge's elevated bench commanded authority.

Inside, the atmosphere was hushed, with long, polished corridors and security checks at every entrance. The weight of history hung in the air; this was the same courthouse that had seen tech battles from Apple vs. Samsung to antitrust fights involving Google. For months, this courthouse was a theatre of deception, ambition, and betrayal. It wasn't just about blood tests anymore; it was about the soul of Silicon Valley.

Rows of lawyers hunched over laptops, their screens glowing in the dim light.

Former Theranos employees and investors testified, their voices sometimes trembling.

Elizabeth Holmes, once hailed as the next Steve Jobs, now sat silent under the cold gaze of Judge Davila. Every gavel strike was not just a call to order—it was the echo of a fallen empire.

The prosecutor's words were sharp: "You promised life-saving technology. Instead, you gave lies. You risked lives for valuation. Wasn't it all a fraud?"

"No," the senior defence lawyer jumped to his feet. "It's just that the technology failed."

Judge Davila looked at the defence lawyer. Outside the court, they were friends. "You think we are fools?"

The senior lawyer made a great show of bowing with respect. "Your honour, you have put me in a very difficult situation. If I say 'yes,' that's contempt; 'no,' that's perjury."

The courtroom burst into laughter.

But Elizabeth wasn't laughing. Avoiding eye contact with jurors, her eyes darted across the courtroom, searching for believers. But the silence was damning.

With decades of experience on the bench, Judge Edward Davila was calm and deliberate. He stared straight into the eyes of Elizabeth.

Reporters became alert in the gallery, hanging on to each word of the Judge.

She was convicted on four counts of fraud. The woman, once worth $4.5 billion, now faced the prospect of years behind bars in a federal women's prison in Bryan, Texas.

*

The Lesson

Theranos was never about science—it was about the power of belief.

Investors wanted to believe in the next Jobs.

Patients wanted to believe in painless healthcare.

Elizabeth wanted to believe in herself so badly that she built a castle out of illusion.

But science is merciless. Technology does not bend to charisma.

And when the curtain lifted, there was no magic—only broken promises and wasted blood. A lie can raise billions, but it cannot heal a single drop of blood.

*

Timeline of Theranos' Failure

Theranos Timeline : Rise and Fall

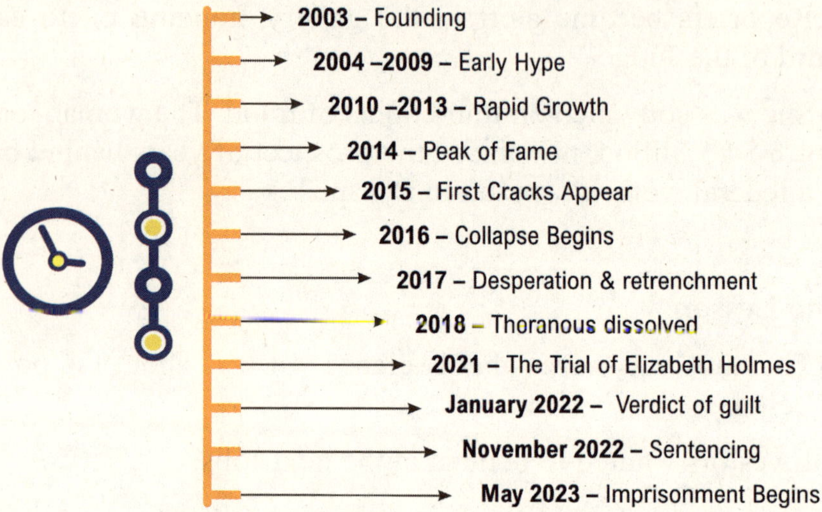

Years Later

Theranos once promised to revolutionise blood testing with a single drop. It raised billions, attracted statesmen and generals to its board, and turned Elizabeth Holmes into the youngest self-made female billionaire in history. But when the science collapsed, so did the myth.

By 2018, Theranos had dissolved, its technology exposed as unworkable. Elizabeth Holmes was convicted in 2022 on four counts of fraud and sentenced to 11 years in prison. Her partner and COO, Sunny Balwani, received a 13-year sentence. Investors lost nearly $1 billion. Patients who relied on faulty tests were left with broken trust.

*

The building at 1701 Page Mill Road that served as Theranos's headquarters was acquired by Kilroy Realty Corp. in early 2017 for around $130 million.

By 2019, Fortress Investment Group, which inherited Theranos's patents and assets following its dissolution, used the building as office and medical lab space. It appears it was repurposed by Stanford University School of Medicine for both administrative and research functions.

*

Today, Theranos survives only as a cautionary tale—a reminder that charisma and storytelling can never substitute for science and substance.

***

Chapter 10
FTX—The Crypto Mirage

Bahamas, 2022. Earlier: Hong Kong, Silicon Valley. Later: Washington, DC.

Fraud ☑ Startup Failure ☑ Money Laundering ☑

> FTX, once hailed as the world's fastest-growing crypto exchange, built by wunderkind Sam Bankman-Fried, promised trust and innovation in a volatile industry. Behind the curtain, however, billions in customer funds were secretly funnelled to sister firm Alameda Research. When the truth surfaced in 2022, the empire imploded almost overnight, erasing $32 billion in value and shaking global confidence in cryptocurrency.

The Cryptic Cryptocurrency

The Bahamas sun blazed outside the glass windows of a sprawling luxury penthouse, but inside, the scene was a strange mix of chaos and genius. Cables snaked across the floor, monitors stacked in uneven rows glowed with charts of coins, arrows, and red-green tickers that danced like casino lights. Empty cans of Diet Coke and crumpled Doritos packets littered the desk.

In the middle of this digital shrine sat Sam Bankman-Fried, hunched in a worn-out gaming chair, his mop of messy hair haloed by the flickering blue light of multiple screens. He wasn't wearing a suit or even shoes—just gym shorts and an oversized T-shirt, his bare feet tapping nervously against the floor. On one screen, billions of dollars' worth of cryptocurrency floated in columns of numbers, shifting by the second.

Sam's fingers flew across the keyboard, his lips moving faster than his thoughts. "It's all safe. We have liquidity. They trust me. They have to." Behind him, the balcony doors stood ajar, letting in the salty Caribbean breeze, almost mocking the suffocating tension of the room.

In the next room, Caroline Ellison, his confidante and head of Alameda Research, scrolled anxiously through spreadsheets of leveraged trades that looked more like a gambler's ledger than financial records. The numbers bled red. She called out hesitantly, "Sam… we can't cover this much longer."

He didn't turn around. His gaze was locked on the flashing screen—billions moving in and out like ocean tides. He adjusted his glasses and whispered to himself, "One more deal. Just one more inflow. They'll never know."

Far away, in homes across the globe, ordinary investors refreshed their FTX apps, believing their savings were safe. They had no idea that in the heart of paradise, inside that messy penthouse, their trust was already slipping into the abyss.

*

Hong Kong

Star Studios I, 8-10 Wing, Fung Street, Wanchai, 2019

The conference hall smelled faintly of coffee and ambition. Bankers in grey suits and developers in hoodies mingled under the neon glow of "Crypto Futures Summit." The expensive chandeliers coruscated with the glitter of the enthusiasm in the eyes of the bankers. Amid the crowd, a young man shuffled awkwardly: messy hair, oversized T-shirt, cargo shorts. He didn't look like a billionaire—or even like someone who had done his laundry in weeks.

This was Sam Bankman-Fried, or SBF, as the crypto world affectionately called him. An MIT grad, former Jane Street trader, and a self-proclaimed adherent of "effective altruism." As of November 2022, FTX was the third-largest digital currency exchange, boasting an active trading volume of US$10 billion and a valuation of $32 billion. Incorporated in Antigua and Barbuda and headquartered in the Bahamas, FTX was closely associated with FTX.US, a separate exchange available to US residents.

SBF spoke quickly, almost too quickly, about arbitrage opportunities, digital asset flows, and building an exchange that would “change finance forever.”

Investors chuckled at his appearance, but listened. Beneath the slouch was a savant. And beneath the savant, as the world would later learn, was something darker.

*

Silicon Valley, 2020

FTX was growing like wildfire. Its sleek app, intuitive for retail traders and powerful for professionals, positioned it as the “Goldman Sachs of crypto.” While Coinbase courted regulation, FTX courted risk. Leveraged tokens, exotic derivatives, and high-stakes bets lured millions.

Sequoia Capital, the legendary VC firm, was smitten. In an internal memo, a partner gushed, “Talking to SBF is like speaking to the future of money.” They invested $213 million after a single Zoom call.

At the same time, Tom Brady and Gisele Bündchen grinned from TV ads, telling America to “trade crypto safely with FTX.” Stadiums were renamed. Politicians posed with SBF. On Capitol Hill, his mop of hair became a familiar silhouette in hearings.

By mid-2021, FTX was valued at $32 billion. SBF, once eating vegan burritos in anonymity, was now hailed as “the J.P. Morgan of crypto.”

*

Nassau, New Providence

Bahamas, 2022

The headquarters didn't look like Wall Street. It was a luxury penthouse in Nassau, filled with bean bags, gaming consoles, and polyamorous entanglements between employees. The staff worked, lived, and partied together, running billions from laptops while overlooking turquoise waters.

Behind the tropical paradise, a hidden relationship festered: FTX and Alameda Research, SBF's trading firm. Money flowed between them in invisible pipes. Customer deposits on FTX were secretly funnelled to Alameda, used for high-risk bets. To the outside world, it was invisible. To insiders, it was "just how Sam wanted it."

When asked why the two entities were so entangled, SBF once mumbled, "Well… it's… complicated."

Complicated was an understatement. It was fraud with a smile.

*

The Collapse

November 2022

It began with a scoop. CoinDesk, a niche crypto news site, published a balance sheet leak showing that Alameda's assets were largely FTT tokens—FTX's own in-house coin. The revelation spread like wildfire. If Alameda's value depended on FTX's token, then the empire was built on vapour.

The crypto world panicked. Binance, a rival exchange, announced it would sell its FTT holdings. The token's price nosedived. Customers rushed to withdraw billions. FTX had no money.

On Twitter, SBF tried to sound calm: "Assets are fine. Withdrawals are fine." But behind closed doors, executives were frantically calling investors, begging for cash. Employees stared at computer screens as numbers went from green to blood red.

Within days, $8 billion had vanished. The once-mighty exchange filed for bankruptcy.

*

Washington, DC, Aftermath

In Congress, lawmakers who once praised SBF now refer to him as a criminal mastermind. Regulators raced to investigate. Celebrities scrubbed endorsements. Tom Brady's smile turned into a lawsuit.

When arrested in the Bahamas, SBF looked less like a financial genius and more like a bewildered college kid caught cheating on an exam. He told reporters, "I didn't knowingly commit fraud."

But for the millions who lost savings, that excuse was worth less than the FTT token itself.

*

Lessons from FTX

FTX wasn't just a startup failure; it was just a mirror reflecting the worst of the new financial frontier—a classic case of charisma masking chaos. Venture capitalists blinded by the fear of missing out… Regulation lagging behind innovation… public too eager to believe in miracles.

The FTX collapse showed how quickly digital dreams could evaporate—how billion-dollar empires could be built on little more than trust, and how trust could vanish in 72 hours.

*

Closing Scene

A Parallel in India

As SBF awaited trial in India, another young fintech giant was facing questions, not about crypto, but about whether growth without profit was just another kind of illusion.

The stories were different… the volume of funds involved was different too, but the lesson was always the same: When foundations are built on hype, no castle survives the tide.

*

Years Later

The glass towers in Nassau stand half-empty now, their faded FTX logos like scars on the skyline. What was once a kingdom of billions is now only silence.

In Washington, whispers linger of the donations—millions flowing into campaigns, blue and red alike. Donald Trump, once dismissive of crypto, invoked FTX's collapse in rallies, calling it proof of a rigged system. Yet behind the scenes, some of Sam Bankman-Fried's checks had touched his orbit too.

When the crypto markets have moved on to chase the next wave of speculation… FTX is not just a warning, but also a caution—how quickly trust can vanish, and how loudly innocence can masquerade as innovation.

***

Chapter 11

HDIL: Skyscrapers of Sand

HDIL Towers, Anant Kanekar Marg, Station Road, Bandra East, Mumbai, India

Over-Valuation ☑ Fraud ☑ Litigation ☑ Alleged Money Laundering ☑

> Housing Development and Infrastructure Ltd. (HDIL), once a leading Mumbai real estate developer, rose rapidly on the back of extensive slum rehabilitation and housing projects. However, mounting debts, stalled projects, and alleged financial irregularities led to a crisis. The company's links to the PMC Bank fraud (2019), where massive loans to HDIL went unpaid, exposed the rot. From being valued in thousands of crores, HDIL collapsed into bankruptcy, symbolising the excesses and risks of India's real estate boom.

The Birth of Grandeur

It was the mid-2000s in Mumbai, the city that never sleeps, forever hungry for land. In a candlelit ballroom of a five-star hotel, the Wadhawans unveiled their newest dream.

The miniature skyscraper model glistened under chandeliers; each balcony carved with precision. Rakesh Wadhawan, silver hair brushed back, basked in applause. His son Sarang whispered, "Baba, we're building more than towers—we're building Mumbai's future."

Investors nodded, charmed. Real estate in India was not just booming—it was a gold rush. HDIL (Housing Development and Infrastructure Limited) rode the wave like kings. Their land bank stretched wide, their projects gleamed on glossy brochures.

That night, under champagne fizz and applause, no one imagined the skyscraper was being built on sand.

*

The Bank That Wouldn't Say No

Dreams Mall, L B S Marg, Bhandup West, Mumbai

At Punjab & Maharashtra Cooperative Bank's (PMC) headquarters, the air was thick with worry.

"Another loan?" one director asked hesitantly.

MD Joy Thomas tapped his pen on the mahogany table. "Gentlemen, HDIL has never let us down. They're family."

"But ₹6,500 crore is not small. What if …"

"What if?" Thomas snapped. "Look around this city. Whose name is on half the hoardings? HDIL's. This is temporary. Markets bounce back. We must support them."

And so, loan after loan was sanctioned. Paper trails turned into a web of evergreening accounts, cover-ups, and creative accounting. The bank became less of a lender and more of an accomplice.

*

The Queue of Broken Dreams

September 2019

A PMC Bank branch in the Mumbai suburbs.

Hundreds of depositors banged at the glass doors. Men in sweat-soaked shirts, women with tears in their eyes, pensioners clutching passbooks as if they were their last hope.

"Only one thousand rupees withdrawal," the manager repeated, his face pale, voice breaking.

“Sir, I need to pay hospital bills,” a man cried.

An old woman whispered, “My pension, *beta*. My medicines. How do I live?”

Inside, employees looked away, ashamed. The RBI’s order had turned savers into beggars overnight. And behind every withheld rupee was HDIL’s empire of debt.

*

The Fall

Wadhwan House, Bandra (West), Mumbai

Police jeeps arrived at the Wadhawan residence one humid evening. Sarang opened the door, trying to look calm. Cameras flashed as officers read the charges.

The same hands that once cut red ribbons at mall openings were now handcuffed behind his back. Neighbours peered from balconies, murmuring like spectators at the fall of royalty.

For years, the Wadhawans had been kings of real estate. That night, they became prisoners of their own empire.

*

The Ghost Towers

Months later, across Mumbai, half-finished HDIL towers stood abandoned. Concrete skeletons rose against the skyline, windows gaping like hollow eyes.

A child flew a kite in the shadow of one such tower. His father, once a depositor at PMC, muttered bitterly, “That building ate our savings.”

Billboards still promised “Luxury Living from ₹2 crore onwards.” But the paint peeled, the dreams faded, and stray dogs made homes in unfinished lobbies.

These towers, meant to symbolise prosperity, became monuments of betrayal.

*

The Courtroom Theatre

Special Court—Prevention of Money Laundering Act, 2002

Before the Special PMLA Judge, Greater Mumbai

The bells of the courtroom did not ring—they thudded. The doors groaned open as if to let the whole city lean in. Cameras crowded the corridor like scavenging birds; inside, the Special Court's oak-panelled chamber felt smaller than the scandal that had carried the men there. Morning light cut across the benches in a pale, merciless blade. Dust motes floated through it like questions.

The special judge arrived late, but the room was already in session: whispers gave way to silence, phones slid face down, and the gallery leaned forward as if to catch a single stray word. When the magistrate spoke, the voice filled the room—not loud, only precise—and the air seemed to calibrate itself to the measure of each syllable. Charging documents were read aloud with a monotone that turned figures into verdict; the numbers—crores, clauses, annexures—hung in the air like ornaments of a ruined celebration.

The charge sheet was long: fraud, money laundering, conspiracy. Each count was another nail in HDIL's coffin.

Joy Thomas of PMC sat on the other side, the banker who said "yes" too easily. Now he was just another man in the dock, his legacy shattered.

Rakesh Wadhawan's shoes sounded hollow on the marble as he was led in, shoulders steady, the weight of years and headlines visible in the stoop of his silhouette. Beside him, Sarang's jaw was set so tight it trembled; the youthful sharpness that had once sold towers now read as fatigue. Their lawyers moved like chess masters—calm, deliberate—palms slick with the papers that would decide everything. Across the aisle, a row of prosecutors watched with the patient, thin smile of those who have rehearsed outrage in courtrooms a hundred times.

The drama played out like a slow opera. Prosecutors thundered, defence lawyers pleaded, and the Wadhawans sat stoic, their empire's ruins reflected in their tired eyes.

The charge sheet was long: fraud, money laundering, conspiracy. Each count was another nail in HDIL's coffin.

Every witness took a breath as if under a tide; every angle of the case was prodded with a light that left no shadow untouched. When the bail motions were argued, the lawyers' words collided and sparkled, then settled like ash. For the Wadhwans, the courtroom was no longer a place where deals were struck—it had become a theatre where past deeds waited to be defined by law.

The ceiling fans hummed with a tired persistence, but the courtroom was electric. The long trial had narrowed to this single hour—closing arguments.

The prosecutor rose first. He adjusted his black gown as if to draw strength from it, then stepped into the centre like an actor entering his mark. His voice was clipped, relentless, every word hammering into the silence: "This is not a case of business misfortune. This is betrayal—of banks, of depositors, of trust itself." He wielded figures like weapons: crores siphoned, shell accounts, empty collateral. Each exhibit flashed on the judge's mind like a crime scene photograph. The gallery murmured; the gavel cut them down.

When he finished, there was no applause—only the hollow echo of finality.

Then the defence. Sarang Wadhawan's counsel stood, leaner in presence but sharper in tone. He did not thunder; he carved. "My Lords, speculation has been dressed up as certainty. Risk-taking is not a crime. A downturn is not fraud." He gestured lightly toward the accused—not pleading, not begging, but pointing out men who, in his telling, had built half of Mumbai's skyline. He painted the prosecution's story as convenient hindsight, a tale without proof.

The judge listened without expression, pen scratching notes that betrayed nothing.

And then—silence. The defence sat down, the files closed, the tension hung like a storm that had not yet broken. Both sides had played their last cards. The only sound was the shuffle of the judge's robe as he leaned forward, eyes steady, and said:

"Order reserved."

In that moment, the room exhaled—some in relief, some in fear. Outside, Mumbai's traffic roared on, but inside, destiny had slipped from argument into judgment's hands.

*

Epilogue

Lessons Written in Dust

Though real, the story of HDIL reads like fiction, with flesh and blood, and unravelling emotions, while still retaining its factual essence. It was not just a company. It was a mirage of trust. Investors believed, banks believed, depositors believed. And when it collapsed, it did not take down just a balance sheet—it took down lives.

The towers still stand in Mumbai, but not as homes. They are gravestones of ambition, greed, and misplaced faith.

Skyscrapers of sand. That's all they ever were.

*

Years Later

The Wadhawans, once masters of Mumbai's vertical dreams, now move under a shadow. Rakesh, frail, is allowed home only under police guard; Sarang walks free on bail, but the court orders a fence for each of their journeys. Their wealth—once measured in towers and acres—lies frozen, seized by agencies, auctioned off piece by piece.

Across the city, the carcasses of their empire remain: abandoned skeletons of half-built towers claw at the sky, their hollow windows staring blankly at nothing. Rusted cranes, frozen mid-swing, hang like decaying relics of a lost ambition. Blue tarpaulins flap in the monsoon wind, wrapping silence around promises that will never be fulfilled.

For families who once poured their savings into these projects, the ruins are not abstract—they are daily reminders. Children who should have grown up in promised apartments now pass by the skeletal buildings on their way to rented homes, their parents still fighting cases in consumer courts. In every unfinished corridor lies a story of trust broken, of futures displaced.

The culprits walk in courts, but their ghosts linger in concrete and steel—and in the lives left suspended between foundation and sky.

***

Chapter 12

Enron: The Short-Circuit of the Powerhouse

1400 Smith Street, Houston, 1985

Accounting Fraud ☑ Litigation ☑ Startup Failure ✗ Political Bribe ☑ International Scandal ☑

Enron (founded in 1985) was once America's most admired energy company, praised for innovation in electricity and gas trading. At its peak, it claimed revenues of $100 billion and was hailed as the future of the energy sector. But in 2001, it collapsed spectacularly after revelations of massive accounting fraud and hidden debt. The scandal wiped out thousands of jobs and pensions, destroyed auditor Arthur Andersen, and became a global symbol of corporate deception—forever remembered as "the biggest bankruptcy of its time."

When Power Becomes the Mistress

1600 River Oak Boulevard, Houston, Texas, USA

Crystal chandeliers dripped light over the marble ballroom of River Oaks Country Club. Champagne flutes clinked, the orchestra played softly, and Kenneth Lay moved through the crowd like a statesman rather than a CEO. His tuxedo fit perfectly, his smile was polished, and every socialite in the room seemed to angle their body just slightly in his direction.

Lay thrived in this world of power and charm. He wasn't merely a businessman - he was Houston's patron saint of wealth, philanthropy, and political favour. The whispers followed him, always—about late-night conversations, lingering touches, the indulgences of a man who enjoyed being admired as much as he enjoyed being obeyed.

Drawn to the magnetic blend of authority and soft-spoken Southern courtesy, women in silk gowns leaned closer to him.

He remained unmoved.

The power was his only mistress.

*

A Modest Beginning

1985

The summer heat of Houston pressed against the glass towers when Kenneth Lay walked into his office at Houston Natural Gas. He was genial, smiling, a man who shook hands warmly with both janitors and senators. But behind those gentle eyes, there was something else: ambition.

That year, his company merged with InterNorth to create a little-known pipeline firm—Enron. Most employees shrugged—just another merger in the energy sector. But Lay saw something bigger.

"Why just deliver gas," he mused to a colleague, "when we can trade it?"

Few realised that in that small thought lay the seed of a financial empire—and of the greatest corporate collapse in American history.

*

Enter Skilling

The Prophet of Markets

A few years later, in walks Jeffrey Skilling—brilliant, restless, bursting with theories from his McKinsey consulting days.

Skilling wasn't a man to settle for pipes and gas. He wanted Enron to become the Amazon of energy.

At one meeting, he slammed a hand on the table and declared:

"We don't deliver gas. We deliver ideas. Energy is a commodity, and commodities can be traded. Enron will be the marketplace of the future."

The board stared, sceptical at first. But his confidence was infectious. Soon, Enron transformed itself from a boring pipeline operator into a trading powerhouse.

*

The Smartest Guys in the Room

By the late 1990s, Enron's Houston skyscraper buzzed with energy. Young MBAs in sharp suits sprinted through the trading floors, shouting into phones, chasing deals like predators. Bonuses in six figures were tossed around like confetti.

Employees wore their arrogance proudly. They weren't just smart; they were the smartest guys in the room. Fortune magazine agreed, naming Enron "America's Most Innovative Company" six years in a row.

In the cafeteria, a junior trader once joked, "Here, it doesn't matter if you make money. What matters is if you make numbers."

Everyone laughed. But it wasn't a joke.

*

The Wizard of Finance

Andrew Fastow

If Skilling was the prophet, Andrew Fastow, Enron's CFO, was the wizard. A thin man with sharp features, Fastow spoke the language of finance like poetry.

His office became a laboratory of financial engineering. Special-purpose entities with exotic names: LJM1, LJM2, Raptors, sprang up like mushrooms. Losses were hidden, debts were concealed, and risks were obscured from Enron's balance sheet.

In reality, these partnerships were nothing more than mirrors reflecting smoke. But to Wall Street, Enron looked dazzling. Revenues shot past $100 billion. Its stock price soared.

Investors cheered. Analysts nodded. Politicians smiled.

No one asked too many questions.

*

The Cult of Growth

Inside Enron, fear and ambition ruled. Every year, employees were ranked in a brutal system called "Rank and Yank." The bottom 15% were fired—no excuses, no mercy.

"You make the numbers, or you're out," one manager barked at his team.

This system bred ruthlessness. People bent rules, ignored red flags, and worshipped quarterly earnings. Growth was God. Stock price was religion.

And Lay, Skilling, and Fastow were its high priests.

Perfect. Let's stage Dabhol not just as history, but as a drama—with voices, scenes, and cinematic tension. Think of it as if you're walking inside the story, seeing Enron's hubris and India's caution clash.

*

The Dabhol Gamble (1992–2001)

Behind Closed Doors of a Five-Star Hotel, Mumbai

It was a perfect place for a late-night rendezvous between the power giant's emissaries and the nation's political gatekeepers…

a place to exchange promises of investment, whispers of profit-sharing, or something less noble. The truth would always remain locked behind closed doors, but the shadows might linger.

Curtains were drawn, and the table was littered with coffee cups. Rebecca Mark, Enron's fiery dealmaker, leaned across to an Indian bureaucrat. She knew the hierarchical order of this man. In the smoky lounge of the hotel, she had spotted men in dark suits with firearm bulges on their hips in these odd hours.

"You see," she said, her Texan drawl softened into charm, "India doesn't need to wait decades for electricity. We'll build you the fastest and largest power plant. We'll bring in the fuel, the expertise, the capital. All we need… is the permission."

The bureaucrat hesitated. He knew the tariff was outrageous, the terms skewed. But the promise of billions in foreign investment was intoxicating. A pen scratched across the contract.

Rebecca whispered, "Look, the math is simple. Dabhol can't run on charity. If the plant must survive, the tariffs need to reflect the investment. We're talking not cents… but rupees that matter."

The bureaucrat smiled faintly. "And the people? Already, they grumble. Four rupees a unit, when the state pays barely half for others? You'll have them marching on the streets."

Rebecca leaned back. "Then call it a premium—for reliability, for technology, for power that never fails. Frame it as progress. Frame it as a necessity."

A pause. Papers slid across the table—projected rates, capacity clauses, sovereign guarantees.

Politician's Aide (after a long silence): "We can push this through… but the wheels of government, you know, need oiling. Consider it… facilitation."

Rebecca put the file inside her briefcase. "Done. Just make sure the signatures appear where they should. Dabhol must shine, whatever the cost." Her briefcase looked ordinary, but it contained many clandestine documents at times.

Outside, the monsoon lashed the Arabian Sea, as if nature itself knew the storm that was being scripted.

*

And just like that, in 1993, Enron secured its deal—a Power Purchase Agreement with the state of Maharashtra.

On paper, India had secured its future. In reality, it had mortgaged it.

Dabhol was less about kilowatts and more about influence.

*

The Resistance (1995)

The monsoon clouds rolled heavily over the Konkan coast. Dabhol was a sleepy fishing town; its people were accustomed to the rhythm of the tides, not the rumble of machines. And yet, in the early 1990s, whispers began: An American giant is coming. A plant like no other. Power for millions.

By 1995, the mood had shifted. Across Maharashtra, banners were unfurled.

"Enron Go Back!"

"Power at Golden Prices, People in Darkness!"

Villagers marched through the narrow roads of Ratnagiri. Fishermen, their nets still damp with the morning catch, chanted against the behemoth that had fenced off their coast.

At a rally in Mumbai, Shiv Sena leaders thundered from the stage: "They are selling us our own power at prices ten times higher! This is not an investment. This is exploitation!"

The Maharashtra government caved to the fury. The project was halted.

In Enron's Houston boardroom, the reaction was disbelief. Kenneth Lay, the suave chairman, reportedly frowned and told his executives, "India needs power. They'll come crawling back. Just wait."

Rebecca Mark flew back to Mumbai, her heels clicking against marble floors as she stormed into meetings. Enron wasn't leaving. Not yet.

*

The Comeback

India (1996–1999)

The political winds shifted again. Deals were renegotiated. More promises were made. Enron sweetened the rhetoric, though not the price.

By 1999, Phase I of the Dabhol Power Plant was ready. Its chimneys rose above the Arabian Sea like sentinels of a new age. The turbines roared to life. Electricity crackled into the grid.

For a moment, it felt triumphant. Newspapers hailed it as the "gateway to India's modernisation."

But the bills came due. The Maharashtra State Electricity Board stared at invoices it could never pay. The cost of Dabhol's power was astronomical. The poor state treasury bled, while consumers rioted at rising tariffs.

The dream was unravelling.

*

The Collapse (2001)

In 2001, the payments stopped. Maharashtra State Electricity Board refused to buy Enron's costly power. The gates of Dabhol shut, guarded by silence and security men.

Rebecca Mark had already exited Enron, her empire-building dreams crumbling. In Dabhol, workers who once laboured under

Enron's cranes wandered jobless. The once-proud project was a fortress of rust and concrete.

In December that year, news thundered across the world: Enron had collapsed in the U.S., due to accounting fraud—fake profits. Greed exposed. Houston burned with scandal, and in Dabhol, the sea wind carried the echoes.

The villagers of Ratnagiri looked at the abandoned chimneys and whispered, "We told them. We told them this would end in ashes."

*

The First Visible Cracks

By early 2001, whispers began. Analysts asked: "How exactly does Enron make its money?"

One dared to ask Skilling during a conference call why Enron's financial statements were so opaque. Skilling snapped: "You, sir, are an asshole."

The line made headlines, but investors laughed it off. Surely the genius of Enron didn't need to explain itself to mortals.

But behind closed doors, even employees were growing uneasy. One mid-level accountant confided to a colleague:

"Every day, I ask myself—where is the cash? We show billions in revenue, but I don't see the cash."

Her colleague shrugged. "Don't ask. Just keep working. Or you'll be next on the chopping block."

*

The Fall Begins: Sherron's Memo

August 2001

The summer of 2001 weighed heavily on Houston. Inside Enron's gleaming glass towers, the energy giant was still dazzling Wall Street, its stock price climbing on promises of endless growth. But behind the façade, Sherron Watkins, a Vice President in corporate development, was staring at numbers that refused to add up.

She wasn't part of the inner circle of accountants engineering the complex partnerships, but she knew enough finance to sense danger. Special Purpose Entities—opaque structures with names like Chewco and LJM—were bleeding losses away from Enron's books, hiding billions in debt. What executives hailed as "innovative" accounting looked to her like a house built on air.

Alone in her office, Sherron drafted a memo that would become part of corporate history. The words were blunt, almost brutal: "Enron could implode in a wave of accounting scandals." She compared the company's position to a "house of cards" ready to collapse.

It was not easy. Speaking truth inside Enron was dangerous; careers and reputations had been crushed for less. She knew Ken Lay, the CEO, cherished Enron's image as untouchable. To challenge that narrative was to question the emperor in his own court. Yet Watkins pressed on, delivering her memo directly to Lay.

*

The Boardroom

Failed Appeasement of Sherron Watkins

The mahogany-panelled boardroom of Enron's Houston headquarters was unusually tense that morning. The windows looked out over the skyline, but the mood inside was anything but lofty. Kenneth Lay, the patriarchal chairman, sat at the head of the long, gleaming table, his gold cufflinks catching the light as he adjusted his glasses. Around him were a handful of trusted executives, silent, shifting uncomfortably in their leather chairs.

The heavy door opened, and in walked Sherron Watkins, the quiet, determined vice president whose memo had sent ripples through the executive floor. Her face betrayed no fear, but her heartbeat thudded louder than the clicking of her heels on the marble.

"Sherron," Lay began with a warm, almost fatherly smile, gesturing for her to sit. "We appreciate your… candour."

The word candour hung in the air, heavy, almost mocking. She sat, meeting his gaze firmly.

"I only did what I felt was right for the company," Watkins replied, her voice steady. "Our accounting practices—if they come to light—could destroy everything Enron has built."

Her voice became soft. "I am sitting in the boardroom not to destroy Enron but to save it—to request the consolidation of the fragile foundation before it shatters."

Lay leaned back in his chair, folding his hands. The executives around the table exchanged nervous glances. "You're loyal. I know that. But these are complicated matters. The markets wouldn't understand the creativity of our structures. What you see as risk, Wall Street sees as innovation."

Sherron shook her head. "No, Ken. This isn't innovation. It's deception. And the longer we hide it, the harder the crash will be."

For a moment, the room fell utterly silent—the kind of silence where even the air seemed to pause. Then Lay leaned forward, his tone soft, almost soothing, but edged with warning.

"Sherron, you've built a good career here. Let's not get lost in technicalities. Leave the bigger picture to us. We'll review your concerns… quietly. For now, keep faith in Enron."

Her jaw tightened. She realised then that this wasn't a dialogue; it was an appeasement, a gentle dismissal wrapped in polished charm. She glanced around the table, but saw only lowered eyes. The room was full of men who had already made their choice.

Watkins rose from her chair slowly. "Faith," she said, her voice steady but cold. "Faith won't save us when the truth comes out."

As she walked out, the door closed behind her with a dull thud—the sound of a warning unheeded.

*

The echo of the door shut behind Watkins lingered in the vast, polished room. For a moment, Kenneth Lay sat motionless, his hands steepled beneath his chin. The other executives avoided eye contact, their silence betraying the unease that Watkins' blunt words had stirred.

Finally, Lay broke the quiet, his voice measured, but his eyes sharp.

"She's loyal… but dangerously naïve," he said, almost to himself. Then, turning to the group, "We cannot let paranoia derail the momentum we've built. Wall Street doesn't reward caution—it rewards confidence. Remember that."

Jeff Skilling, always eager to assert his swagger, smirked and leaned back. "Ken, she's overreacting. Everyone on the Street bends numbers. We just do it better. We're smarter. That's why we're Enron."

A few chuckles rippled around the table, though nervous, strained.

CFO Andrew Fastow cleared his throat, fiddling with a stack of papers. "Her concerns are… technically accurate. The SPE structures, the mark-to-market numbers—they could raise eyebrows if the SEC pokes too hard." He paused, sweat collecting at his temple. "But as long as our stock stays strong, no one will care."

Lay fixed his gaze on Fastow, his voice calm, almost paternal. "Exactly. The market believes in us. The analysts worship us.

That is our shield. If we show doubt—even a flicker—we invite ruin."

Another executive muttered, "And if she goes outside?"

Lay's jaw tightened. His genial smile vanished for a fleeting second. "She won't. Watkins knows her future depends on Enron's future. And Enron's future depends on us maintaining the illusion."

The word hung heavy in the air—illusion. None dared repeat it, but all understood it.

Lay rose slowly, straightening his jacket, restoring his grandfatherly composure. "Gentlemen, our job is to keep the dream alive. Leave the worrying to the worriers. Let's give the Street another quarter of magic."

The executives nodded, some reluctantly, others with forced conviction. As they shuffled their papers and gathered their things, the boardroom felt colder, as though the truth Watkins had carried in had been locked out with her departure.

Her warning was filed away; her concerns smothered under layers of denial. Enron continued its parade, Wall Street still dazzled, and analysts still applauded.

Behind the closed doors, Enron's leadership had chosen denial over disclosure, bravado over honesty—and in doing so, sealed their fate.

*

Resignation

A shockwave hit Houston: Skilling was fired."

Employees whispered in hallways. Something was wrong.

By October, Enron announced huge quarterly losses—$618 million—and admitted to wiping out $1.2 billion in shareholder equity. The partnerships Fastow created were finally coming into the light.

Investors panicked. Credit agencies slashed Enron's rating. Banks circled like sharks. The once untouchable empire was bleeding.

On the trading floor, a young employee stared at the falling stock price on his screen:

"Ninety… eighty… seventy… oh God, it's fifty…"

His colleague muttered, "My entire 401(k) is in Enron stock."

They exchanged a hollow look. Silence filled the room.

*

Collapse

December 2, 2001

By December 2001, just four months after the memo of Sharon Watkins, the company imploded in bankruptcy, the largest in American history at the time.

Enron filed for bankruptcy—the largest in U.S. history at that time.

Employees poured out of the Houston towers carrying cardboard boxes—family photos, coffee mugs, diplomas. The air outside was cold, but what chills them more is despair.

A woman whispered to a reporter: "I worked here 15 years. My retirement, my savings, everything was Enron. Now it's gone."

Arthur Andersen, Enron's mighty auditor, began shredding documents in panic. Within months, the venerable accounting firm, once a pillar of trust, collapsed too.

The blast radius of Enron's implosion spread worldwide. Markets trembled. Washington shook. The myth of the "New Economy" lay in ruins.

*

The Reckoning

Trials followed. Fastow, once celebrated, was now vilified.

Sherron Watkins's words resurfaced in hearings; her memo transformed from a private alarm into a public prophecy.

Skilling stood in court, insisting he had never intended to commit fraud, his arrogance finally broken. Lay, the fatherly chairman, died of a heart attack before sentencing—escaping justice, but not infamy.

Kenneth Lay initially wrestled with prosecutor John Hueston, who grappled over Lay's lavish lifestyle. When Hueston asked about his withdrawal of $70 million in cash from Enron the year it slid into bankruptcy, Lay surrendered.

The U.S. government responded with the Sarbanes-Oxley Act of 2002, which tightened corporate governance and held CEOs personally responsible for financial statements.

Enron had become the cautionary tale of a generation.

*

The Ghost of Enron

Years later, in business schools, professors still ask: "What killed Enron?"

Some say greed. Some say arrogance. Some say the failure of auditors, regulators, and analysts who looked away. But perhaps it was simpler. Enron forgot the oldest rule of capitalism: profits must be real, not imaginary.

As one former employee put it: "We thought we were building the future. Turns out, we were just building smoke."

For India, the Dhabol project was a scar—a reminder that, in the glitter of globalisation, one must always read the fine print. Dabhol was more than a failed power plant. It was a parable. A story of boardrooms and villages, of contracts written in haste and protests shouted in the rain. It showed how ambition can be blind, how greed can disguise itself as progress, and how even billion-dollar dreams can sink into the sea.

*

The Legacy

In many business schools, Enron is still being taught as a corporate thriller. It wasn't just a run-of-the-mill corporate failure. It was a cultural one. It revealed how a story—if told with enough conviction—can seduce Wall Street, Washington, and the world.

It showed that when ambition outruns ethics, collapse is inevitable.

And it left behind a question that still haunts boardrooms today:

How many other Enrons are out there, waiting to fall?

*

Power Failure of Enron: Infographic

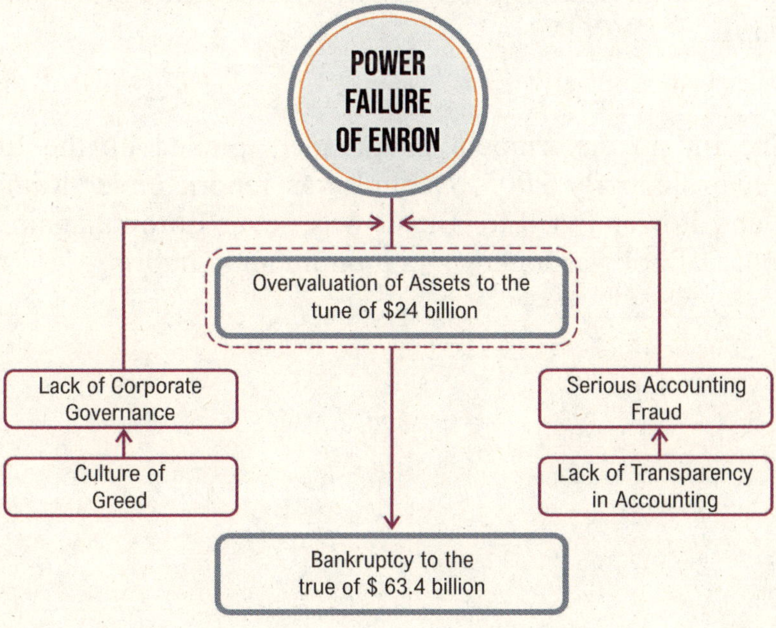

Years Later

The Houston skyline has moved on. New companies light up the towers once branded with Enron's name, their glass façades polished to erase memory. Yet for those who watched the collapse, the reflection still cuts like broken glass.

The accountants are gone, the executives long scattered, but the shadow lingers in every annual report and audit. Wall Street still chases its quarters, still bends its numbers, but always with a flicker of unease.

Enron is no longer a brand, but a ghost haunting balance sheets, a permanent reminder that illusions can glitter brighter than truth.

*

Sherron Watkins, the whistleblower, was named one of *Time* magazine's Persons of the Year (2002), alongside WorldCom's Cynthia Cooper and FBI agent Coleen Rowley, for courage in speaking truth to power. In 2003, she authored a memoir with Mimi Swartz: *POWER FAILURE: The Inside Story of The Collapse of ENRON.*

*

The Indian government and lenders picked up the Enron power project. By 2005, Dabhol was reborn under Ratnagiri Gas and Power Pvt. Ltd. But it was never Enron's again. For Enron, Dabhol was a ghost—a monument to hubris.

***

Chapter 13

The House of Cards—Satyam's Fall from Grace

Madhapur, Hyderabad, Telangana, India

Auditing Fraud ☑ Litigation ☑ Technology Failure ✗ Startup Failure ✗ Deception ☑

> The Satyam scandal (2009) was India's largest corporate fraud, in which founder Ramalinga Raju admitted to inflating revenues, profits, and cash balances by over ₹7,000 crore. Once celebrated as India's fourth-largest IT company, Satyam collapsed overnight, earning the title "India's Enron." The case exposed deep cracks in corporate governance, auditing, and investor trust.

The Jog on Necklace Road

The early morning sun glistened over Hussain Sagar Lake in Hyderabad. On Necklace Road, joggers and walkers traced the curve of the shimmering waters, the air filled with the rhythm of sneakers hitting pavement and the distant honk of buses starting their day.

Among them was a man in his fifties, his face calm yet clouded, his footsteps slower than the others. Ramalinga Raju, founder of Satyam Computer Services, moved with an aristocratic air, but his mind was anything but serene.

To the world, he was the architect of one of India's IT crown jewels, a visionary who had put Hyderabad on the global technology map. To the everyday joggers crossing his path, he was just another man with a determined stride. But inside, he was fighting battles invisible to them all.

He slowed down, his breath heavy, not from exhaustion, but from the weight of deception. Each stride felt like running away from a truth that always managed to catch up.

He looked across the lake where the Buddha statue stood tall, unmoved, timeless. In its silent gaze, Raju felt both judged and comforted.

How much longer can I keep running? he wondered, adjusting his pace. The city around him was waking up to a new day of business, optimism, and opportunity—but for Raju, the dawn carried only shadows.

He stopped, resting his hands on his knees, the sweat trickling down his brow. A black car waited discreetly nearby to take him to the Satyam headquarters. Straightening up, he took a deep breath.

It was time to face the boardroom, as if that alone could solve the storm raging inside him.

*

The Rise of the "Fourth IT Giant" (1987–2000s)

The late 1980s were a time of quiet revolution in India. While politicians debated reforms, a wiry, soft-spoken man named B. Ramalinga Raju sat at a modest office in Hyderabad, drafting a vision.

He named his company Satyam, meaning "truth."

Employees would later joke about the cruel irony of the name, but in those early years, there was nothing ironic about it. Clients signed on, projects rolled in, and Satyam rose. It joined the pantheon of Indian IT giants alongside Infosys, Wipro, and TCS.

At town halls, Raju spoke of integrity, hard work, and India's place in the global economy. Employees clapped. Investors nodded. Hyderabad, then a sleepy tech hub, began calling him the city's own Narayana Murthy.

But in the quiet corridors of power, Raju had already started his other obsession: land.

*

The Shadow of Greed

By the early 2000s, the IT business was thriving, but Raju was restless. Real estate in Andhra Pradesh was booming. His family set up Maytas Infrastructure and Maytas Properties.

During closed-door conversations with confidantes, Raju's tone shifted.

"IT services are stable," he would murmur, "but land... land creates dynasties."

But land required cash—mountains of it. And while Satyam was profitable, it couldn't quench the Raju family's appetite.

That's when the "adjustments" began.

*

Cooking the Books (2001–2008)

It started small. A few inflated invoices here, a few fake entries there. Enough to polish the quarterly reports. The stock climbed, analysts applauded, and Satyam's place in the global IT pecking order grew stronger.

Inside the finance department, however, accountants whispered nervously. "Sir... the deposits don't reconcile."

"Just adjust them," came the order from above.

Soon, the "adjustments" became a parallel empire. By 2008, the company's books showed ₹5,040 crore in non-existent cash.

Fake employees were added to the payroll. Bank statements were forged.

The fraud was so elaborate that even PwC, the auditors, failed to question it.

But as the hole deepened, Raju confessed to a close aide one evening over scotch:

"It's like riding a tiger. I cannot dismount now. The tiger will eat me."

*

The Fatal Misstep

December 16, 2008

The fateful board meeting at Satyam's Hyderabad headquarters was supposed to be routine. Mahogany tables gleamed, directors shuffled papers, and Raju entered calmly, holding a neat folder.

He cleared his throat. "Gentlemen, today I propose a strategic acquisition: Maytas Infrastructure and Maytas Properties."

Some directors raised eyebrows. He continued, voice smooth: "This will diversify Satyam into infrastructure. The deal is worth $1.6 billion."

Silence hung in the room. A director finally asked, "Ramalinga… aren't these companies controlled by your family?"

"Yes," Raju replied evenly, "but this is in the shareholders' interest. A visionary step."

But outside that room, the news sent shockwaves. Shareholders revolted. Within hours, the stock plunged by more than half. Angry calls flooded the board. Independent directors resigned.

The move intended to save Satyam exposed the cracks in its foundation. The mask was slipping.

*

The Confession

January 7, 2009

The boardroom air was heavy with disbelief. After Ramalinga Raju laid down his letter, the directors sat frozen, caught between fury and shock. A secretary rushed in: "Sir… the press is waiting."

Raju nodded slowly. The time for private revelations was over. Now came the public fall.

Minutes later, the glass doors of the conference hall slid open. Flashbulbs exploded. Microphones pushed forward like spears. Raju, flanked by pale-faced executives, walked to the podium. His hands clutched the same letter he had just read to his board.

He cleared his throat. "Ladies and gentlemen… I stand before you with a heavy heart. For years, the financial statements of Satyam Computer Services have not reflected reality. Revenues were overstated. Profits were fabricated. Cash balances were falsified. The gap today stands at more than ₹7,000 crore."

Reporters shouted, "Are you admitting fraud? How long has this gone on? Who else knew?"

Raju's voice wavered but did not falter. "The responsibility is mine alone. No one else in management had prior knowledge. This deception began as a small adjustment, a temporary measure, but it grew until it consumed everything. It was like riding a tiger—every day I hoped to dismount, but the fear of being devoured kept me on."

The line hung in the air. The room erupted with frantic typing, camera flashes, and whispered disbelief.

Behind him, his executives stared down at the floor, unwilling to meet the press or the founder's eyes.

Raju folded the letter, placed it on the podium, and stepped back. "I am sorry," he said. "Satyam was my dream. Today, I confess, it has become my greatest failure."

The conference hall thundered with questions, but he spoke no more. Security guided him away as the headlines were already being written:

"India's Enron: Satyam Founder Admits ₹7,000 Crore Fraud."

*

Panic engulfed Dalal Street. Employees huddled in cafeterias, staring at television screens in disbelief. One young engineer whispered,

"My father bought Satyam shares for my marriage fund... It's all gone."

The stock collapsed 78% in minutes. A company once hailed as a jewel was now branded India's Enron.

*

The Fallout

Kiran Karnik Takes Over

The Indian government acted with urgency. Satyam's board was dissolved overnight. A new interim board was formed, led by respected figures like Kiran Karnik.

Investigators swarmed Hyderabad. CBI, SEBI, SFIO—all hunting for evidence. PwC, the auditor, was ridiculed worldwide.

Raju was arrested, along with his brother Rama Raju and CFO Vadlamani. Cameras flashed as the once-revered founder was led into custody, head bowed.

In homes across India, trust in corporate governance was shattered. For many, the word "Satyam"—once synonymous with truth—became shorthand for betrayal.

*

Resurrection of a Fallen Giant

The Company Survived, the Name did not

But unlike Enron, Satyam was too large to be liquidated. Clients worldwide depended on it.

In April 2009, the government auctioned the company. Tech Mahindra emerged as the winner, paying ₹2,900 crore. Slowly, the rebranded Mahindra Satyam regained stability before merging fully into Tech Mahindra in 2013.

The company survived. Its name did not.

*

The Verdict (2015)

India is a country known for delayed justice. After a marathon trial, on April 9, 2015, a Hyderabad court sentenced Raju and nine others to seven years in prison.

The courtrooms were packed. Investors sat shoulder-to-shoulder with journalists. When the verdict was read, a survivor of the fraud muttered, "Seven years? He stole seven thousand crores. Where is justice?"

*

Epilogue

Lessons from the Tiger

Satyam was not merely an accounting fraud. It was the collapse of faith.

Faith in numbers, in boards, in auditors, in the word trust. It showed how unchecked ambition can mutate into deception, and how silence in boardrooms can be as dangerous as fraud itself.

Today, the glass towers of Satyam still glisten in Hyderabad, now bearing Tech Mahindra's name. They stand as reminders that empires built on lies eventually crumble, no matter how tall they rise.

And in the echoes of Raju's own words—"riding a tiger"—lies the simplest, starkest lesson of all: *"Once you begin to feed a lie, the lie soon begins to feed on you."*

*

Rise and Fall of Satyam

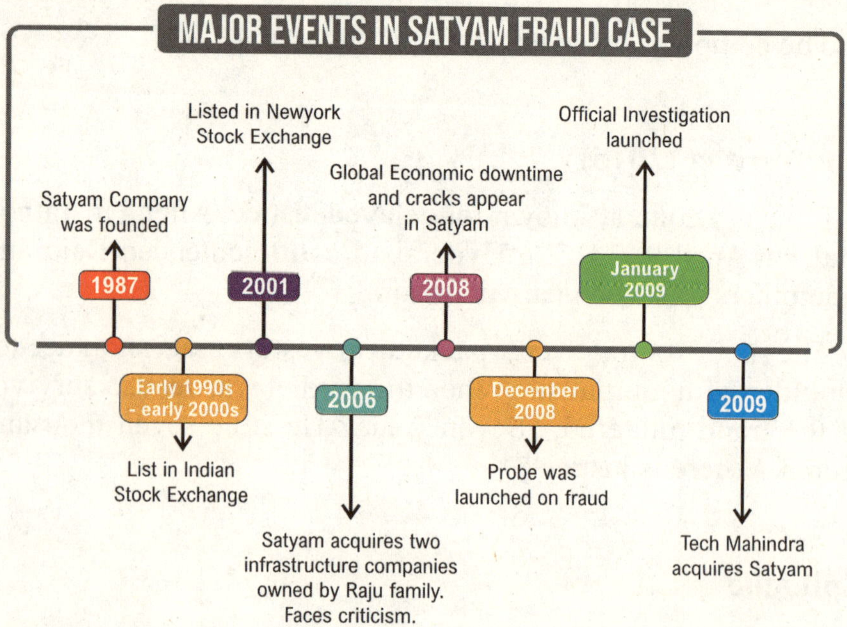

Years Later

Tech Mahindra stepped in, salvaging what could be saved, rebuilding trust brick by brick. But history has a memory longer than the markets. In the DNA of Indian boardrooms, the word Satyam lingers—not as software, not as innovation, but as a parable of ambition corroded by deceit.

The Satyam towers no longer carry the name. Fresh logos gleam across Hyderabad's skyline, and the campus hums with new employees who may scarcely recall the scandal. Yet, in every discussion of corporate governance in India, the shadow of Satyam still drifts through the room.

It was not merely a balance sheet fraud. It was a betrayal of India's global ambition—a reminder that even the country's most celebrated companies could be hollow at the core. Investors lost fortunes, employees carried the stigma, and regulators were forced to confront uncomfortable truths.

*

After being convicted in 2015 for the Satyam fraud, Raju was granted bail and has since maintained a very low public profile. He continues to guide and mentor family ventures behind the scenes. He is linked to a Hyderabad-based IT firm, Brane Enterprises (formerly Fractal Enterprises), where he is referred to as a "mentor." He's not overtly named, but reportedly holds influence—even conducting periodic "mentoring sessions" for employees.

His family remains active in real estate and healthcare. Ventures like CallHealth, promoted by his daughter-in-law, Sandhya Raju, continue to operate—though he maintains no official position in them.

The Enforcement Directorate has attached around 4,000 acres of land belonging to Raju and his family, citing links to proceeds from the Satyam scam. This includes properties in Ranga Reddy district, while their Hyderabad residence remains under legal seizure.

Raju now lives a reserved life, primarily confined to his home in Hyderabad, attending societal functions sparingly and devoting much of his energy to ongoing legal paperwork and family business affairs. His health has reportedly been fragile.

***

Chapter 14

The Subprime Mortgage: The Promise of the American Dream

Calabasas, California, USA

Over Valuation ☑ Bankruptcy ☑ Bubble Burst ☑

> The Subprime Mortgage Crisis (2007–2008) began when U.S. banks flooded the market with risky home loans to borrowers with poor credit, packaging them into complex securities sold worldwide. When housing prices collapsed, defaults surged, triggering a chain reaction that wiped out trillions in wealth, bankrupted major financial institutions like Lehman Brothers, and ignited the global financial crisis.

The Bubble That Was About to Burst

The summer sun glinted over rows of identical suburban houses, each one painted in optimism. A young couple, barely out of college, sat across a mortgage broker's desk. He slid the papers forward with a grin too broad to be trusted.

"Don't worry about the details," he said. "House prices only go up. Sign here, and your dream begins today."

They signed. Somewhere in that moment, the first crack of disaster echoed—though no one heard it yet.

*

Wall Street's Alchemy

High above Manhattan, in towers of glass that kissed the clouds, traders laughed over champagne. On their screens, fragile mortgages from middle America were bundled, sliced, and reborn as "triple-A" magic.

"It's like turning lead into gold," one banker said, tapping his glass. They believed they had outsmarted the laws of risk itself.

In the vaults below, greed hummed louder than reason.

*

Cracks in the Foundation

The laughter turned hollow in 2006. On the same street where children once rode bicycles, foreclosure signs sprouted like weeds. Adjustable-rate mortgages reset, and families who had been promised heaven now stared into hell.

A father tore open the envelope: the new payment was double. His hands trembled. His wife wept in the kitchen. The American Dream had just sent them an eviction notice.

*

The Collapse Begins

On Wall Street, September 15, 2008, the morning began with silence. At Lehman Brothers' headquarters, employees carried cardboard boxes, their careers collapsing into dust.

Traders stared at screens glowing red. Numbers plummeted so fast that even seasoned veterans muttered prayers. A billion vanished here, another there. The market wasn't falling anymore—it was in free fall.

The empire of illusions had finally met gravity.

*

A Global Contagion

In London, bankers stormed out of offices clutching their belongings. In Iceland, a nation watched as its entire banking system drowned overnight. In China, factory gates were locked, and workers dismissed without warning.

The world was choking on America's toxic mortgages. The disease of greed had spread, and no continent was immune.

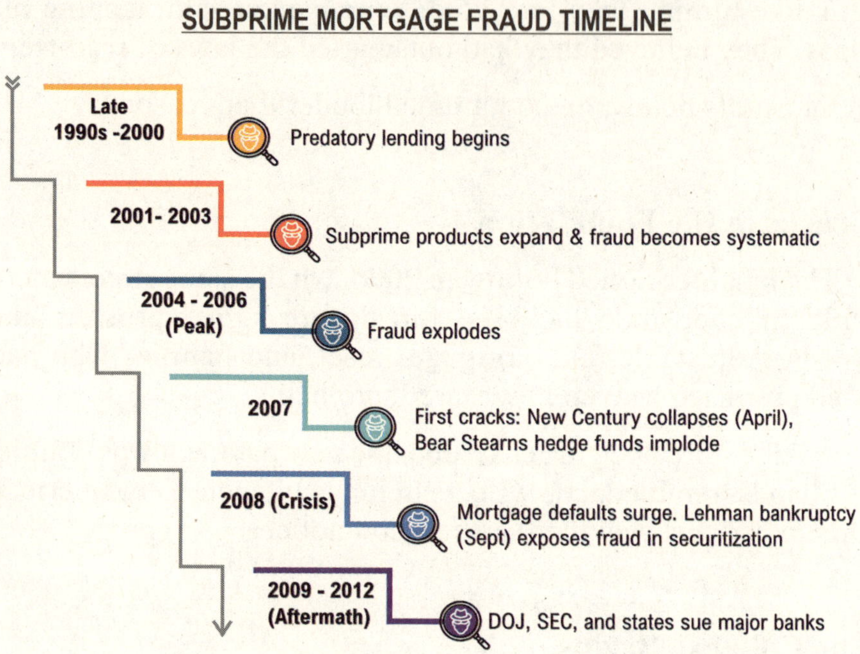

The Government Steps In

Washington, D.C.

The air was thick with anger. Senators shouted. Protesters outside roared: "They bailed out Wall Street—but who will bail out Main Street?"

Yet the ink dried anyway. Trillions were unleashed to save the very banks that had gambled with lives. Justice was absent; survival had taken its seat.

*

The Aftermath—Lessons in Hubris

Years later, empty homes still stood like skeletons across America's suburbs. Families never returned. Dreams once mortgaged were now ashes.

The crisis left a scar deeper than numbers—it left mistrust. A generation learned that when greed dresses up as innovation, it can topple the world.

And still, somewhere in the glittering towers, another scheme was already being born.

*

Years Later

The ruins of 2008 never truly disappeared; they were paved over, landscaped, and repackaged as progress. Shiny new condos now rise where foreclosed homes once stood, boarded and silent. The bankers returned to their bonuses, regulators returned to their revolving doors, and the world moved on—or at least pretended to.

But memory has a way of seeping through balance sheets. For the families who lost homes, the children who watched moving vans carry away their lives, the word subprime is not jargon. It is a wound.

In Washington, the hearings faded into archives, and the grand promises of "never again" softened with time. In Wall Street boardrooms, however, the mood was different: lessons were filed, not learned. Risk, like a stubborn weed, grew back in new forms - private credit funds, fintech lending, algorithmic trading. The names changed, but the appetite remained the same.

Even now, investors whisper about "the next bubble." Is it student debt? Is it shadow banking? Is it crypto? They never ask if—only when.

The subprime mortgage crisis endures as a ghost in the global financial system. Every rally carries a flicker of doubt, every crash a reminder of fragility. And in quiet conversations among old traders, one phrase returns with chilling certainty: "It will happen again. The only question is how."

*

Chapter 15

The Bitter Brew: Starbucks' Valuation Misfire

Seattle, Washington, USA

Fraud ✗ Over Expansion ☑

> Starbucks, the global coffeehouse chain, faced severe setbacks during the 2008 financial crisis, with plummeting sales and store closures worldwide. Many analysts predicted its decline, calling it a victim of overexpansion and waning consumer demand. Yet, through bold restructuring, renewed focus on quality, and digital innovation, Starbucks staged a dramatic comeback, reasserting itself as the undisputed global leader in coffee culture.

The Burnt Brew

There was a time when Starbucks was more than coffee. It was culture. It was an aspiration. It was the warm glow of an inviting café on a cold morning, the place where laptops hummed, friendships blossomed, and a simple paper cup bore the weight of status. The green siren logo was no longer a brand; it was a lifestyle.

By the early 2000s, Starbucks had become unstoppable. Stores mushroomed across continents, not just in big cities but in small towns, airports, train stations—even inside bookstores and grocery aisles. Wall Street cheered the growth, analysts forecasted limitless expansion, and the aroma of rising stock prices intoxicated investors. The valuation soared, and Schultz's empire seemed immune to the laws of gravity.

But in its race to conquer every street corner, Starbucks forgot the soul of its own brew.

*

The Quiet Shift

Inside a store in Chicago, a longtime customer frowned as a barista handed over a latte. The coffee was hot, yes, but it lacked the aroma of freshly ground beans. Why? Because in the quest for efficiency, Starbucks had started pre-grinding coffee. What once was a ritual of freshness had become the dull buzz of industrial routine.

At another store in California, customers noticed the machines towering over counters, blocking the baristas' smiles. The theatre of coffee-makingthe hiss of steam, the artistry of pouring—was gone. Starbucks had become efficient, yes, but sterile.

Somewhere, between cost-cutting and expansion, the magic had vanished.

*

The Overstretch

By 2007, the empire had grown obese. More than 13,000 stores dotted the map. In some neighbourhoods, you could stand in one Starbucks and see another across the street. Real estate became reckless—any vacant lot was a potential store, any city a battleground.

But the crash came swiftly. The 2008 financial crisis struck like a cold winter storm, and suddenly, people who once paid $4 for a cappuccino now chose cheaper alternatives. Disposable incomes shrank. Foot traffic dropped. Investors panicked.

By 2008, Starbucks announced the closure of over 600 stores in the U.S. alone—the first real admission that the dream had overexpanded. The stock, once flying high, tumbled nearly 50%.

*

The Return of Schultz

Howard Schultz, the founder who had stepped aside, returned in 2008 to rescue his creation. The scene was almost Shakespearean: the fallen king reclaiming his throne amidst fire and ruin. He confessed in boardrooms, "We lost sight of our core."

Schultz ordered sweeping reforms. Stores closed. New strategies were written. The company relearned the art of coffee, retrained its baristas, redesigned its stores, and embraced the digital future with mobile apps and loyalty programs.

Yet the return was not immediate glory—it was survival, a slow rebuilding, like nursing a burnt brew back into something drinkable.

*

The Stock Market Trial

Analysts turned Starbucks into a courtroom case. Charts projected in financial conferences showed the fall in valuation, the evaporation of billions in shareholder wealth. "Was it greed?" one questioned. "Was it hubris?" asked another.

The answer, as always, lay somewhere in between. Starbucks wasn't killed by competition alone—its own ambition wounded it. The myth of infinite growth had blinded it.

*

Years Later

Years later, the phoenix rose again from ashes. Starbucks stock rebounded, its stores regained relevance, and China emerged as its biggest bet. But even in triumph, the scars remained. Investors still whispered about the 2008 collapse, and Schultz himself admitted: "We became everything we swore we'd never be."

The world moved on from the crisis, but Starbucks endured. By the mid-2010s, the green mermaid once again shimmered across skylines from New York to Shanghai. Yet the aura was different now—less of a conquering empire, more of a weathered veteran that had tasted defeat and clawed its way back.

Jim Donald, CEO 2005–2008, after being ousted from Starbucks, went on to lead several other companies, including Extended Stay Hotels and Haggen grocery stores. In 2018, he briefly became CEO of Albertsons Companies (a big U.S. supermarket chain). He's now semi-retired but still active as a business advisor.

Howard Schultz, greyer and slower, stood on stages not with the bravado of a visionary but with the humility of a survivor. "We lost our way," he admitted in interviews, a rare confession among corporate titans, where failure is often disguised as "temporary turbulence." His honesty became part of Starbucks' redemption arc.

In China, new Starbucks Reserve stores gleamed like temples of coffee culture, while in the U.S., mobile orders buzzed through smartphones faster than the hum of espresso machines. The stock rebounded, investors returned, and Starbucks was once again hailed as a "case study in resurrection."

But if you looked closely—past the glossy annual reports and aromatic brews—there lingered a faint scar—the memory of shuttered stores, of baristas laid off, of valuations that once mocked reality. Starbucks had survived, yes. It had even thrived. But like a strong cup of coffee, its story carried a bittersweet aftertaste: a reminder that even the most celebrated brands are one crisis away from collapse.

Now, Starbucks is being run by Laxman Narasimhan, the current CEO. He is originally from India. Previously led Reckitt Benckiser (consumer goods) and worked at PepsiCo. Based in Seattle, he is focused on stabilising Starbucks amid union disputes and global expansion challenges.

This saga reminds us: a brand can conquer the world, but if it forgets its essence, it risks losing everything. Starbucks today stands not just as a coffee chain but as a parable—that ambition without restraint is bitter, but resilience, if brewed right, can still taste sweet.

***

Chapter 16

Waste Management Inc.—The Empire of Trash

800 Capital Street, Houston, Texas, USA

Overvaluation ☑ Accounting Fraud ☑ Startup Failure ✗

> The Waste Management accounting scandal (1998) involved the company's top executives inflating profits by $1.7 billion through deceptive bookkeeping. Led by CEO Dean Buntrock and later exposed under successor Maurice Myers, the fraud misled investors for years and became one of the largest accounting scandals of its time. The case ended in massive shareholder lawsuits and SEC penalties, cementing Waste Management as a cautionary tale of corporate deception.

The Garbage of Spreadsheets

The irony was hard to miss. Waste Management, the company that hauled away America's garbage, had hidden its own financial trash in the neat columns of accounting spreadsheets. And for years, no one noticed.

The company's Houston headquarters, with its bland corporate façade and manicured lawns, looked ordinary—almost too ordinary for a firm that handled the messiness of millions of households. But behind its beige walls, a corporate drama unfolded that would rival the stench of any landfill.

*

The Illusion of Growth

In the late 1990s, Waste Management's boardroom smelled faintly of cigar smoke and ambition. Dean Buntrock, the founder and chairman, sat at the head of the table. He was old-school, a man who had built his empire truck by truck, landfill by landfill.

"We're the backbone of America," he told his executives, slamming a palm on the polished table. "Trash doesn't stop. Recessions, wars, elections—people will always need us. And Wall Street needs to see growth. We don't disappoint."

The CFO, James Koenig, shifted in his chair. "We've pushed depreciation schedules as far as they can go," he said cautiously. "The numbers don't lie. Landfills are filling up faster, equipment is ageing, and recycling isn't yielding the returns we projected."

Buntrock's eyes narrowed. "Numbers don't lie, but accountants can adjust them. Extend asset lives. Capitalise expenses. Smooth the earnings. No one looks too closely at a garbage company. We're invisible. Use that."

The room fell quiet. Invisible. That was the word.

*

The Accounting Trick

What followed was an elaborate game of financial smoke and mirrors. Garbage trucks that should have been written down as scrap metal were kept on the books as if they were brand new. Landfills, whose useful lives were nearing expiration, were magically extended in the ledgers. Costs that should have been reflected in the bottom line were buried under "capital improvements."

Every quarter, the executives presented glossy reports, growth curves pointing skyward. Analysts applauded. Investors cheered. Waste Management looked unstoppable—an empire built on trash, now gilded with gold.

But deep inside the accounting department, whispers grew. Junior accountants stared at numbers that didn't add up. "How can this truck still be worth millions when it's rusting in the yard?" one asked quietly. The response came with a glare: "Do you want a career here or not?"

*

The Reckoning

Maurice Myers—The Reluctant Cleaner

The illusion lasted until 1997, when the truth became too large to bury. When A. Maurice Myers walked into Waste Management's headquarters in 1997 as the new CEO, he wasn't expecting to play detective. A seasoned executive with a reputation for discipline, Myers had been hired to steer the giant through a turbulent market.

He opened the books and recoiled.

What he discovered instead was a corporation built on a landfill of lies.

The books looked too neat, too polished for a company in such a volatile industry. Trucks were depreciating at impossibly slow rates. Assets appeared on paper long after their usefulness had ended in reality. Revenue sparkled with an unnatural shine. Myers's instincts told him that Waste Management's empire had been dressed up for Wall Street's eyes.

He pushed deeper, and what unravelled was staggering: more than $1.7 billion in inflated earnings spanning years. The fraud wasn't a small accounting trick; it was systemic, crafted at the very top by founder Dean Buntrock and his circle of loyal executives. They had stretched numbers, manipulated depreciation, and bent accounting rules to keep profits climbing.

For Myers, the decision was brutal, but clear. In 1998, he announced a massive restatement, admitting to the deception and shattering investor confidence. Waste Management's market value plunged by billions overnight. Shareholders filed lawsuits, the SEC intervened, and the company's glossy reputation deteriorated in the public eye.

Myers became both villain and saviour. To investors, he was the bearer of bad news, the man whose leadership began with catastrophe. Yet history remembers him differently: the executive who dared to face the rot, rather than bury it deeper.

Ironically, Myers himself would later resign in 2004 under a cloud of unrelated allegations about personal misconduct at the company. But his role in pulling back the curtain on Waste Management's grand illusion remains an indelible part of corporate history. Without Myers, the scandal might have remained hidden, festering until the collapse became too big to contain.

What he found was staggering.

Over $1.7 billion in overstated earnings.

Asset lives inflated like balloons.

Expenses treated as investments.

In one dramatic board meeting, Myers laid the evidence on the table. "This isn't creative accounting," he thundered. "This is fraud. We've been selling garbage to Wall Street—and now it's rotting."

The silence was suffocating. Faces turned pale. Dean Buntrock avoided eye contact, staring instead at a spot on the mahogany table.

When the news broke, the market erupted. Shares plummeted. The SEC descended. Waste Management became a headline, not for its trucks or landfills, but for orchestrating the largest accounting scandal in U.S. history at the time.

*

The Courtroom

The federal courtroom in Chicago was packed. Rows of reporters scribbled in notebooks as the defendants filed in: Buntrock, Koenig, and other executives who had once ruled the empire of trash. Now they looked smaller, diminished, their power stripped by subpoenas and indictments.

The prosecutor rose, voice echoing against the wood-panelled walls: “Ladies and gentlemen, Waste Management promised Wall Street growth. But growth was an illusion—fabricated by false numbers, hidden liabilities, and deliberate lies. Trucks that belonged in junkyards were treated as assets. Landfills that were overflowing were given longer lives. They built an empire on deception.”

The defence lawyer countered, his tone smooth, rehearsed. “These men didn’t steal a dime. They worked tirelessly to keep the company afloat in a competitive industry. Accounting is interpretation, not an exact science. Were mistakes made? Perhaps. But fraud? No.”

The jury watched as evidence was projected onto screens: falsified depreciation schedules, emails instructing accountants to “find earnings,” memos demanding “smooth numbers at any cost.” The paper trail was damning.

In a quiet moment, Buntrock was asked directly: “Did you order these adjustments?”

He hesitated, his voice barely audible. “We wanted to protect the company. Wall Street doesn’t forgive weakness.”

The courtroom held its breath. Protecting the company—or protecting themselves?

*

The Fallout

Waste Management was forced to restate its earnings by nearly $2 billion. The executives settled with the SEC, paying hefty fines, though none served prison time. Investors lost billions. The name that once stood for steady, unglamorous reliability now carried the taint of scandal.

The boardroom, once a place of bravado, had become a cautionary tale. "Garbage," an SEC official remarked, "is hard to hide. Even in the books."

*

Years Later

The company survived. Rebranded and reorganised, it leaned into environmental sustainability, recycling, and renewable energy. Its green trucks still rumble down American streets, hauling away yesterday's refuse.

But in the annals of corporate history, the Waste Management scandal endures as a reminder: even garbage leaves a trail. And when it's hidden too long, the stench will eventually reach the courtroom.

***

Chapter 17
The WorldCom Collapse—When Valuation Ignores Reality

Ashburn, Virginia, USA

Accounting Fraud ☑ Litigation ☑ Startup Failure ✗

Once the second-largest long-distance telecom company in the U.S., WorldCom collapsed in 2002 after revelations of a $11 billion accounting fraud—one of the biggest in corporate history. The scandal led to bankruptcy, massive investor losses, and the downfall of CEO Bernard Ebbers, making WorldCom a defining case of deception and inflated valuations.

Many Years Ago

Alberta

In the quiet farming town of Edmonton, a lanky boy delivered newspapers at dawn, his breath visible in the freezing Canadian air. The son of a travelling salesman and a devout family, Bernard grew up with little money and even less certainty. He worked odd jobs, scraped through school, and found solace only on the basketball court, where his height gave him the confidence life otherwise denied him.

But deep inside, young Bernie nursed a fire—a gnawing determination that one day, he would never be small, poor, or overlooked again.

*

A Tower of Numbers

The Office of the CEO

The ticker glowed in the corner of Bernard Ebbers' office, red and green digits flickering like a heartbeat. WorldCom's stock—his empire, his lifeline—was slipping again.

Bernard leaned back in his leather chair, cowboy boots propped on the desk, staring at a framed photograph of his sprawling Canadian ranch. Horses galloped across the fields in frozen perfection. He sighed. Those fields were mortgaged, just like his hockey team, just like everything else he owned.

He slammed his fist on the table, cowboy ring clinking against the polished wood: *As long as the stock holds, it all holds.*

Down the hall, the boardroom was tense. Executives whispered about rising line costs, declining revenues, and the cracks widening in the telecom giant's glittering façade.

Sullivan, the CFO, stepped in—tall, commanding, radiating a preacher's confidence.

Ebbers snapped to attention.

The CFO slid a folder across the table. Inside, in red ink: "Line Cost Adjustments—Proposed."

A hush fell—adjustments—a polite word for a dangerous game.

Bernard's eyes lingered on the folder. "Great! Wall Street wants growth, and we'll give it to them. Don't let the stock fall. No excuses!"

Behind his calm smile, the truth gnawed: *if the stock price fell, the loans would be called, and his empire—the ranches, the hockey team, the one he had built from dust—would vanish overnight.*

Outside, the ticker kept pulsing, oblivious to the storm that was about to engulf WorldCom—and the man who refused to face his own limits.

*

The Rise

In the late 1990s, America's corporate sky was lit with the glow of telecom revolutions. Fibre optic cables crisscrossed the nation like arteries of a new economy. At the centre of it all stood WorldCom, a Mississippi-based telecom that grew from obscurity to dominance, swallowing competitors in billion-dollar acquisitions.

The stock soared, analysts cheered, and Wall Street crowned CEO Bernard Ebbers as the cowboy-turned-telecom-king.

Peak Valuation: Over $180 billion market cap

Employees: More than 80,000 worldwide

Claim: The largest provider of long-distance telecom services in America

But as the dot-com bubble burst, the tide began to recede. And what it revealed was more sinister than anyone had imagined. The WorldCom collapse was one of the most dramatic valuation and accounting scandals in history, second only to Enron in its infamy… the sheer collapse of trust.

*

The First Cracks

WorldCom's revenues were flattening. The once sky-high ARPU (Average Revenue Per User) began to slip. Competitors like AT&T and Sprint slashed prices, and demand projections collapsed.

By early 2001, analysts were pressing: "Where is the revenue growth?"

"Why does your capex not align with cash flow?"

"Why are your margins out of sync with peers?"

Inside WorldCom, CFO Scott Sullivan faced the impossible task: report declining earnings, or find a way to "massage" them. He chose the latter.

*

The Boardroom

The mahogany-panelled boardroom at WorldCom's Clinton, Mississippi headquarters was tense. Spreadsheets projected on the wall glowed with numbers that did not add up.

The CFO cleared his throat: "Ladies and gentlemen, if we expense our line costs—the payments to third-party telecom networks—our EBITDA margin drops below 20%. Wall Street expects 30%. Our share price will collapse."

An auditor from Arthur Andersen shifted uncomfortably: "But line costs are operating expenses. Capitalising them on the balance sheet as investments… that's not GAAP. You're turning expenses into assets."

Sullivan's voice hardened: "Wall Street rewards EBITDA. Investors don't care about the accounting nuance. They care about growth. We'll spread these costs over the years. By capitalising, we preserve EBITDA. Our EV/EBITDA multiple stays attractive, and our stock holds."

The room fell silent.

Bernard Ebbers, leaning back, his eyes fixed on the table, finally spoke: "I built this company on acquisitions. If our stock collapses, our entire strategy unravels. Do it. Make the numbers work."

A mid-level finance manager, visibly uneasy, whispered: "But sir… this is billions in misclassification. If the auditors dig —"

Ebbers cut him short. "No auditor will dig if we don't invite them to. This is about survival. About valuation. About keeping the Street on our side."

The order was sealed.

*

The Mirage

Over the next five quarters, WorldCom quietly capitalised over $3.8 billion in line costs, transforming losses into profits.

Reported EBITDA margins: 30%+

Actual margins: barely 15%

DCF models analysts ran showed healthy free cash flows, but the cash was an illusion.

Price target upgrades kept coming; the Street was fooled.

Employees received congratulatory emails. Investors bought more stock. Analysts wrote glowing notes: "WorldCom remains undervalued at 12x EBITDA compared to AT&T at 15x."

But in the quiet corners of the finance department, unease grew. The spreadsheets told a story of fraud.

*

Cynthia's Watch

June, 2002

The office was almost deserted, its fluorescent lights humming faintly over rows of empty desks. It was past midnight, but Cynthia Cooper was still there, surrounded by stacks of binders and endless printouts. The numbers stared back at her like riddles, taunting her with their inconsistencies. Line items that should have been reconciled weren't. Expenses that should have dragged the bottom line into the red had somehow disappeared. Profits, impossibly, had bloomed where there should have been none.

Being the Vice President of Internal Audit at WorldCom, she had been auditing for years, and she knew the difference between an error and a scheme. These were not mistakes—they were deliberate moves, carefully stitched together to create the illusion of strength.

In the small hours, she called in two trusted members of her internal audit team. They huddled in the cramped back office, whispering as though the walls themselves might be listening. Every recalculation, every spreadsheet rechecked, only confirmed their fears: billions of dollars had been shifted into the shadows. Expenses had been capitalised, losses disguised, balance sheets engineered not to reflect truth, but to maintain the illusion of growth.

The deeper they dug, the heavier the air became. Each discovery was a step closer to danger. They were not just accountants now; they were detectives in a crime scene where the suspects were their own bosses. One wrong move and their careers could vanish overnight. Cynthia felt the weight of it: responsibility pressing on her chest, fear gnawing at her resolve.

Yet she could not ignore what was before her. As she wrote in her notebook, the words seemed to tremble on the page: Fraud. Systematic. Deliberate. Three words that, if spoken aloud, could bring down a giant.

Her mind flashed to the possible consequences: executives imprisoned, investors ruined, employees stripped of pensions. And yet, the alternative—staying silent—would be worse. It would mean complicity.

*

The world was yet to know that the summer of 2002 would uncover Cynthia Cooper's persistence in one of the largest accounting scandals in history: a $11 billion fraud at WorldCom. The company would crumble; its name forever tied to deception. She would become a whistleblower, celebrated by some, feared by others. But on that quiet night, she was simply an auditor staring into the abyss, deciding whether truth was worth the personal cost.

There was a thin line between an early reckoning and a catastrophic collapse.

*

The Boardroom

WorldCom HQ

The boardroom was unusually tense. Heavy drapes muted the Mississippi night outside, while the long mahogany table glowed under harsh white lights. At its head sat the directors, men accustomed to dominance, their cufflinks gleaming, their expressions stiff with unease.

Cynthia Cooper entered quietly, clutching a stack of files. Her audit team followed, their faces pale with exhaustion from weeks of secret midnight work. The chair of the board gestured curtly.

"Ms Cooper," he said, "we're told you have something urgent."

She didn't sit. Instead, she placed the first folder on the table and opened it with deliberate calm.

"We've uncovered irregular entries," she began. Her voice was steady, but the weight of the moment pressed down on every syllable. "Billions of dollars moved out of expenses… into capital accounts. Adjustments made in the dead of night. This isn't an error. It's deliberate."

A director leaned forward, brows furrowed.

"Billions, you say? That seems… exaggerated."

Cynthia clicked her remote. The projector lit up the screen with a slide of numbers cascading downward - entries highlighted in red.

"$3.8 billion so far," she said. "And that is only what we've verified. Every line item can be traced back to concealment. If we dig further, it will be worse."

The silence was thick. Someone coughed. Another drummed his fingers nervously against the table.

Finally, the CFO, his face flushed, broke the quiet.

"You don't understand how competitive this industry is. Adjustments like these—"

"Fraud," Cynthia cut in sharply, her voice slicing through the room. "Call it what it is. Fraud."

A gasp escaped one of the junior directors. The chair cleared his throat, visibly shaken.

"Are you certain, Cynthia? You realise the implications?"

She stepped closer to the table, locking eyes with him. "These are not allegations. They are facts. Documented, traced, confirmed. Every day we delay, the fraud grows. If we do not act, it won't just be numbers that collapse—it will be this company, and every person tied to it."

She strode out of the boardroom.

*

The heavy oak doors clicked shut behind Cynthia Cooper. For a moment, the Enron boardroom was frozen, the silence so thick that even the air-conditioning hum felt deafening.

Stacks of files lay open on the polished mahogany table, the damning evidence staring back in black and red ink. Numbers that once told stories of growth now revealed ghosts of manipulation.

Kenneth Lay leaned back in his chair, eyes unfocused, his usually confident frame suddenly sagging. His hand reached for the water glass, but it trembled, spilling a few drops onto the table.

A Board Member whispered: "If this gets out... we're finished."

The auditor was shaken inside out. "These are not mistakes. These are deliberate reclassifications. If disclosed, we face SEC action, restatements, and potential bankruptcy."

Another Board Member snapped: "Not if. When. She's got the numbers. She's got the proof."

Jeffrey Skilling shifted uneasily, drumming his fingers against the table, a nervous rhythm echoing in the silence. He broke it with forced bravado.

Skilling smiled tightly. "We manage the message. We've done it before. Wall Street trusts us. The market trusts us. This... this is noise."

The auditor slammed a fist on the table. "Noise? This is billions hidden off the books! Shell companies, fake revenues, debt buried under layers! We can't spin this forever!"

Lay finally spoke, voice low, measured—the tone of a man still trying to keep control of a crumbling empire. "Gentlemen, let's remember who we are. Enron is too big to fail, too admired to be doubted. Cooper may have her spreadsheets, but power... power is perception. And perception can be managed."

No one replied. They all knew the truth: perception had already slipped out the door with Cynthia Cooper, tucked under her arm in neat binders.

The men in the boardroom sat in silence, each staring into the abyss that was once their empire, hearing only the echo of the door Cynthia had closed—perhaps forever—on Enron's illusions.

The room fell silent, but this time the silence was different. It wasn't dismissal—it was fear. The empire of illusion had been named, and no one could unhear it.

Sullivan, the CFO, thundered, "You don't understand—if we don't, the company collapses anyway."

The board looked at Ebbers. His silence said it all.

*

The Collapse

Within weeks, the scheme unravelled. WorldCom admitted to $3.8 billion in fraudulent entries, which later ballooned to $11 billion—the most significant accounting scandal in American history at the time.

On July 21, 2002, WorldCom filed for bankruptcy.

$180 billion to nearly zero Market Cap Wiped Out: $180 billion to nearly zero.

17,000 employees were laid off. The investor lost billions.

CEO Bernard Ebbers was sentenced to 25 years in prison.

CFO Scott Sullivan pleaded guilty, cooperated, and received 5 years imprisonment.

The "telecom revolution" had ended not in innovation, but in accounting fraud.

The case fuelled the passage of the Sarbanes-Oxley Act (2002), which reformed corporate governance and audit practices in the U.S.

*

The Anatomy of WorldCom's Valuation Fraud

An Autopsy of EBITDA, June 2002

A dimly lit office. Midnight. An internal auditor stares at the glowing screen.

The rows whisper their betrayal. Billions paid to other telecom networks to carry calls. Accounting rule says: Expense them immediately - they're operating costs.

WorldCom's trick was to reclassify them as capital expenditures. Pretend they were "investments" to be depreciated slowly over the years.

The effect?

They inflated EBITDA. By removing billions of expenses from the income statement, EBITDA margins magically jumped from 15% to 30%.

They distorted DCF. In discounted cash flow models, free cash flow to the firm (FCFF) looked stronger. Capex appeared stable. Operating margins looked world-class. The intrinsic value appeared 20–30% higher than reality.

They created the Balance Sheet Mirage. Assets ballooned with "capitalised line costs." The company looked bigger, stronger, and more asset-rich than it really was.

It was as if a patient with failing organs had been painted with makeup, dressed in fine silk, and paraded before the world as healthy. The numbers on the sheet sang a tune of growth, but behind the melody lay silence, decay, and inevitable collapse.

When auditors pulled the fine threads apart, the fabric tore apart. $11 billion in false assets unravelled. The EBITDA multiple collapsed to dust. The DCF terminal value evaporated. The fraud at WorldCom was not hidden in complex derivatives or exotic swaps. It was buried in plain sight, in the most widely used metric on Wall Street: EBITDA.

WorldCom had not just fooled Wall Street—it had weaponised valuation metrics to extend its life.

*

The Lesson

The WorldCom crash was not merely about one company's failure. It was a reminder that valuations built on manipulated EBITDA are mirages. If EBITDA is the song, always ask: who is writing the notes? Numbers can be orchestrated, but cash flow never lies.

Capitalisation tricks distort DCF models and fool even seasoned analysts. Corporate governance failures allow such fraud to fester when no one dares challenge the CEO. Silence in the boardroom can be as damning as complicity.

*

Closing Scene

In the empty boardroom, the projection screen still glowed faintly with rows of numbers - EBITDA margins, cash flow charts, growth curves. They looked perfect, pristine, flawless.

But behind them lay silence, fraud, and the ghosts of billions lost.

WorldCom's voice had carried across continents. But when the truth emerged, the line went dead.

*

Years Later

At its peak in the late 1990s, WorldCom was the darling of Wall Street—boasting more than $39 billion in annual revenue, serving tens of millions of phone and internet customers, and briefly becoming the second-largest long-distance telecom company in the U.S. Investors believed it was a giant destined to reshape global communications.

Then came 2002, when the accounting scandal unravelled. WorldCom admitted to inflating its assets by over $11 billion, making it one of the largest corporate frauds in history at the time. Within months, the company collapsed into bankruptcy, wiping out $180 billion in market value and the retirement savings of thousands of employees and investors.

The aftermath was devastating. WorldCom's CEO, Bernie Ebbers, once hailed as a visionary, was sentenced in 2005 to 25 years in prison for securities fraud and conspiracy. For many, his downfall became as infamous as the scandal itself—a portrait of unchecked ambition turned into hubris. After serving nearly 13 years, he was released in late 2019 on compassionate grounds due to ill health. Just two months later, in February 2020, Ebbers died at the age of 78, his name forever tied to one of corporate America's darkest chapters.

Today, WorldCom exists only in fragments, its networks having been absorbed by Verizon Communications in 2006. What remains is a cautionary echo, a reminder that inflated valuations and hidden numbers can bring even the mightiest giants to their knees.

*

Cynthia Cooper, the whistleblower, was named one of *Time* magazine's Persons of the Year (2002), alongside Enron's Sherron Watkins and FBI agent Coleen Rowley, for courage in speaking truth to power. Later, she authored a memoir, *Extraordinary Circumstances: The Journey of a Corporate Whistleblower (2008).* Today, she works as a speaker and consultant, focusing on ethics, leadership, and corporate accountability.

***

Chapter 18

Nikola Motors SPAC: The Truck That Rolled Downhill

Phoenix, Arizona, United States

Over Valuation ☑ SPAC Mania ☑ Corporate Fraud ☑ Deception ☑

Nikola Motors, once hailed as the "Tesla of trucks," skyrocketed to a $30+ billion valuation in 2020 on promises of revolutionary hydrogen-powered vehicles. But a short-seller report exposed that its showcase truck had rolled downhill in a demo video, and many of its claims were grossly exaggerated. Founder Trevor Milton was later convicted of fraud, and Nikola's stock collapsed, making it a textbook case of hype-driven valuation deception in clean tech.

The Truck That Didn't Roll

The summer of 2020 was a fever dream for Wall Street. SPACs—those mysterious "blank-check companies"—were the hot ticket, raising billions from investors hungry for the next big thing. And into that frenzy roared Nikola Motors, a company that promised to revolutionise trucking.

The backdrop of the stage depicted Trevor Milton leaning against the gleaming shell of his hydrogen-powered truck prototype. At the centre of it all stood Trevor Milton, a brash, charismatic founder with the swagger of a Silicon Valley messiah. He spoke with the conviction of a messiah, even though he knew the truck behind him could not move an inch on its own.

Cameras were flashing.

To the crowd, it was the future of transport. To Trevor, it was theatre. He declared that Nikola would outpace Tesla, that its hydrogen-powered trucks would replace diesel forever, and that a nationwide network of hydrogen fuelling stations would blanket America. The vision was intoxicating.

Nikola didn't crawl onto the market through a cautious IPO. No, it exploded onto the NASDAQ through a SPAC merger, bypassing the scrutiny of traditional vetting. Overnight, Nikola's valuation rocketed past $30 billion—making it more valuable than Ford, a century-old titan that had built millions of cars.

Investors cheered. Media headlines screamed: "The Tesla of Trucks is Here." And Trevor Milton? He became a billionaire almost instantly.

But behind the glossy decks and bold promises, cracks were already forming.

*

The Illusion Unravels

In September 2020, a bombshell report from short-seller Hindenburg Research dropped like a thunderclap: "Nikola is an intricate fraud built on dozens of lies."

The most damning revelation was almost absurd in its simplicity. The much-hyped Nikola One prototype truck, the star of its promotional video, was not actually self-propelled. Instead, it had been quietly towed up a hill and left to roll down while cameras tilted the angle to make it appear as if the truck was cruising on its own power.

The so-called miracle of hydrogen? It was little more than gravity in disguise.

Wall Street, which had been drunk on the vision, suddenly sobered up. Shares plummeted. Investors who had poured retirement savings, pension funds, and family wealth into Nikola watched their fortunes evaporate.

*

U.S. District Court, Southern District of New York

Manhattan

The illusion ended in a place far removed from Wall Street's glass towers: a federal courtroom in Manhattan. Trevor Milton's trial was held in 2022, before Judge Edgardo Ramos. The SDNY courthouse is famous for handling high-profile financial fraud cases—from Wall Street scams to crypto collapses—and Milton's case fit perfectly into its long legacy.

The marble halls of the U.S. District Court for the SDNY stood heavy with history. Here, where Wall Street's titans and fraudsters alike had once faced judgment, another name was about to be etched into infamy: Trevor Milton, the self-styled prophet of hydrogen, now a defendant in a federal fraud trial. As the Manhattan skyline glittered outside, inside the courtroom, the illusions of Nikola Motors were being dismantled, piece by piece.

The oak-panelled chamber was packed. Journalists filled the back rows, sketch artists readied their pencils, and investors, some hopeful, some bitter, waited for the delivery of justice. At the front sat Trevor Milton, no longer the confident showman of glossy roadshows, but a man diminished, staring at the polished wood of the defence table.

The prosecutors spoke with cutting precision: "This was not visionary exaggeration. This was deception. Trucks that didn't move. Stations that didn't exist. Technology that never worked."

On the giant screen, the infamous truck video was replayed for the jury. The semi glided majestically across the desert highway. For a moment, the courtroom was silent—awed, even seduced—until the prosecutor froze the frame and delivered the fatal line: “Ladies and gentlemen, this was not innovation. This was gravity. The truck was rolling downhill.”

Gasps spread through the room. A former engineer, called to testify, spoke with a mix of regret and quiet fury: “We tilted the camera. We knew it was wrong. But we were told—it had to look real.”

Investors took the stand, recounting how they had trusted Milton, how they had believed in his dream. A retired teacher spoke of losing her pension. A small trucking business owner admitted he mortgaged his future on Nikola shares.

Milton’s defence argued that he was a visionary, guilty only of enthusiasm, not deceit. But the jury had seen enough. The judge’s words sealed the atmosphere: “Markets can forgive failure. They cannot forgive fraud.”

When the verdict came, it was like a hammer blow: “Guilty.”

Trevor Milton slumped, his once fiery eyes dulled. The same man who had been hailed as the pioneer of hydrogen highways was now another fallen figure in the long list of valuation mirages.

*

Epilogue

Nikola Motors still exists, limping forward under new leadership, trying desperately to prove it is more than its founder’s lies. But the aura of invincibility is gone. The story of Nikola is no longer about a truck of the future—it is about the dangers of unchecked hype, of billions thrown at dreams built on sand.

And so, the legend of the truck that rolled downhill became not just an exposé, but a parable—a reminder that in the world of valuations, gravity always wins.

*

Years Later

The years rolled on, but Nikola never escaped the shadow of its fallen prophet. The once-hyped "Tesla of Trucks" became a cautionary tale, whispered in investment circles whenever SPACs or startup promises surfaced.

Trevor Milton, once a billionaire on paper, now carries the weight of a criminal conviction. In 2022, a jury found him guilty on multiple counts of fraud. By 2023, he was sentenced to four years in federal prison, his empire reduced to legal briefs and appeal filings. The man who once spoke of reshaping America's highways now walked under the watch of prison guards.

Nikola's stock, which had soared past $60 at its peak, crashed to mere pennies on the dollar. Investors who once dreamed of a hydrogen revolution were left holding scraps of paper, reminders of faith misplaced.

The company itself limped forward under new management, still trying to sell trucks, still struggling with credibility. The hydrogen stations Milton had promised never materialised at scale. In boardrooms and classrooms, Nikola's story was dissected as a case study in valuation deception, market mania, and the price of exaggeration.

On Wall Street, the joke became bitter: "The only thing Nikola trucks ever ran on… was gravity."

And so, like Enron, Theranos, and Kingfisher before it, Nikola Motors earned its place in the museum of corporate illusions—a reminder that, in finance, as in physics, what rolls downhill rarely rolls back up.

*

Nikol Tesla: Watching From the Seventh Cloud

From the silence of the seventh cloud, Nikola Tesla could only watch the strange afterlife of his name. His first name, borrowed by Nikola Motors, soared briefly on hype before crashing into scandal, leaving his legacy stained by fraud he never touched. Yet his last name, Tesla, was etched into history as the emblem of a new electric revolution, a company that reshaped industries and rivalled empires. Between ruin and triumph, his name was split—one half dragged into the dust, the other lifted into the stars.

***

Chapter 19
Yes Bank: When "Yes" Meant Disaster

Yes Bank House, Santacruz East, Mumbai, India

Bad Loans ☑ Valuation Misfire ☑

Once celebrated as India's fastest-growing private lender, Yes Bank collapsed in 2020 under the weight of bad loans, inflated balance sheets, and alleged quid pro quo deals led by founder Rana Kapoor. With exposures running into tens of thousands of crores, the crisis triggered a bailout by the RBI and SBI. The scandal became a defining case of how aggressive lending and hidden corruption can bring down a financial giant.

The Mirage of Confidence

Samudra Mahal, Worli, Mumbai, India

The chandeliers in Rana Kapoor's sea-facing penthouse glittered almost as brightly as the priceless canvases on his walls—works by M.F. Husain, S.H. Raza, and Tyeb Mehta. To Kapoor, they weren't just art; they were trophies, proof that he had arrived.

That evening, he stood in his signature tailored suit, gazing at one of his favourite paintings, a glass of vintage wine in hand. His phone buzzed incessantly—updates on the bank's ballooning loan book, the regulator's probing questions—but Kapoor ignored them. The art, the skyline, the sense of power… this was his true intoxication.

Hours earlier, in Yes Bank's glass boardroom, the story had been the same. Slick presentations, rising graphs, applause that drowned out the whispers of unease. Kapoor had basked in it all, his voice booming with confidence.

"We are not just building a bank—we are building a legacy. India's most iconic institution."

But beneath the gloss, the truth festered. Risky loans to troubled corporates had already begun to rot the foundations. The applause was hollow, the charts a mirage.

Back in his penthouse, Kapoor raised his glass to his reflection in the window—a man who mistook art for stability, glamour for strength, illusion for immortality.

Outside, Mumbai's night glittered. Inside, the empire was already cracking.

*

It Began with a Promise

"Yes."

A word of optimism.

A word of ambition.

A word that promised Indian banking a bold new chapter.

When Rana Kapoor co-founded Yes Bank in 2004, he wasn't just opening another financial institution. He was opening a dream. A bank that would say "yes" where others hesitated. To borrowers. To investors. To India's rising middle class.

And for a while, it worked.

By 2017, Yes Bank wasn't just growing—it was soaring. Skyscraper headquarters gleamed in Mumbai. Financial dailies splashed headlines of record profits. The stock climbed past ₹400. Dalal Street worshipped Kapoor as a visionary. His sharp suits and confident smile became the face of a "new India."

Investors believed. Depositors trusted. Analysts cheered.

But beneath the polished marble of Yes Bank's towers, termites were at work.

*

The Mirage of Success

Loans were flying out of Yes Bank's coffers like confetti at a wedding. Real estate tycoons, infrastructure giants, shadowy NBFCs—all found open doors and quick approvals. Where other banks said no, Yes Bank said yes.

It was reckless.

It was dangerous.

It was brilliant—until the music stopped.

By 2018, India's economy was slowing. Projects stalled. Borrowers defaulted. The glossy loan book began to rot. What Yes Bank had called "assets" were now time bombs ticking beneath its balance sheet.

Rana Kapoor, the master illusionist, continued to smile for the cameras. The annual reports gleamed with optimism. Numbers were polished. Risk was buried. The show went on.

But whispers began. "Bad loans." "Underreporting." "Cooking the books." The RBI was watching.

*

Art in the Midst of Ruin

The Valerian Gallery, New York City

The auction hall shimmered with quiet opulence. Chandeliers spilt light across gilded frames and polished marble floors. The crowd was hushed, its whispers carrying the perfume of old money and nouveau ambition.

In the front row sat Rana Kapoor, impeccably dressed, his tie a precise Windsor knot, his cufflinks reflecting the golden gleam of the room. The world outside might have been talking about the storm gathering over Yes Bank—mounting NPAs, worried regulators, analysts raising red flags—but inside the gallery, Kapoor appeared untouched, almost regal.

The auctioneer's gavel struck. "Lot number 42—an untitled work by F. N. Souza. We begin at two crores."

Kapoor's hand rose, calm and confident. A rival bidder hesitated, then countered. Kapoor lifted his hand again, almost lazily, as though money were no more than air. Around him, collectors watched with fascination—this was the banker with the golden touch, the man who had built Yes Bank from scratch. His hunger for art was legendary; his collection, already vast, was spoken of in hushed reverence.

"Sold! To Mr Rana Kapoor." The gavel fell, and applause followed.

But even as the room celebrated, his phone buzzed relentlessly on the velvet seat beside him. Messages he didn't read: a warning from RBI, anxious notes from his compliance officers, whispers of an investigation brewing. Kapoor ignored them all. His eyes were fixed on the next canvas being unveiled, his pulse quickening not at balance sheets but at brushstrokes.

The irony was cinematic. Outside, depositors were beginning to worry. Inside, Kapoor was still bidding, chasing art as though each acquisition could insulate him from the unravelling reality of his empire.

In that moment, the gallery wasn't merely a marketplace of paintings. It was a theatre of denial. The banker, once hailed as visionary, now resembled Nero—collecting beauty while the fires of finance grew closer to his own doorstep.

Kapoor was happy. He had won. But beyond the gilded doors, the storm had already broken.

*

The Boardroom

The polished glass table at Yes Bank's headquarters reflected the nervous faces of its directors. It was late evening, but the city lights outside could not brighten the gloom inside.

Stacks of papers lay untouched; numbers circled in red ink. Non-performing assets had begun to accumulate, hidden for too long beneath layers of optimism and creative accounting. The air conditioning hummed louder than the men in suits.

"Rana," one director finally broke the silence, his voice trembling with a mixture of respect and fear, "these exposures… IL&FS, DHFL, even Jet Airways… the risk is becoming unmanageable. We cannot keep pretending."

Rana Kapoor leaned forward, his cufflinks catching the boardroom light. He spoke with his trademark bravado, the salesman's charm never leaving him: "Gentlemen, Yes Bank is not a follower, it is a pioneer. Risk is the price of growth. We don't hide from it—we harness it."

Another director shifted uneasily. "But the RBI is asking questions. Our balance sheet doesn't add up. If the market catches wind —"

Rana slammed his palm on the table, startling everyone. "The market believes what I tell it to believe. Numbers are only stories—and I am the storyteller. Do you understand?"

A heavy silence followed. The directors exchanged glances but said nothing. Outside, the Mumbai skyline glittered—oblivious to the cracks spreading within.

In that moment, Yes Bank wasn't just a financial institution. It was a stage. And Rana Kapoor, with his silken tie and rehearsed confidence, was still trying to play the hero—even as the walls began to close in.

*

The Implosion Inside Out

March 2020

The curtain fell.

Yes Bank, once valued at ₹80,000 crore, was suddenly staring at bankruptcy. The RBI swooped in, imposing a moratorium. A chilling order hit the news:

"No depositor shall withdraw more than ₹50,000."

The panic was instant.

Outside Yes Bank branches, queues of terrified depositors stretched for hours. Mothers wept, unable to pay hospital bills. Shopkeepers cursed, unable to access working capital. Middle-class families clutched their passbooks, staring in disbelief. Their savings—their lives—locked behind a bank's glass doors.

ATMs went silent.

Dalal Street howled.

Yes Bank's stock crashed to ₹5.

For investors, it was not just a fall. It was a freefall into betrayal.

*

The Rescue Operation

India held its breath. A bank this size could not be allowed to fail. The collapse of Yes Bank wasn't just a corporate disaster—it was a systemic risk, a threat to the financial bloodstream of the nation.

In a dramatic midnight manoeuvre, the Reserve Bank of India summoned India's banking giants. State Bank of India and others were ordered to step in, injecting capital to keep Yes Bank alive.

The government referred to it as a "rescue." Depositors called it a "theft of trust."

Meanwhile, Rana Kapoor's empire crumbled. Once a billionaire banker, he was arrested on charges of money laundering and bribery. The man who built Yes Bank's glass palace now sat behind iron bars.

*

The Valuation Misfire

Yes Bank's story is not just about one bank. It is about the madness of valuations.

How did investors ignore the warning signs?

How ambition disguised as growth misled an entire market?

How a ₹400 stock could become worthless almost overnight?

Yes Bank wasn't a failure of banking alone. It was a failure of belief.

*

Lesson

Across two decades, the triggers change—dot-com hype, emerging market euphoria, SPAC mania—but the roots remain constant.

The future was overestimated while ignoring present weaknesses. The investors and banks believed in the charismatic founders without challenging the numbers. Capital availability was confused with business viability.

Valuation failures are not accidents; they are symptoms of optimism unchecked by discipline. History doesn't just rhyme—in finance, it replays on a loop.

*

Years Later

Today, Yes Bank limps along under new management, scarred but alive. Its logo still glows on branch signboards, but it carries a ghostly weight. Investors trade its stock, but cautiously, as if touching a flame that once burned them.

And Rana Kapoor? He fights case after case, once a king in skyscrapers, now a prisoner of his own greed.

In the Indian Parliament, his name occasionally resurfaces in heated debates—“Who let this happen? Who looked away? Who said yes when they should have said no?”

The Yes Bank survives, but it will forever remain a cautionary tale. A reminder that in finance, a single word can be both a promise and a curse.

Yes.

***

Chapter 20

Smoke and Mirrors—The Volkswagen Dieselgate Scandal

Technology Fraud ☑ Startup Failure ✗ Litigation ☑

> Volkswagen's Dieselgate erupted in 2015 when regulators discovered the company had secretly installed "defeat devices" to cheat emissions tests. Nearly 11 million cars worldwide were affected, spewing pollutants far above legal limits. The scandal triggered a stock market collapse, forced CEO Martin Winterkorn's resignation, and cost Volkswagen over $30 billion in fines and settlements. Once a symbol of German engineering pride, the brand became synonymous with deception—its clean image revealed as nothing more than smoke and mirrors.

Wolfsburg—The Throne of Power

Sebastian Rudolph, Volkswagen AG, Berliner Ring 2

The Volkswagen headquarters loomed like a modern fortress, all glass and steel under the grey German sky. Inside, a high-level boardroom was in session. Charts and projections flickered on the wall: "World's No. 1 Automaker by 2018."

Martin Winterkorn, precise in his tailored suit, leaned forward with the intensity of a chess master.

"We will dominate the U.S. market," he said, voice clipped. "Clean diesel is our weapon. Toyota has hybrids, but we—" he tapped the table, "—we have German engineering."

Around him, executives nodded, though unease flickered in their eyes. Everyone knew the emissions standards in America were brutal. Meeting them without sacrificing performance was like squaring a circle. Yet in this culture, saying no was not an option.

Somewhere far below, in the engineering floors, coders and designers quietly deployed the "defeat device." Software lines were buried deep in the engine's brain. A secret whispered in code.

*

Michigan—The Lab

Ann Arbor Lab

The International Council on Clean Transportation (ICCT) is a non-profit organisation. Its mission is to provide unbiased research to environmental regulators.

Rows of fluorescent lights hummed in a modest emissions lab at the University of West Virginia. A diesel Jetta sat strapped onto the testing rollers. Graduate students in lab coats watched the monitors.

One frowned. "The numbers don't match," he muttered.

When tested in the lab, emissions looked clean. But out on the road, the portable testing equipment told another story—nitrogen oxides spiking like a heartbeat under stress.

The students exchanged puzzled glances. One finally whispered what none dared to believe: "This car knows when it's being tested."

The data was passed to the EPA. The quiet storm had begun.

*

Washington, D.C.—The Leak

September 2015

At the Environmental Protection Agency, officials gathered for an urgent press briefing. The room was sterile, beige, bureaucratic—yet the announcement would shake the corporate world.

"Volkswagen has admitted to installing defeat devices in its diesel vehicles," the spokesperson said evenly. "These devices alter performance to pass emissions tests. Nearly eleven million cars worldwide are affected."

No dramatic flourish. No raised voice. Just cold, bureaucratic precision. Yet outside, the statement detonated across news networks. Tickers screamed:

VOLKSWAGEN CHEATED. WORLD IN SHOCK.

*

Frankfurt Stock Exchange—The Crash

Late September 2015

The trading floor erupted into chaos. Phones rang endlessly, brokers shouted across the room, and Volkswagen's stock graph plummeted like a stone dropped from a cliff.

A trader with sweat beading his forehead muttered into the phone: "We're watching thirty billion euros evaporate in real time."

The symbol VOW3.DE blinked in red, flashing warnings across the globe. Investors who once believed in German reliability now dumped shares like burning coal.

*

Wolfsburg—The Fall of a Titan

Back in Wolfsburg, Winterkorn stood before the press. Cameras clicked like machine guns. His jaw was set, but his voice faltered.

"I am shocked by the events of the past few days," he said. "Above all, I am stunned that misconduct on such a scale was possible in the Volkswagen Group."

For a man who built his reputation on micromanagement, the words rang hollow. Days later, he resigned. The titan had fallen.

*

The People's Betrayal

Across Europe and America, owners of Volkswagens—teachers, nurses, young families—sat staring at their keys with a mixture of disbelief and anger. They had bought the promise of "clean diesel." Some had paid a premium for it.

Now they realised: they had been pawns in a corporate deception. Late-night comedians mocked the brand, and Das Auto became a punchline.

One American owner looked into the camera during a news interview and said bitterly, "I thought I was helping the environment. Turns out, I was choking it."

*

Courtrooms and Settlements

Lawyers in crisp suits shuffled papers as judges delivered rulings. The numbers grew monstrous: $30 billion in fines, settlements, and buybacks. Criminal charges followed. Executives faced questioning. The scandal became a case study in corporate ethics—or the lack thereof.

*

Redemption Attempt

Years later, Volkswagen unveiled a sleek electric car under blazing spotlights. The CEO of a new era stood tall, promising reinvention.

"Dieselgate will never happen again," he declared. "We are driving into an electric future."

Applause filled the hall, but somewhere in the crowd, a journalist scribbled in her notebook: Smoke and mirrors have not vanished—they've only changed form.

*

Closing Montage

The pristine showroom cars, the smoky exhaust on highways, the panicked trading floors, the courtroom gavels, the disappointed faces of customers.

Dieselgate was never just about emissions. It was about ambition without restraint. About a culture where no one dared to say the truth aloud. About what happens when the drive to be number one outruns integrity.

And like the cars themselves, Volkswagen's story looked clean under test conditions. But out on the open road—it was something else entirely.

***

Chapter 21

The $100 Billion Vision: SoftBank's Gamble

Tokyo Port City Takeshiba Office, Minato-ku, Tokyo, Japan

Valuation Misfire ☑ Massive write-offs ☑ Fraud ✗

SoftBank Vision Fund (2017) was backed by Saudi and Abu Dhabi wealth. Masayoshi Son launched the world's largest tech fund with $100 billion, betting that flooding startups with capital would create global monopolies. It poured billions into Uber, WeWork, OYO, Paytm, and others, driving valuations to dizzying heights. But hype soon unravelled—WeWork imploded, OYO bled cash, and Uber stumbled, leading the fund to post record multi-billion-dollar losses. Once hailed as a bold vision, the experiment became a symbol of excess capital, inflated dreams, and the thin line between vision and delusion.

The Boardroom

Tokyo, Japan

The boardroom was bathed in late-afternoon light. Masayoshi Son, a visionary, gambler, and prophet of technology, stood before a wall of screens, his hand gripping a laser pointer as if it were a sword. Behind him glowed a single number in bold white:

$100,000,000,000.

"This," he said, pausing for effect, "is not a fund. This is a revolution."

The room erupted in murmurs.

Advisors from Goldman Sachs, lawyers from New York, emissaries from Riyadh—all present to witness the birth of what would become the SoftBank Vision Fund, the largest technology investment fund the world had ever seen. Saudi Arabia's Public Investment Fund (PIF) had agreed to pour in $45 billion, while Abu Dhabi's Mubadala was to invest another $15 billion, with the remaining funds sourced from Apple, Foxconn, Qualcomm, and SoftBank itself.

The idea was simple yet audacious: flood startups with capital so massive that competition would suffocate. Market domination, Son believed, could be bought.

*

The Cult of Masa

In Tokyo, Masayoshi Son paced his study, walls lined with samurai swords and calligraphy scrolls. A single word echoed in his mind: Vision. His bets weren't just investments; they were destiny-defining gambles, each stroke as bold and reckless as a warrior charging into battle.

He was no stranger to risk. He had lost billions in the dot-com bust, only to bounce back with a single bet on a Chinese startup called Alibaba. That stake, worth $20 million in 2000, would one day be valued at over $100 billion. The legend of Masa was born in that gamble—he was the man who saw the future before anyone else.

The Vision Fund, launched in 2017, was his most ambitious wager yet. At the launch, Son invoked the words of the Meiji-era samurai: "Only those who risk going too far will know how far they can go."

Behind closed doors, however, boardroom sceptics whispered: Was this boldness or madness?

*

Money Without Discipline

The floodgates opened. Billions cascaded into startups across the globe. Uber, WeWork, DoorDash, OYO Rooms, Grab, Paytm, Slack, Fair, Zume Pizza—the list was dizzying. Pitch decks barely lasted 15 minutes before receiving term sheets.

In a glass tower in Manhattan, a SoftBank executive once told a founder: "Don't think small. If you want $200 million, ask for $2 billion. Masa likes scale."

And so, scale became the mantra. WeWork's Adam Neumann strutted barefoot into SoftBank's offices, muttering about elevating human consciousness. He walked out with a check for $4.4 billion. At OYO Rooms in India, Ritesh Agarwal spoke of conquering global hospitality. SoftBank pumped in over $3 billion, even as rooms went empty and quality collapsed.

Inside the Vision Fund boardroom, reports piled up—loss-making units, ballooning expenses, valuations that defied logic. But dissent rarely survived. Masa would point at charts projecting hockey-stick growth curves. "You see? You have no vision!" he would thunder, silencing doubters.

*

The Cracks Appear

By 2019, the first tremors were visible. WeWork imploded after its failed IPO, wiping out tens of billions in paper wealth. The Wall Street Journal ran headlines questioning SoftBank's judgment. Uber struggled to turn a profit. OYO bled cash. Even Paytm, once India's golden fintech unicorn, faltered in public markets.

In one tense Tokyo meeting, an advisor dared to ask: "Masa-san, what if growth cannot be bought?"

Son's reply was icy: "Then we double down."

But reality refused to bend. The Vision Fund reported a record $18 billion loss in 2020, one of the largest ever for an investment vehicle. The pandemic accelerated the reckoning. Analysts began calling it "the house of cards built on cheap money."

*

The Reckoning

In 2022, SoftBank announced another staggering loss—over $23 billion in a single quarter. The Saudi backers grew restless. Mubadala trimmed commitments. Founders once hailed as visionaries became cautionary tales.

The same boardroom that once cheered $100 billion now echoed with silence. Advisors spoke in hushed tones about "discipline," "consolidation," and "capital recycling." Words alien to the Vision Fund's original ethos.

Masayoshi Son, the man who had once declared he would invest in 10,000 unicorns, appeared sombre. At a press conference, he admitted, "I am embarrassed. Past successes may have intoxicated me."

The emperor of overcapitalisation had confessed his fallibility.

*

Years Later

The Vision Fund survives, but it is no longer the unstoppable juggernaut of 2017. Its legacy is written not just in numbers, but in the cautionary whispers across Silicon Valley and beyond: Too much money, too fast, can destroy even the best of ideas.

And in that Tokyo boardroom, the ghost of that glowing number—$100,000,000,000—still lingers, a reminder of the thin line between vision and delusion.

***

Chapter 22

AOL—Time Warner: The $165 Billion Mirage

AOL Way in Sterling, Virginia; Time Warner HQ: New York

Corporate Merger ☑ Dot-Com Bubble ☑

At the dawn of the millennium, two giants shook hands in New York. America Online (AOL), the darling of the internet boom with thirty million dial-up subscribers, joined forces with Time Warner, owner of Hollywood studios, cable networks, and glossy magazines. The union was sealed in a $165 billion stock-swap deal, hailed as the largest merger in history.

The dream was simple yet seductive: marry the speed of the internet with the prestige of old media, and create an empire that would dominate the digital century. For a brief moment, it seemed unstoppable. Within two years, however, the deal would unravel into a $99 billion loss—a mirage of the dot-com bubble that had dazzled Wall Street before vanishing into dust.

The Wedding of the Century (January 2000)

The Hilton ballroom glowed with flashbulbs, a cathedral of optimism. On stage stood Steve Case, the boyish visionary of AOL, and Gerald Levin, the seasoned baron of Time Warner.

Case beamed as he declared: "Together, we will create the world's first fully integrated media and communications company for the Internet century."

The crowd erupted. Headlines the next day dripped with superlatives: "The deal of the century," "A marriage made in heaven." At $165 billion, it was the largest merger in history. AOL, fuelled by stock market frenzy, was paying with its inflated shares, and Time Warner's board—caught between awe and fear of irrelevance—said yes.

Investors cheered. Wall Street raised glasses. To the outside world, it was the dawn of a digital empire. Inside, a fault line was already forming.

*

The Honeymoon of Illusions (2000)

For a brief moment, the dream looked real. AOL, master of dial-up internet, had 30 million subscribers, while Time Warner controlled magazines, Warner Bros., and CNN. The promise: deliver movies, news, and music instantly to every household via the internet.

But cracks showed quickly.

AOL's core—dial-up-subscriptions—were already waning. Broadband lurked on the horizon.

Time Warner's executives, proud of their legacy, bristled at being told how the future should work by "kids in khakis" from AOL.

Cultures clashed: Silicon Valley optimism against New York conservatism.

Board meetings grew tense. Time Warner's old guard muttered that AOL's valuation was "pixie dust." AOL's young team whispered that Time Warner was "dinosaurs in suits."

The marriage that Wall Street had hailed began to feel more like a forced union.

*

Collapse of the Mirage (2001–2002)

The dot-com bubble burst like glass under pressure. AOL's stock, once the high-flying currency of the merger, cratered. What had been a $165 billion dream shrank to a bitter illusion.

In 2002, the merged company announced a $99 billion write-down—the most significant corporate loss in U.S. history. The boardroom turned toxic.

Levin resigned under fire.

Case stepped aside, his "visionary" label tarnished.

Analysts, once cheerleaders, now sneered.

A director is said to have sighed during a tense meeting:

"We didn't merge a digital future with old media. We just doubled our problems."

The empire that was supposed to rule the 21st century was now the poster child of hubris.

*

The Divorce (2009)

Years of bitterness followed. AOL became a shell of its former self, overtaken by Google and broadband rivals. Time Warner, once proud, carried the dead weight of the failed merger like an albatross.

In 2009, after nearly a decade of decline, Time Warner spun off AOL in a quiet separation. No flashbulbs, no grand statements—just a silent retreat from a marriage that had once promised immortality.

The $165 billion mirage had vanished into dust.

*

Epilogue

The AOL–Time Warner deal stands as a monument to the intoxicating power of inflated valuations. It wasn't just a merger—it was a mirror of the dot-com bubble itself: dazzling, irrational, and destined to collapse.

What began with champagne toasts ended with whispered regrets.

***

Chapter 23

The $11 Billion Mirage: HP's Autonomy Gamble

Palo Alto, California, USA

Overvaluation ☑ Alleged Corporate Fraud ☑ Merger ☑ Litigation ☑

In one of tech's most infamous deals, Hewlett-Packard acquired UK-based software firm Autonomy for $11.1 billion, hoping to reinvent itself beyond hardware. Within a year, HP accused Autonomy of accounting fraud and inflated revenues, leading to an $8.8 billion write-down. Founder Mike Lynch denied wrongdoing, but years of lawsuits and trials followed. The deal, meant to transform HP, instead became a cautionary tale of overvaluation, failed due diligence, and shattered boardroom dreams.

The Acquisition

Palo Alto, 2011

The Hewlett-Packard boardroom was unusually tense that summer. The long mahogany table was lined with directors, advisors, and bankers. At the head sat Léo Apotheker, HP's newly minted CEO, pacing with a restless energy.

Behind him, the projector glowed with three bold words: "Strategic Shift. Autonomy. Future."

Apotheker raised his voice, gesturing at the slides.

"HP cannot survive as a hardware company. Printers, servers—these are commodities. Our future lies in software. And Autonomy is our ticket."

Autonomy, a Cambridge-based software firm led by its charismatic founder Mike Lynch, specialised in "big data" analytics. At a time when Silicon Valley buzzed with talk of harnessing the explosion of digital information, Autonomy was pitched as a crown jewel—a way for HP to reinvent itself against Oracle, IBM, and Microsoft.

The bankers from Goldman Sachs nodded eagerly. Advisors spoke of synergies. Valuations were justified with hockey-stick graphs. Lynch himself had dazzled the HP board earlier, invoking phrases like "meaning-based computing" and "unlocking unstructured data."

The price: $11.1 billion, nearly ten times Autonomy's revenue.

"Expensive?" Apotheker admitted, leaning in. "Yes. But this is not an acquisition. This is a transformation."

*

The Dream Deal

On August 18, 2011, HP announced the acquisition with great fanfare. Press releases declared it a landmark moment. "The most strategic move in HP's history," Apotheker told analysts.

Inside Autonomy's Cambridge offices, champagne corks popped. Employees cheered. Lynch assured his engineers they were joining the "world's greatest technology company."

But not everyone was convinced. Oracle's Larry Ellison mocked the deal openly, comparing it to "buying a used car at new-car prices." Some HP insiders whispered about overpayment. Yet, in the boardroom, dissent was drowned out by the euphoria of a "bold vision."

*

Trouble in Paradise

Barely a year later, the mirage began to crack. HP's finance team pored over Autonomy's books, and what they saw chilled them. Revenues seemed inflated, costs buried, deals misclassified. Hardware sales had been disguised as high-margin software revenue. Channel stuffing and aggressive accounting lurked in the shadows.

By late 2012, the HP board convened in an emergency session. The atmosphere was grim. Meg Whitman, who had replaced Apotheker as CEO, addressed the room: "Ladies and gentlemen, we have a problem. A very big problem."

She revealed findings of forensic auditors: billions in accounting irregularities. HP alleged that Autonomy's management had employed dubious practices to inflate its value before the sale. The dream deal had become a nightmare.

The boardroom fell silent. One director muttered, "We've been had."

*

The $8.8 Billion Write-Down

In November 2012, HP stunned Wall Street by announcing an $8.8 billion write-down on Autonomy, most of it attributed to "serious accounting improprieties." The news wiped billions off HP's market value in a single day.

Headlines screamed: "HP's Worst Deal Ever." Analysts called it one of the most significant corporate write-offs in tech history. Apotheker's vision was now derided as hubris. Mike Lynch, meanwhile, denied wrongdoing, accusing HP of mismanagement and scapegoating.

In HP's Palo Alto boardroom, the mood was apocalyptic. Directors grilled executives, lawyers outlined litigation strategies, and investors fumed. The words "fraud," "betrayal," and "negligence" hung heavy in the air.

*

The Legal Battles

What followed was a decade-long legal war. HP accused Lynch and Autonomy CFO Sushovan Hussain of orchestrating fraud. Lynch, defiant and combative, insisted HP had destroyed Autonomy after the takeover.

Courtrooms in London and the U.S. became battlegrounds. In 2022, Lynch was extradited to the U.S. to face charges of wire fraud and securities fraud. Sushovan Hussain was convicted earlier and sentenced to five years in prison.

The once-proud founder who had stood in HP's boardroom promising a revolution now stood in court, accused of orchestrating one of the biggest frauds in tech history.

*

Years Later

HP never fully recovered from the Autonomy debacle. The company's identity crisis deepened, leading to spin-offs, restructurings, and missed opportunities. The deal that was meant to save HP became the symbol of its decline.

In Cambridge, Autonomy's name faded into obscurity, its legacy reduced to footnotes in legal briefs. For Mike Lynch, the story shifted from tech visionary to defendant, fighting to clear his name.

And for the world of corporate governance, the $11 billion mirage of Autonomy became a stark reminder: in the heat of boardroom ambition, due diligence is often the first casualty.

***

Chapter 24
Jet Airways: From Runway to Freefall

Siroya Centre, Sahar Airport Road, Andheri (East), Mumbai

Alleged Money Laundering ☑ Aggressive Expansion ☑

Failure of Low-Cost Aviation Model ☑

> Jet Airways, once India's most glamorous private airline, founded in 1993 by Naresh Goyal, soared with over 120 aircraft and a 22% market share at its peak. But mounting debts, fierce competition, and financial mismanagement grounded the carrier in 2019, leaving unpaid employees, stranded passengers, and a legacy of ambition turned turbulence.

Many Years Ago

Sangrur, Punjab, India

A thin boy stood barefoot in a dusty lane, clutching his schoolbooks tighter than his stomach, which often went empty. His father was gone, the family home lost to creditors, and nights were filled with hushed conversations about survival rather than dreams.

Yet, whenever he heard the distant roar of an airplane cutting across the sky, his eyes lit up. To everyone else, it was just noise. To young Naresh, it was a promise—that one day, he would not just fly, but command the skies.

*

The Sky Belonged to Jet

Mumbai, 2005

At a private hangar, the spotlight shone on a brand-new Boeing 777 draped in the royal blue and gold livery of Jet Airways. Inside the aircraft, the seats gleamed with fresh leather, the champagne sparkled in crystal glasses, and Bollywood stars smiled for the cameras. It wasn't just an airline launch; it was a spectacle of India's new ambition.

Naresh Goyal, dressed immaculately in a navy suit, stood in the aisle with folded hands, greeting guests as though welcoming them into his palace in the sky. Models in mustard-yellow saris glided through the cabin with rehearsed elegance, embodying luxury and charm. The photographers clicked relentlessly.

That evening, newspapers across India carried the same images: Jet Airways was no longer just an airline. It was glamour, aspiration, and the very definition of India's rise.

What nobody knew then was that behind the champagne bubbles and smiles, the seeds of turbulence had already been sown.

*

The Golden Take Off

The morning sun glinted off the windows of the Siroya Centre in Andheri, Mumbai, Jet Airways' headquarters. Inside, the walls were adorned with framed photographs of Jet's glory days—smiling cabin crew in mustard-yellow saris, gleaming Boeing 777s on international runways, and Naresh Goyal shaking hands with global leaders.

In the late 1990s and early 2000s, flying Jet Airways meant status. For India's new middle class, it was luxury they had only seen in films: champagne in business class, glossy inflight magazines, and a service culture that rivalled Singapore Airlines. At its peak, Jet commanded over 22% of India's market share, carrying more than 20 million passengers annually with a fleet that touched 120 aircraft.

Naresh Goyal, who had once worked as a cashier at a small travel agency, had risen to become the undisputed king of Indian skies. To employees, he was a patriarch; to ministers, a close confidant; and to passengers, a symbol of aspiration.

But even the smoothest flights encounter turbulence.

*

Acquisition of Air Sahara

The First Cracks Appear

By 2007, Goyal made his boldest move yet: acquiring Air Sahara for $500 million and rebranding it as JetLite. It was meant to secure Jet's dominance, but instead it bled cash. The low-cost revolution was coming, led by Indigo and SpiceJet. Passengers who once paid for glamour now demanded cheaper fares. Jet, with its high-cost structure and debt-fuelled expansion, was suddenly on the back foot.

By 2010, whispers began to circulate in Nariman Point and Bandra-Kurla Complex: Jet's debts were rising, profit margins shrinking. Creditors wanted answers. Employees noticed delays in reimbursements.

Yet in public, the airline maintained its sheen. Glossy ads continued to run, celebrities still endorsed it, and Goyal's signature half-smile reassured everyone that Jet was untouchable.

*

The Boardroom Storm

2018. The atmosphere inside Jet's boardroom was tense, the kind of tension you could slice with a knife.

The CFO projected numbers onto the screen, each figure like a dagger. "Debt has crossed ₹8,500 crore. Market share is down to single digits. Our net losses this quarter alone are ₹636 crore. We've delayed salaries for pilots and crew for the third month running."

The room fell silent. Goyal, his face pale but defiant, spoke slowly. "Jet Airways is not just another airline. It is India's airline. We carried 20 million passengers at our peak. We have 22,000 employees. The government cannot let us fall."

One director whispered, "Etihad is no longer interested. They've lost too much already. Lessors are repossessing aircraft daily. We are down from 120 planes to just 16 operational this week."

Another added, "Sir, banks have stopped extending credit. Even fuel suppliers have cut us off."

Naresh slammed the table. "We are Jet Airways. We cannot stop flying!"

His words rang with conviction, but in the silence that followed, everyone knew they were nothing more than echoes of a fading empire.

*

The Grounding

By March 2019, the inevitable happened. Lessors reclaimed aircraft overnight, leaving Jet with barely five planes in the sky. Airports across India saw Jet counters shuttered, passengers holding useless tickets, and employees begging for months of unpaid salaries.

On 25 March, Naresh Goyal resigned as chairman, stepping down from the very airline he had built from scratch. He left quietly, no cameras, no applause—just silence. The once-mighty Jet Airways had been grounded.

*

Epilogue

The Dream That Fell from the Sky

For employees, it was betrayal. For passengers, it was nostalgia. For bankers, it was a nightmare of bad loans and unpaid debts. Jet Airways, once the crown jewel of Indian aviation, had collapsed under the weight of debt, mismanagement, and hubris.

In the glittering world of Indian business, the fall of Jet was more than a corporate failure - it was the end of an era. The lesson was clear: in aviation, as in valuation, even the brightest dreams cannot defy gravity forever.

*

Years Later

The once-proud blue-and-gold bird no longer graces Indian skies. Its fleet scattered, offices locked, and employees dispersed, Jet Airways lives only in memory and litigation. For passengers, the name still evokes nostalgia—the warm service, the mustard-yellow saris, the aura of flying first-class. But in the balance sheets of creditors, Jet remains a symbol of broken promises and unpaid billions.

*

Naresh Goyal, once the smiling face of Jet Airways, was arrested in 2023 in a ₹538 crore fraud and money laundering case. After months in Mumbai's Arthur Road Jail, he was granted medical bail in 2024 to undergo cancer treatment. Today, he lives quietly in Mumbai, his empire gone and his legacy under a long shadow.

***

Chapter 25

Hanbo Steel: The Empire of Borrowed Steel

Godae-ri, Songak-myeon, Dangjin-gun, Chungcheongnam-do, South Korea

Corporate Corruption ☑ Political Favouritism ☑

Hanbo Steel, once South Korea's second-largest steelmaker, collapsed in 1997 after revelations of massive corruption and political favouritism. The company had secured billions in loans through bribery and government pressure on banks, despite weak fundamentals. Its bankruptcy not only exposed deep ties between business and politics but also became a key trigger in South Korea's financial crisis during the Asian meltdown.

Steel and Silk

Seoul, Spring of 1995

The ballroom of the Shilla Hotel glittered under chandeliers as the who's who of South Korea's political and business elite gathered for Hanbo Steel's gala. Waiters in white gloves floated across the room, pouring champagne into crystal flutes while a jazz band played softly in the corner.

At the centre of it all stood Chung Tae-soo, the founder of Hanbo Steel, his silk tie perfectly knotted, his handshake firm, his smile magnetic. To the ministers and bankers clustered around him, he was more than an industrialist—he was a visionary who promised to make South Korea a steel superpower.

"Hanbo will not just rival POSCO," Chung declared with confidence, raising his glass. "It will surpass it. We will build the backbone of Asia."

Applause erupted, glasses clinked, and cameras flashed. In that moment, Hanbo seemed invincible—an empire of steel forged by ambition and blessed by the powerful.

But beyond the chandeliers and champagne, in the shadow of the steel mills, the truth was far less glamorous. Hanbo's furnaces were inefficient, its debts spiralled out of control, and its glittering rise was built not on profits but on politics, bribes, and borrowed time.

The empire of steel was already rusting.

*

The Illusion of Power

Seoul, 1995. The lights in Hanbo Tower never seemed to dim. From its sleek glass façade, executives watched over a country drunk on growth—South Korea's economy was roaring, chaebols were expanding like unstoppable dynasties, and credit flowed like a river.

Chung Tae-soo, the charismatic founder of Hanbo Steel, was treated not just as an industrialist but as a kingmaker. Dressed in immaculate suits, his smile disarmed bankers, and his connections reached the highest levels of government. Politicians bowed to him, bureaucrats took his calls at midnight, and banks—both public and private—extended him credit lines that defied logic.

His boardroom was a theatre of ambition. Every Monday morning, Chung entered with a swagger, spreading glossy reports across the polished mahogany table.

"Gentlemen," he would declare, "Hanbo will rival POSCO. We will be Asia's steel giant."

Nods followed. Applause sometimes. No one dared question him.

What the bankers and politicians didn't see—or chose not to—was that Hanbo's steel mills were drowning in inefficiency, bleeding cash, and over-leveraged to the point of collapse.

*

The Corruption Engine

Hanbo Steel's expansion was not funded by market success but by political patronage. Bribes flowed in envelopes and whispered promises. Politicians approved massive loans from state-controlled banks. In return, Chung ensured campaign funds and discreet favours.

Inside the boardroom, some executives whispered. Numbers didn't add up, inventories were inflated, and production capacity was exaggerated. But dissent was dangerous. Chung's fury was legendary; those who resisted found themselves sidelined or forced into silence.

By 1997, Hanbo had accumulated more than $6 billion in debt. The façade cracked. Creditors began circling, demanding payments that couldn't be met.

Still, Chung insisted, "Steel is the backbone of the nation. The government won't let Hanbo fall."

But the tide was turning. The Asian Financial Crisis was tightening its grip. Investors grew suspicious.

And the inevitable happened: Hanbo Steel collapsed.

*

The Scandal Unveiled

January 1997

The fall sent shockwaves through South Korea. Investigators uncovered a tangled web of corruption—loans forced through by bribed officials, banks pressured to ignore red flags, and politicians shielding Hanbo in exchange for favours.

Courtrooms replaced boardrooms. Chung Tae-soo was arrested and sentenced to 15 years in prison for corruption and bribery. Senior bankers and politicians were indicted. The scandal exposed the fragile foundations of South Korea's growth miracle and became one of the largest corporate scandals in its history.

The mighty illusion of Hanbo Steel had turned into a national disgrace.

*

Years Later: Hanbo Steel

Today, Hanbo exists only in case studies and legal archives. Its steel plants were sold off, its assets dismantled, and its once-proud headquarters fell silent. The scandal forced South Korea to confront the dark side of its chaebol system—unchecked growth fuelled by crony capitalism.

Chung Tae-soo, once toasted in elite circles, died in 2003, a broken man with a tarnished name. His empire, once projected to rival global giants, became a synonym for corruption.

Yet, Hanbo's fall also became a turning point. It spurred reforms in banking oversight, corporate governance, and the curbing of political favouritism in South Korea's financial system.

For many Koreans, the name Hanbo still evokes a bitter lesson: that ambition without discipline, and power without accountability, can melt even the strongest steel.

***

Chapter 26

BluSmart: The Silent Ride to Nowhere

1515 3rd Street in San Francisco, California, USA

Startup Failure ☑ Weak Financial Model ☑

> Founded in 2019, BluSmart set out to be India's first all-electric ride-hailing service, positioning itself as a green alternative to Ola and Uber. Despite early investor enthusiasm and a futuristic vision, the company struggled with high operating costs, limited charging infrastructure, and intense competition. Once hailed as the "Tesla of Indian mobility," BluSmart became a cautionary tale of ambition outpacing financial sustainability.

Electric Dreams

Gurugram, India, 2019

The corporate office of BluSmart gleamed like a tech temple—glass walls, bean bags in corners, young executives buzzing with excitement. On the whiteboard was scrawled a single phrase in bold letters:

"India's First All-Electric Ride-Hailing Revolution."

Investors leaned forward in leather chairs as the founders clicked through their pitch deck. The numbers sparkled—zero emissions, zero surge pricing, a market hungry for sustainable transport. Outside the window, the honking chaos of Delhi's traffic felt like a perfect metaphor: millions waiting for a better way to move.

"The future," one founder declared, "is not Uber. It is not Ola. The future is green. BluSmart will be the Tesla of India's mobility."

Applause followed. Commitments were made. Capital flowed. The electric cars rolled out, their blue logos glowing like promises of a new tomorrow.

For a brief moment, BluSmart wasn't just a startup. It was hope —wrapped in lithium batteries and venture money.

*

Boardroom of High Voltage

2021. The conference room buzzed with tension. Spreadsheets were projected on the wall—rising revenues, but losses that rose faster.

"The average ride is too cheap," the CFO said, his voice tight. "We subsidise every trip. We need higher fares."

"But if we hike fares, Ola and Uber will crush us," a director shot back.

Silence. Everyone knew the truth. Ola and Uber were burning cash too, but they had deeper pockets. BluSmart was running on the goodwill of ESG-focused funds and green dreams.

The founder tried to calm the storm. "Gentlemen, this is not just about profit. This is about climate. This is about India's future. Investors will stay patient."

But patience, like capital, had limits.

*

Charging Empty

By 2022, problems multiplied. Charging stations promised as BluSmart's competitive edge turned out to be bottlenecks. Cars lined up for hours, batteries drained faster than expected in

Delhi's punishing summers, and drivers complained of wasted time.

"We are running an airline with no fuel," muttered a manager during one crisis meeting.

Meanwhile, Ola and Uber had quietly begun testing their own electric fleets. The green monopoly BluSmart dreamed of was evaporating.

*

The Last Ride

By 2024, cracks became canyons. Investors started asking sharper questions. Losses mounted. Expansion slowed. In town halls, drivers whispered about delayed incentives. Some quit.

At one fateful board meeting, the lead investor leaned forward, fingers steepled.

"We believed in your dream," he said, his voice cold. "But the dream must meet the balance sheet. Without profit, BluSmart will not be the Tesla of India. It will be another story of ambition without discipline."

The founders argued that more time and more money would make the EV future inevitable. But inevitability was not the same as solvency.

The blue cars continued to run, but the company's future was on fumes.

*

Years Later

Delhi, 2028. The BluSmart logo, once seen on every second sedan in Gurugram, had faded. Ola Electric dominated the EV fleet market. Charging stations with the BluSmart brand had either been taken over or dismantled.

Former employees recalled the early days with a mix of pride and bitterness.

“We were ahead of our time,” one said. “But being first is not enough. You need to last.”

On a deserted lot outside Gurugram, a row of dusty electric cars stood abandoned, their batteries dead, their promise broken.

BluSmart had promised a silent ride into the future. Instead, it became a cautionary tale of silence.

***

Chapter 27

Thomas Cook: The Collapse of a Travel Empire

200 Aldersgate Street, London, United Kingdom

Startup Failure ✗ Outdated High-Street Model ☑ Corporate Failure ☑

Thomas Cook, founded in 1841, was once the world's most trusted travel brand, pioneering package holidays and carrying millions abroad. But weighed down by £1.7 billion in debt, an outdated high-street model, and failure to adapt to digital disruption, it collapsed in 2019, triggering Britain's largest peacetime repatriation of 150,000 stranded tourists and marking the end of a 178-year-old travel empire.

The Golden Holiday Dream

It was the summer of 1978, and the beaches of Mallorca glistened under the Mediterranean sun. Rows of chartered jets touched down one after another, their cabins filled with British families clutching straw hats, sunscreen, and Thomas Cook brochures promising "the world within reach."

At the heart of it all, a Thomas Cook tour representative in a crisp yellow blazer waved his clipboard high, calling out names, shepherding excited tourists into waiting buses bound for seaside resorts. Children pressed their noses to the glass, eyes wide with wonder at the turquoise waters. Parents sighed in relief, knowing that every detail—from flights to hotels to meals—had been taken care of.

This was the golden age of Thomas Cook—a company that didn't just sell holidays, it sold dreams. From honeymoon packages in Greece to rail journeys across Europe, the Thomas Cook name meant freedom, escape, and the luxury of a world suddenly opened to the everyday traveller.

What no one knew was that decades later, those very brochures would gather dust, the yellow blazers would be folded away for good, and the empire of holidays would collapse in the dead of night, leaving thousands stranded under foreign skies.

*

The Boardroom

200 Aldersgate Street, London

Early 2019

The oak-panelled boardroom of Thomas Cook's London headquarters was unusually tense on the morning. The company's brass plate, once a proud marker of British travel heritage dating back to 1841, still gleamed on the entrance door. Yet behind it, the empire that had once pioneered the modern package holiday was gasping for breath.

At the head of the table sat Peter Fankhauser, the CEO, his face drawn, eyes bloodshot after yet another sleepless night. A stack of documents lay before him—debt schedules, emergency funding requests, last-minute rescue plans. He looked around at his colleagues: senior executives, bankers, lawyers, government liaisons. Each wore the same strained expression.

"Gentlemen," Fankhauser began, his voice breaking slightly, "unless we secure £200 million by tonight, Thomas Cook will cease to exist."

The words fell like a guillotine. A murmur swept across the room, but no one seemed truly shocked. The signs had been there for years—bloated debt, outdated business models, rising competition from online travel agencies like Booking.

com and Expedia, and the do-it-yourself revolution brought by Skyscanner and Airbnb.

The company's physical network of 500+ high-street travel shops now seemed like relics of a bygone age.

*

The Illusion of Stability

For decades, Thomas Cook had been a household name—synonymous with honeymoons in the Mediterranean, family trips to Spain, and package tours across the globe. It had ferried generations of British holidaymakers abroad, offering the promise of comfort, safety, and affordability.

But inside the company, cracks had begun to show long before the world noticed. In the 2010s, as debt piled high (nearly £1.7 billion by 2019), executives gambled on expanding hotels and airlines rather than investing in digital platforms. They clung to a model that thrived in the 20th century but looked fragile in the 21st.

The boardroom discussions turned desperate. Bankers demanded fresh collateral, governments hesitated to intervene, and shareholders grew restless. Fankhauser tried to rally the team: "We are not just a company," he said, pounding the table. "We are an institution. Millions of customers trust us. We cannot let them down."

But trust alone could not keep planes flying or hotels paid.

*

The Longest Night

September 22, Sunday, 2019

The city wore its season like a melancholy cloak—a low ceiling of grey clouds pressed over Aldersgate Street. The air was damp from an earlier drizzle. The temperature hovered in that uneasy balance—neither warm nor cold—just enough to make a man pull his coat tighter as the evening wind found its way through the city's alleys.

Inside Thomas Cook's headquarters that Sunday, however, the weather was the least of their worries. The air was thick with dread. The boardroom lights illuminated faces etched with fatigue and fear. On the table lay contracts, bailout proposals, and coffee cups gone cold.

For 178 years, Thomas Cook had carried travellers across seas and continents, but now, as the drizzle intensified outside, the company itself was stranded—waiting for a rescue umbrella that would never arrive.

Chairman's voice was heavy: "If the money doesn't come through by morning, we're finished."

An executive nervously shuffled the papers. "We need £200 million. Without it, planes won't fly. Hotels will lock out our customers."

Negotiators dialled into calls with Chinese investors, hedge funds, and UK government officials. The phones buzzed endlessly—creditors, government officials, desperate hotel partners from Spain and Greece demanding answers. Each call felt like a nail in the company's coffin.

Each conversation ended the same way: no deal.

The Finance Director's tone was grim, "The lenders won't extend further. The government won't step in. We're out of options."

The room went silent, broken only by the hum of air-conditioning and the weight of history pressing on everyone present. Thomas Cook—the company that had invented modern tourism and once symbolised adventure and aspiration—was staring into the abyss.

At 2 a.m., the final blow landed. A message flashed across the screen: the rescue deal had collapsed.

Peter Fankhauser, the Chairman for the last five years, said quietly: "A hundred and seventy-eight years… ended in one night."

"Notify the authorities," were his last words.

The directors sat frozen.

Outside, the city slept. But across the world, some 15,000 travellers—honeymooners, families, pensioners on holiday—were about to wake up stranded, their dream vacations turned into logistical nightmares.

Amid the drizzle, one of Britain's proudest companies died on Sunday.

*

The collapse triggered the largest peacetime repatriation in British history. Stranded tourists had to be brought home. Airport departure boards flashed CANCELLED as bewildered families queued, clutching holiday documents now rendered worthless. Staff wept as shops shuttered overnight, their uniforms still neatly pressed. A 178-year-old company—older than Coca-Cola, older than many nations—was gone.

Thomas Cook's end was not just a corporate failure. It was the sudden shattering of trust in a brand that had promised safety, escape, and certainty for generations. The longest night had ended, but the dawn brought chaos.

*

Years Later

The collapse of Thomas Cook became a textbook case of how legacy giants fall—not because the world turned against them, but because they failed to evolve with it.

Years later, travel itself bounced back with digital-first startups, budget airlines, and platforms powered by algorithms. But for millions, the name "Thomas Cook" remained etched in memory as both a symbol of golden holidays and a reminder of corporate complacency.

*

After liquidation, the brand was revived by the Chinese conglomerate, Fosun Tourism Group. However, instead of restoring it as a traditional brick-and-mortar travel company with physical shops and in-person services—the model Thomas Cook had pioneered for over 178 years—Fosun relaunched it as a digital-only travel platform.

That shift meant the legacy of Thomas Cook as a trusted, traditional travel agency with high-street presence, package tours, and personal service was effectively lost. What survived was only the brand name, not the historic business model or its cultural significance.

*

In September 2024, eSky Group (a Polish travel tech company) acquired the Thomas Cook UK business from Fosun (excluding China). The CEO currently leading Thomas Cook under that revived business is Alan French.

*

On quiet afternoons, passersby still pause outside shuttered storefronts that once bore the iconic yellow globe logo. For them, Thomas Cook was not just a traditional travel company—it was an emotion, a part of Britain's cultural fabric. Its end was more than bankruptcy; it was the closing of a chapter in the story of how the world once travelled.

***

Chapter 28

HIH Insurance: When Trust Became Dust

Sydney, Australia

Reckless Expansion ☑ Corporate Failure ☑

HIH Insurance, once Australia's second-largest insurer, collapsed in 2001 under a staggering A$5.3 billion deficit, making it the country's biggest corporate failure: reckless expansion, underpriced policies, and the disastrous FAI acquisition exposed years of mismanagement and weak oversight. The fallout left thousands uninsured, employees jobless, and founder Ray Williams imprisoned—cementing HIH as a cautionary tale of hubris and regulatory failure.

The Glittering Façade

Sydney, Australia, Late 1990s

The lobby of HIH Insurance's headquarters was a cathedral of glass and chrome, where visitors were greeted by tall banners proclaiming:

"HIH—Protecting Australians at Home and Abroad."

The company was everywhere—insuring cars, homes, businesses, even hospitals. It had become the second-largest insurer in Australia, its name synonymous with stability and trust.

Ray Williams, the charismatic co-founder, loved to walk the halls, pausing to shake hands with young employees, offering them the kind of paternal smile that inspired loyalty. He often boasted at industry dinners that HIH wasn't just an insurer—it was a guardian of the Australian way of life.

But behind the handshakes and banners, HIH was bleeding quietly, its foundation hollowed out by reckless expansion, underpriced policies, and disastrous acquisitions.

*

Boardroom Unease

The boardroom on Level 12 had once been a place of triumphs—deals signed, acquisitions toasted with champagne. But by 2000, its walls had absorbed a different energy: hushed arguments, worried glances, and the quiet scratching of pens over balance sheets that didn't add up.

At one tense meeting, a director pushed a file across the table. "The FAI acquisition is dragging us down. Loss reserves are underestimated. If these claims hit at once, we're finished."

Ray Williams bristled. "Gentlemen, these are temporary setbacks. The market believes in HIH. Our shareholders believe in us. What we need is confidence, not doubt."

But the numbers told another story. Reserves were grossly inadequate, reinsurance deals were complex, and losses were mounting in overseas markets, particularly in the U.S. and U.K. The empire looked strong from the outside, but inside, it was a crumbling cathedral of paper promises.

*

The Cracks Widen

In late 2000, whispers began to circulate in Sydney's financial district. Analysts questioned HIH's ability to meet future claims. Credit agencies grew uneasy. Even brokers, long loyal, began shifting clients quietly to rivals.

Regulators raised red flags, but HIH's reassurances sounded convincing—on paper. The market carried on, even as the storm gathered.

Employees noticed strange signs: delayed payments to vendors, executives holding more "closed-door" meetings, and auditors demanding yet another round of clarifications. Some whispered that HIH had become "too big to be questioned."

*

The Collapse

March 15, 2001

The inevitable happened: HIH Insurance was placed into provisional liquidation.

The scale of the collapse was staggering—an estimated A$5.3 billion hole in its books, making it the largest corporate failure in Australian history.

Across the country, panic erupted. Families called frantically to ask whether their home and health policies were worthless. Small businesses discovered overnight that their coverage had vanished. Hospitals wondered how to pay bills that HIH had promised to settle.

News anchors spoke with hushed tones. One headline screamed:

"Australia's Insurance Giant Collapses—Millions at Risk."

The boardroom that once echoed with confidence was now occupied by liquidators, investigators, and lawyers flipping through mountains of contracts, unravelling years of deception and denial.

*

The Reckoning

The collapse led to a Royal Commission, exposing not only HIH's reckless leadership but also systemic failures. Regulators had been slow. Auditors had signed off on misleading accounts. Advisors had looked the other way.

Ray Williams, once celebrated as a visionary, became a symbol of corporate greed and incompetence. In 2005, he was sentenced to prison for misleading investors and failing in his duties as a director. The image of the once-proud founder, head bowed in court, contrasted starkly with the confident man who had once claimed HIH would "secure Australia's future."

Employees lost jobs. Shareholders lost fortunes. Policyholders lost peace of mind. The name HIH became shorthand for betrayal.

*

Years Later

Two decades later, the HIH collapse remains etched in Australia's corporate memory. It reshaped governance laws, tightened solvency rules, and became a permanent case study in universities worldwide.

Ray Williams, released from prison a broken man, faded into obscurity, a living reminder of ambition turned to ash.

Yet the damage lingered. Thousands of Australians never fully recovered from the shock of finding themselves uninsured overnight. The sight of shuttered HIH offices, their logos stripped from buildings, stood like tombstones for years—a reminder of how quickly trust can vanish.

In business circles, when executives speak of risk, they invoke HIH with a shudder. The scandal was more than a balance sheet failure; it was a betrayal of public faith, proof that even giants can fall when vision turns to hubris and oversight turns to silence.

***

Chapter 29

Saradha Group: Bronze that Glittered Like Gold

Financial Scandal ☑ Ponzi Scheme ☑

The Saradha Group scam (2008–2013) was a massive Ponzi scheme in West Bengal that lured millions of small investors with promises of high returns, but collapsed in 2013, wiping out savings worth an estimated ₹20,000 crore. Led by Sudipto Sen, the group expanded into media, real estate, and film, but its model was unsustainable. The fallout devastated poor households, triggered suicides, and dragged politicians, celebrities, and journalists into controversy—leaving behind one of India's most infamous financial scandals.

The Glitter of Easy Riches

Kolkata, early 2010s. In the humid air of Bengal's bustling towns, posters and billboards shouted promises of prosperity. Glossy leaflets fell into eager hands:

"Double your money in just three years."

"Safe, secure, and government-backed."

The name Saradha Group became a talisman of hope. From small farmers to schoolteachers, from housewives saving for their daughter's wedding to retired pensioners looking for a steady income—everyone seemed to trust Saradha.

At the centre of it all was Sudipto Sen, the empire's enigmatic chairman. He was not flamboyant like Vijay Mallya, nor visionary like Gautam Adani. Instead, he cultivated the image of a benevolent guardian—soft-spoken, approachable, almost paternal. To the common man, Sen was the man who would make dreams come true.

But beneath the polished offices and the promises, Saradha was no fortress. It was a Ponzi scheme; a sandcastle built on shifting tides.

*

The Expansion of an Illusion

Saradha was not just about "chit funds." Soon, it sprawled into media, real estate, tourism, and even film production. Bengali movie stars endorsed it, journalists defended it, and politicians attended its glittering functions.

In villages, local agents—often respected community members—went door-to-door, collecting small savings from ordinary families. In city offices, smartly dressed executives reassured investors with glossy brochures and confident words.

The group boasted of employing over 1,500 agents and serving millions of depositors. The money poured in, and with it came luxury: plush cars, expensive gifts, celebrity endorsements. To many, Saradha looked like Bengal's answer to Reliance.

But in the boardroom, the reality was grim. The money coming in was not invested in productive ventures. It was used to pay old investors while luring new ones—classic Ponzi mechanics hidden behind the mask of diversification.

*

The Day the Bubble Burst

By 2013, the tide began to turn. Regulators had begun sniffing around chit fund operations. Payments slowed. Investors grew restless.

One hot April morning, agents who had once been greeted with folded hands now found themselves chased down narrow lanes by furious depositors. The offices of Saradha were mobbed, shutters pulled down in haste. Whispers spread like wildfire: "The company has collapsed."

In the boardroom, panic reigned. Sudipto Sen, realising the net was closing in, typed out a desperate, rambling 67-page confession letter before fleeing Kolkata in a white SUV. His empire, once glittering, had crumbled overnight, exposing losses estimated at ₹20,000 crore, one of India's largest financial scams.

The collapse devastated millions. A farmer in Nadia who had trusted Saradha with his life savings hanged himself. A widow in Cooch Behar fainted on learning her deposit was gone. Entire families were ruined.

The political fallout was explosive. Allegations flew that Saradha's money had funded election campaigns and bought media silence. The scandal spread its dark shadow into the corridors of power.

*

Courtrooms and Chains

Sudipto Sen was finally arrested in Kashmir, a fugitive no more. Images of him, dishevelled and handcuffed, splashed across television screens. In courtrooms, as evidence piled up, his soft-spoken demeanour gave way to weary silence.

For many, he was less a criminal mastermind than a man who rode a tiger he could not dismount. Yet for the millions who lost everything, he was nothing less than a betrayer of trust.

*

The Human Toll

What made the Saradha scam particularly tragic was its widespread impact. It did not simply hurt wealthy investors or speculative traders—it devoured the savings of the poor.

Housewives lost their gold, rickshaw pullers their rainy-day funds, farmers their harvest money.

And the agents—many of them simple villagers who had believed in Saradha themselves—found their lives destroyed too, branded as fraudsters by the very communities they had once served.

The scandal was not just financial—it was deeply social, a scar on Bengal's collective psyche.

*

Years Later

A decade on, the ruins of Saradha still haunt Bengal. The CBI continues to investigate, names of politicians still surface, and trials crawl slowly through India's overburdened legal system.

For many investors, justice feels distant, and compensation schemes have been too little, too late. The offices, once buzzing with agents, now stand abandoned, their signboards faded and peeling in the monsoon rains.

Sudipto Sen remains in custody, a fallen emperor of illusions. His name evokes anger and sorrow—a reminder of broken promises and destroyed lives.

In business schools, the Saradha Group is taught not as a corporation but as a warning: how unchecked greed, political complicity, and the hunger of the poor for security can combine into catastrophe.

For Bengal, Saradha was more than a scam. It was a betrayal of trust, a wound that, years later, still aches whenever someone knocks on a villager's door, offering an "investment scheme."

The House of Sand had fallen, but its dust still lingers.

***

Chapter 30

Bharatpe: The Unicorn That Burned Too Bright

Sadhna Enclave, Malviya Nagar, New Delhi, India

Allegations of Financial Mismanagement ☑
Governance Failure ☑

BharatPe, once hailed as a fintech unicorn revolutionising digital payments, imploded in 2022 after allegations of financial mismanagement and governance failures against co-founder Ashneer Grover. A leaked audio clip triggered audits that uncovered forged invoices and misuse of funds, leading to Grover's dramatic ouster. The scandal tarnished BharatPe's brand, serving as a cautionary tale of unchecked ambition and inadequate oversight in India's startup ecosystem.

Indian Institute of Management

Ahmadabad, Gujarat, 2005

The neon lights of the IIM Campus flickered against the evening sky as a restless young man, Ashneer Grover, sat with his friends on the steps of a college canteen. He was sharp, witty, and armed with an arrogance that made him impossible to ignore. Where others saw exams and safe jobs, Ashneer saw shortcuts, loopholes, and a faster road to success.

Years later, at the glittering offices of BharatPe, that same restless energy had transformed into raw ambition. Grover paced the glass-walled boardroom in a designer jacket, speaking in the same blunt, biting tone that once unsettled his professors.

Investors leaned in, half-impressed, half-intimidated. Every sentence carried both vision and threat.

His colleagues admired him, feared him, envied him—often all at once. Behind the charisma lay something darker: a man who could not slow down, who lived on confrontation, who thrived on control.

In that moment, as BharatPe grew into a fintech darling, it seemed nothing could stop him. But in the shadows, the same traits that had propelled him—pride, defiance, audacity—were already sowing the seeds of collapse.

*

BharatPe: The Dream of Ashneer Grover

Gurugram, 2021

The plush conference room was buzzing with energy. It was the peak of India's startup boom, and BharatPe was riding the wave. Posters on the wall screamed "India's fintech revolution is here". On the table sat investors from Sequoia, Tiger Global, and Coatue, their eyes glistening with the promise of India's next big unicorn.

At the head of the table was Ashneer Grover, the co-founder with a sharp tongue, a restless energy, and the swagger of a man who believed he was untouchable. "We are not just building a payments company," he declared, pacing like a showman, "We are building the backbone of Bharat's financial system. BharatPe will outgrow Paytm, PhonePe, even Google Pay."

The room erupted in applause. Term sheets were signed. Valuations skyrocketed. In just three years, BharatPe was valued at $2.8 billion, a rocket ship defying gravity.

*

Cracks in the Unicorn Armour

But behind the glittering numbers, cracks had begun to appear. Vendors whispered about delayed payments. Employees complained of a toxic culture, fearing the wrath of Grover's infamous temper. Still, nobody dared speak openly; BharatPe was the darling of the ecosystem, and dissent was drowned out by valuation frenzy.

Then came the leak—a viral audio clip in early 2022. Ashneer Grover was allegedly heard abusing a Kotak Mahindra Bank employee over IPO share allocations. The clip spread like wildfire, shaking the company's clean image. Soon, internal audits followed.

The results were damning: misuse of company funds, forged invoices, and millions allegedly siphoned off through sham vendors tied to family members. The "fintech revolution" was suddenly under the scanner.

*

The Boardroom Showdown

The boardroom that once echoed with investor cheers now reeked of tension. Ashneer sat across from the independent directors, his trademark confidence replaced by flashes of defiance. "This is a witch hunt!" he barked. "Without me, there is no BharatPe."

But the evidence on the projector screen told another story: irregular vendor payments, lavish personal expenses routed through company accounts, even private jets billed as business development.

An uneasy silence hung over the room.

Finally, one board member spoke: "Ashneer, this is no longer about vision. This is about governance."

*

Fallout

March 2022

Ashneer Grover was forced to resign, stripped of power in the very empire he had built.

The scandal sent shockwaves across India's startup world. BharatPe's brand took a beating; merchants and customers grew wary, rivals seized the opportunity, and regulators began tightening oversight of fintech companies.

Investors who once cheered Grover's bravado now distanced themselves, insisting on stronger corporate governance across their portfolios. Meanwhile, Grover reinvented himself as a media personality, writing a tell-all memoir and appearing on talk shows—turning scandal into yet another stage for his theatrics.

*

Years Later

By 2025, BharatPe still existed, but the sheen of its unicorn glory had dulled. The company focused quietly on its lending business, overshadowed by UPI giants and new-age neobanks. The Grover saga became a case study in business schools: how unchecked ambition, founder hubris, and weak governance could derail even the most promising ventures.

Ashneer himself remained a polarising figure—mocked by some, admired by others for his audacity. The empire he once dreamed of building was no longer his, and yet his name remained inseparable from BharatPe's rise and fall. After leaving BharatPe, Ashneer founded a third unicorn, which launched the fantasy sports platform CrickPe, and is also preparing to launch an app for medical loans called ZeroPe. His first unicorn was Grofers (now Blinkit), where he served as Chief Financial Officer in 2015, before its significant funding and rise to unicorn status. He also hosted the TV show Rise and Fall. These ventures follow his high-profile exit from BharatPe in 2022 and a subsequent legal settlement in late 2024 that severed all ties between him and the company.

In the end, BharatPe was not just a fintech story. It was a mirror held up to India's startup ecosystem, showing how quickly dreams could turn into drama and valuations into scandals.

***

Chapter 31

Videocon: From Living Rooms to Courtrooms

Chittegaon, Aurangabad, Maharashtra, India

Startup Failure ✗ Over Expansion ☑ Bankruptcy ☑

Videocon, once India's leading consumer electronics giant and a household brand in the 1980s and 90s, collapsed under ₹90,000 crore of debt after losing ground to global rivals and overextending into telecom and oil. Its downfall deepened with the ICICI Bank loan scandal involving Venugopal Dhoot and Chanda Kochhar, leading to bankruptcy proceedings in 2018. Once the "TV King of India," Videocon today survives only as a case study in hubris, debt, and governance failure.

Videocon: The TV King of India

The grand headquarters of Videocon Industries in Aurangabad once shimmered like a symbol of middle-class aspiration. In the 1980s and 1990s, it was impossible to enter an Indian home without spotting a Videocon TV set, refrigerator, or washing machine. For millions, Videocon wasn't just an appliance—it was a badge of progress, a signal that India was moving into a new age of modern living.

In those heady days, Venugopal Dhoot, the suave and ambitious founder, was a household name. The "TV King of India," they called him. His advertisements featured cricket stars, film celebrities, and smiling families gathered around their Videocon products.

The company expanded aggressively, moving from consumer electronics into oil, telecom, and real estate. In 2008, it even dared to enter the telecom war with Videocon Telecom, a move that promised to make the Dhoot family a permanent fixture in India's corporate elite.

But beneath the glossy commercials and high-decibel launches, Videocon was walking on fragile ground.

Cracks Behind the Screen

By the late 2000s, global brands like Samsung, LG, and Sony had muscled into the Indian market. Videocon, once the pride of India's manufacturing, struggled to keep up with its technology, design, and aggressive marketing budgets.

Sales declined. Margins shrank. Yet the Dhoots were not ready to give up the glamour of expansion. Loans were taken—massive ones. Banks, dazzled by Videocon's legacy, continued to extend credit.

The debt piled up to ₹90,000 crore.

But the real twist came with the ICICI Bank-Videocon scandal. Allegations surfaced that Venugopal Dhoot had secured loans for Videocon through quid pro quo arrangements with ICICI Bank's CEO, Chanda Kochhar, and her husband, Deepak Kochhar.

What had once been a proud Indian multinational was now entangled in whispers of corruption and favouritism.

*

The Boardroom Storm

The boardroom in Mumbai was thick with unease. Executives shuffled nervously as the financial statements were laid out. Losses were staggering. Debt obligations loomed like vultures circling overhead.

Venugopal Dhoot, still carrying his trademark smile, tried to calm the storm. "Videocon is too big to fail. We have assets across the world. The market will bounce back."

However, the board members knew the truth: assets had been pledged, revenues had collapsed, and creditors were circling. The once-proud king of consumer durables was cornered.

Bankers, who once courted Dhoot, now demanded repayment with icy precision. "Mr Dhoot," one senior banker said, his voice cold, "we need to know—where did the money go?"

No answer could save him.

*

Collapse

By 2018, Videocon was referred to bankruptcy courts. The empire that once dominated living rooms had become one of India's largest corporate defaulters. Factories shut down, employees were left jobless, and the brand that had defined an era vanished from shelves.

The investigation into the ICICI-Videocon loan scandal grew sharper. Chanda Kochhar resigned under a cloud of suspicion, and Venugopal Dhoot found himself in and out of custody, his legacy reduced to courtroom hearings and newspaper headlines about fraud.

*

Years Later

By 2025, Videocon will be remembered only as a relic in the minds of those who grew up in the 1980s and 1990s. For younger Indians, the name barely registered—a ghost of a brand that once ruled their parents' homes.

Venugopal Dhoot's empire was dismantled, his assets auctioned off to repay creditors. ICICI Bank faced reputational scars that took years to heal. Chanda Kochhar's fall from grace remained one of the most dramatic in Indian banking history.

In business schools, Videocon became a case study—not just of debt and fraud, but of hubris, missed opportunities, and the danger of living too long on past glory.

The televisions that once brought joy to Indian families now lie forgotten in scrap yards, their brand logos fading under the dust of time.

Videocon had once promised to light up India's homes. In the end, it only lit up the headlines of financial scandals.

***

Chapter 32
The Great Stock-Market Battle

Dalal Street, Mumbai, India

Stock Market Acumen ☑

> In 1982, Dhirubhai Ambani faced off against a powerful Bear Cartel that tried to crush Reliance by short-selling its shares. While the cartel gloated, Dhirubhai quietly orchestrated a counterattack through loyal brokers, triggering a short squeeze that left his rivals in chaos. The episode transformed Reliance into a stock market powerhouse and cemented Dhirubhai's reputation as a master strategist who outplayed the establishment on Dalal Street.

The Calm and the Storm

The Arabian Sea glistened under the early sun as Dhirubhai Ambani walked along Marine Drive, his pace steady, his white kurta fluttering in the sea breeze. Around him, joggers and morning walkers passed by, but he seemed far away, his mind sharpened not by the waves but by numbers, leverage, and the invisible currents of Dalal Street.

He paused for a moment, looking at the horizon. "Storms don't frighten the ocean," he murmured to himself. "They only prove its depth."

*

A smoky café in Fort, Bombay, not far from the stock exchange. The Bear Cartel was gathered, their laughter cutting through the smell of cigarettes and strong filter coffee. One slammed a newspaper on the table—Reliance shares had slumped the previous day.

"Textile-wala has been taught his lesson," sneered one.

Another raised his cup, "To the end of Reliance! By settlement day, he'll be begging us."

They toasted, confident, their eyes glinting with greed.

*

Back on Marine Drive, Dhirubhai continued his walk. His face betrayed no worry, only a faint smile—the kind a chess master wears before making his final move. The sea wind carried his words, whispered almost like a prayer: *Let them laugh today. By the time the dust settles, it is I who will write tomorrow's price.*

The stage was set. The ocean against the storm.

*

The Great Stock Market Battle

The Trading Ring

It was the Bombay of the early 1980s. The city still smelled of salt, sweat, and ambition. At Dalal Street, the Bombay Stock Exchange was not yet electronic; it was a cauldron of voices, hand signals, and cigarette smoke. Brokers huddled in their coats, shouting prices, their eyes darting to catch the faintest signal of change.

That morning in 1982, there was a strange electricity in the air. A group of powerful brokers—later known as the Bear Cartel—had launched a daring assault. Their target: Reliance Industries, the company of a rising but still underestimated man—Dhirubhai Ambani.

They had short-sold Reliance shares in massive quantities, betting that the stock would tumble. "Ambani's empire is over-leveraged," they whispered in corridors. "It cannot last."

*

The Whispered Wager

Inside a smoky café near Flora Fountain, the cartel celebrated. They had cornered dozens of brokers, convinced them to dump Reliance. One of them raised his glass and sneered,

“Dhirubhai is nothing but a weaver who thinks he can outsmart the markets. Let’s see how he handles this storm.”

But far away, in a quiet office, Dhirubhai sat unflustered. His eyes, sharp behind rimmed glasses, betrayed no fear. He listened to his aides describe the cartel’s moves.

Then, with a calm smile, he said, “They don’t understand. Reliance is not just a company—it's an idea. And I do not lose to whispers.”

He summoned his allies, a group of loyal brokers who would come to be known as the “Friends of Reliance.”

*

Chaos in Dalal Street

The following days saw a scene straight out of a financial war drama.

The Bear Cartel kept selling Reliance shares aggressively, pushing the price down. The trading ring erupted in shouts of “Sell Reliance! Sell!” The ticker board flickered with blood-red numbers.

But then, a counterforce appeared.

The Friends of Reliance began buying every share the cartel dumped, absorbing the shock. Day after day, Reliance shares found unexpected buyers. The cartel grew nervous. “Who is supporting this price? How can the buying be endless?”

By the end of the week, the cartel was in a tight spot. They had sold shares they did not own, and now they had to deliver. However, the Friends of Reliance had acquired nearly every share on the market.

*

The Squeeze

On settlement day, panic struck. The Bears scrambled to find Reliance shares to deliver, but the cupboards were bare. Prices shot up as they begged for deliveries. Brokers screamed, telephones rang incessantly, and fortunes vanished in minutes.

The cartel members, once smug in their confidence, were now pale and sweating.

One of them muttered, "This Ambani… he has turned the market into a theatre, and we are the clowns."

In contrast, Dhirubhai, far from the chaos, walked calmly in his office, his trademark smile intact. He had orchestrated a short squeeze so powerful that the Bear Cartel collapsed under its own arrogance.

*

The Legend is Born

When the dust settled, Reliance emerged stronger than ever. The Bear Cartel was humiliated; some brokers even faced ruin. The public saw Dhirubhai not as a gambler, but as a strategist—a man who could outmanoeuvre the most entrenched elites of Dalal Street at their own game.

The legend of Reliance had begun.

*

Years Later

The 1982 battle became a defining moment in India's financial history. Dhirubhai Ambani's victory signalled a new era—the rise of aggressive, fearless Indian entrepreneurs who could challenge old money and entrenched cartels.

Critics would continue to question the methods, whisper about political support, and debate whether the "Friends of Reliance" were just proxies. But there was no denying one fact: the rules of the Indian stock market had changed forever.

In the corridors of Dalal Street, old brokers still recall that week in 1982 with a shudder. "Reliance was more than a stock that day," one of them once said. "It was a storm. And everyone had to learn to live with it."

*

Dalal Street, Mumbai

It was settlement day, the make-or-break moment.

Dalal Street was a furnace of panic. Brokers shouted themselves hoarse, phones rang endlessly, and clerks ran with slips of paper as if carrying lifelines. The Bear Cartel was in chaos. They had short-sold lakhs of Reliance shares, and now they could not find them to deliver. Prices shot up like a fire out of control.

Inside his office at Maker Chambers IV, Dhirubhai sat like a general in a war room.

His aides rushed in, breathless. "Sir, the Bears are finished. They can't find a single Reliance share for delivery!"

Another whispered with awe, "The price has jumped past 150. They are begging for sellers. What should we do now?"

Dhirubhai leaned back, his fingers tapping on the armrest. His voice was calm, almost soft, but it carried the weight of inevitability: "This is what happens when arrogance challenges conviction. Let them sweat. We hold the shares. They hold only fear."

An aide, barely able to hide his grin, asked, "Sir, shall we release some stock to them?"

Dhirubhai smiled—a sharp, knowing smile. "No. Not yet. Let them learn the value of every share they mocked. Reliance is not paper; it is faith. And today, faith will win."

At the exchange, the Bears were on their knees, calling in favours, offering absurd prices, even begging. Brokers who once laughed at Dhirubhai's "textile empire" now scrambled to survive.

As word spread of Dhirubhai's quiet counterattack, the ring buzzed with awe. A veteran broker muttered, "He is playing chess while the rest of us are playing marbles."

Back at Maker Chambers, when victory was certain, Dhirubhai finally gave the order: "Release a few shares. Not to crush them completely, but to remind them—Reliance does not bow. It never will."

The room erupted in cheers.

*

Years Later

That week in 1982 entered Dalal Street folklore. It was not just a financial skirmish; it was a war for respect. Dhirubhai's quiet defiance, his unshakable confidence, and his ruthless strategy turned him from a textile magnate into a stock market legend.

For the Bears, it was a lesson written in loss: never underestimate the man from Chorwad.

***

Chapter 33
Evergrande: The Skyscraper Mirage

Guangzhou, China (1996-2025)

Changed Government Policies ☑ Over Leverage ☑
Startup Failure ✗

Evergrande, once China's largest property developer, grew on a mountain of debt, fuelled by presales and political connections. When confidence collapsed in 2021, it triggered protests, unfinished cities, and global financial tremors. What was built as a symbol of prosperity became a towering monument to over-leverage and broken promises.

The Banquet

The chandeliers of the Evergrande Banquet Hall blazed with a thousand golden lights, their crystal drops shimmering like falling stars. Waiters in white gloves floated silently, pouring streams of fiery Moutai into crystal glasses. At the head of the grand table sat Xu Jiayin, his silk tie perfectly knotted, a smile carved in steel. Around him: ministers, celebrities, and business tycoons, all laughing as if wealth itself were eternal.

The air smelled of abalone, shark fin soup, and power. A pop star crooned softly in the corner, her voice competing with the clink of glasses. Xu raised his cup, voice ringing with confidence.

"Evergrande is not just a company. It is the pulse of China's rise. We build cities, we build futures, we build dreams."

The hall erupted in applause, champagne bubbling over like promises.

But outside the gilded doors, on the rain-slicked streets of Shenzhen, hundreds of homebuyers huddled under umbrellas. Their placards were smeared with water, their voices hoarse but unyielding: "Give us our homes! Return our money!"

The contrast was brutal. Inside, luxury and laughter. Outside, rage and despair. The music drowned out the cries—for now.

*

The Skyscraper Mirage

The glittering skyline of Shenzhen stood as China's proud symbol of modern ambition—towers piercing the clouds, neon lights reflected in the Pearl River, cranes swaying like mechanical dragons. And at the centre of this architectural frenzy stood Evergrande, the behemoth of real estate, its founder Xu Jiayin hailed as a visionary who transformed farmland into sprawling megacities.

But in the marble corridors of Evergrande's headquarters, ambition had already begun to rot into something darker.

*

The Boardroom

September, 2020

The mahogany-panelled boardroom on the 38th floor overlooked acres of Evergrande's own projects—half-built towers rising in the distance like skeletal giants. Xu Jiayin sat at the head of the long oval table, his presence commanding, his tailored suit a sharp contrast to the sweat-drenched workers labouring below.

Stacks of balance sheets were spread before the directors, their pages bleeding with red ink. Whispered numbers hung in the air like smoke: $300 billion in liabilities.

A finance officer cleared his throat, voice hesitant.

"Chairman Xu… the cash flow from presales is tightening. Buyers are losing confidence. The banks…" He trailed off, unable to finish.

Xu's eyes narrowed. His tone was iron. "Confidence is everything. We build not only buildings but belief. Without belief, China's dream collapses."

Another director ventured, "But the apartments… many are unfinished. Buyers protest in the streets. If deliveries stop —"

Xu slammed his fist on the table. The crystal water glasses rattled. "We will borrow more. Sell assets. Promise more. The Party will not let Evergrande fall. We are too big, too vital. Do you understand?"

The CFO burst out. "No. We can't do it anymore - Three Red Lines bars us from doing so."

In August 2020, China introduced financing restrictions for the real estate sector, known as the "three red lines. This policy curbed the rapid expansion of real estate companies and reduced the share of real estate-related credit in the financial sector.

The room fell silent. Outside, cranes continued to swing, lifting steel into a sky already heavy with debt.

*

The Mirage of Wealth

For years, Evergrande had sold dreams before they were built—glossy brochures, scale models lit like jewels, promises of luxury apartments in cities still under construction. Ordinary Chinese families poured their savings into these presales, convinced that Evergrande was indestructible.

Xu Jiayin himself lived like a sovereign. Banquets of abalone and shark fin soup, private jets, luxury villas, and a lifestyle fit for an emperor. While construction sites halted for lack of funds,

Xu's social calendar glittered with political soirées and celebrity appearances.

The image was intoxicating. But cracks were spreading beneath the glass façade.

*

The Collapse

By 2021, the illusion could no longer hold. Buyers staged mass protests, chanting outside Evergrande offices. Videos went viral of desperate families shouting, "Give us our homes!" Construction workers abandoned sites, leaving behind forests of lifeless concrete pillars.

The boardroom turned into a bunker. Creditors demanded repayment. International investors panicked. The Chinese government, long accused of propping up giants, began to distance itself.

One director whispered the unthinkable: "Chairman… we are bankrupt in everything but name."

Xu stared at the skyline—towers rising like hollow monuments—and for the first time, his voice broke. "Evergrande was meant to be eternal. How could eternity fall so fast?"

*

Years Later

By the mid-2020s, Evergrande's story became a cautionary tale told in hushed tones. The company's once-proud projects dotted China like ghost cities, half-completed, their empty windows staring out like eyes of broken promises.

Xu Jiayin himself was placed under investigation, his empire dismantled piece by piece. For ordinary citizens, the collapse was not just financial but personal—life savings wiped out, homes undelivered, dreams betrayed.

The world realised that Evergrande was not just a corporate failure. It was a mirror reflecting China's debt-fuelled growth, its obsession with scale, and its fragile balance between state control and market greed.

***

Chapter 34

Rajat Gupta: The Fall of A Former MD

New York, USA

Insider Trading ☑

Rajat Kumar Gupta is an Indian-American business executive who, as CEO, was the first foreign-born managing director of McKinsey & Company from 1994 to 2003. In 2012, he was convicted of insider trading and spent two years in prison. Gupta was a board member of corporations including Goldman Sachs, Procter & Gamble, and American Airlines, as well as an advisor to non-profit organisations such as the Bill & Melinda Gates Foundation and The Global Fund to Fight AIDS, Tuberculosis, and Malaria. He is the co-founder of the Indian School of Business, American India Foundation, New Silk Route, and Scandent Solutions.

The Boardroom

McKinsey's New York Headquarters

Somewhere Between 1994-2003

The room glittered under soft white lights. The long mahogany table stretched endlessly, lined with some of the sharpest business minds in the world. At the head sat Rajat Gupta—impeccably dressed, posture regal, his voice calm yet commanding.

He was the man who had rewritten the immigrant dream: orphaned in Kolkata, groomed at IIT Delhi, polished at Harvard Business School, and now, the first foreign-born Managing Director of McKinsey & Company.

As he spoke, his colleagues hung on every word. Gupta wasn't just a consultant. He was a bridge between Wall Street and Silicon Valley, between the West and the rising power of India. He dined with Bill Gates, advised Goldman Sachs, whispered strategy to CEOs, and was on the boards of Procter & Gamble and American Airlines.

In that moment, he looked untouchable.

But power has a way of whispering new temptations.

*

The Whisper in the Boardroom

200 West Street, New York, USA, 2008

The Goldman Sachs boardroom was a fortress of polished wood and steel nerves. The world outside was burning - Lehman Brothers had fallen, banks were collapsing, markets choking. Inside, the directors sat like war generals, plotting survival.

Lloyd Blankfein leaned forward, his voice clipped, carrying both authority and dread. "Gentlemen, Warren Buffett has agreed. Five billion. It will stabilise us."

The room froze. It wasn't just money; it was validation, salvation. This was information worth more than gold—and it had to be guarded until morning.

At the far end, Rajat Gupta adjusted his tie. He nodded along with the others, expression smooth, professional, unreadable. Yet beneath that calm exterior, something twisted inside him. For decades, he had been the consultant's consultant, the man CEOs trusted, the immigrant boy who rose to become head of McKinsey, the pride of a global Indian elite.

But respect was not the same as reverence. He was always the smartest man in the room, but rarely the richest. He could command boardrooms, but not yachts. His peers—the billionaires—lived in a different stratosphere. Gupta wanted that recognition, that belonging, the intoxicating sheen of ultimate power.

As the meeting ended, directors left in silence, the weight of confidentiality etched into their faces. Gupta lingered, footsteps echoing against marble walls. He slipped his hand into his pocket, touching the phone like a talisman. His rational mind whispered restraint. His ego whispered louder.

He dialled. His voice, calm but urgent, cut through the static. "Warren Buffett is coming in. Five billion. Don't wait."

On the other side, Raj Rajaratnam—the hedge fund shark—grinned. The line crackled with opportunity.

That night, Gupta lay awake, Manhattan glittering beyond his window. He told himself it wasn't greed, merely a gesture, a bridge between friends. But deep down, he knew: it was about belonging. About being seen, finally, as one of them.

*

The Seduction of Power

Enter Raj Rajaratnam—billionaire hedge fund manager of Galleon Group, known for his appetite for information, his charm, and his ruthless pursuit of profits. He invited Gupta into a new orbit—where stock tips traded faster than truths, where friendship was blurred with insider whispers.

Over dinners and late-night calls, Rajaratnam dangled promises: influence, wealth beyond consultancy fees, the thrill of being in the inner circle of Wall Street's power game.

Gupta, who had lived most of his career by the book, found himself intoxicated by the access. His phone calls, later captured on wiretaps, revealed moments of weakness. A whisper about

Goldman Sachs' quarterly results—a nudge about Warren Buffett's secret $5 billion investment.

Small leaks. But enough to sink a reputation built over four decades.

*

The Fall

When the FBI raided Galleon's offices, the dominoes began to fall. Rajaratnam was sentenced to 11 years for insider trading. And in a stunning twist, Rajat Gupta—the golden boy of global business—was implicated.

The trial was surreal. The courtroom saw a parade of business titans and old friends, testifying, defending, or watching in silence. Gupta himself remained dignified, composed, denying intent, but the wiretaps were damning.

The jury's verdict was swift: guilty on insider trading charges.

The immigrant dream had cracked under the weight of whispered secrets.

*

The Human Weakness

Gupta was not a fraudster in the Enron sense. He wasn't cooking books or creating phantom companies. His was a weakness of another kind: the temptation to remain relevant in the world of billionaires, the craving for a seat at the innermost circle of power.

It wasn't money he lacked—it was the thrill, the validation, the sense of belonging. And that human weakness became his undoing.

*

Years Later

In 2012, the empire of whispers collapsed. Rajat Gupta was convicted of insider trading. The world saw not the immigrant success story, not the boardroom luminary, but a man who let the hunger to belong eclipse a lifetime of integrity.

After serving two years in prison, Gupta walked out quietly, a free man but forever marked.

He retreated to writing—his memoir Mind Without Fear attempted to reclaim dignity, telling the story of a man who had risen from the ashes of loss to conquer the world, and then stumbled.

In conferences, he spoke softly about resilience, about mistakes, about rebuilding. Yet in hushed corners of Wall Street, his name was invoked as a cautionary tale: how even the most respected, the most polished, the most untouchable—can fall.

The boardroom where he once reigned still exists, the mahogany table polished as ever. But if you lean in close, you might still hear the faint echo of a voice that once commanded the room… and then, a whisper that undid it all.

***

Chapter 35
Wirecard—The Phantom Billions

Aschheim, Bavaria, Germany

Embezzlement ☑

Phantom billions, political protection, and regulatory blindness fuelled Wirecard's spectacular rise and collapse. Once Germany's fintech pride, it became Europe's greatest corporate scandal—ending with a vanished CFO, a jailed CEO, and €1.9 billion that never existed.

The Window at Sunset

The glass façade of Wirecard's Munich headquarters shimmered in the fading light. From his office on the top floor, Markus Braun stood at the window, gazing out at the city skyline. The Alps loomed faintly in the distance, sharp and immovable against the horizon. Munich looked timeless, stable, solid—everything Wirecard was supposed to be.

Braun adjusted his collar, his reflection staring back at him in the glass. For years, he had played the part of the visionary CEO: calm, unflappable, the face of Germany's tech miracle. Politicians had courted him. Investors had trusted him. Journalists, he told himself, were parasites.

Behind him, the boardroom door clicked open. His executives shuffled in, papers tight in their hands, eyes heavier than usual. One of them cleared his throat.

"Markus… the auditors. They can't find it. The €1.9 billion. It's not there."

The words hung in the air like a noose.

Braun didn't flinch. He clasped his hands behind his back, still staring at the skyline. "It's a mistake," he said flatly. "It has to be."

But deep inside, a flicker of fear crept in—a fear he had long buried beneath layers of confidence and denial. The empire he had built on phantom billions was about to collapse, and all of Munich, all of Germany, was about to watch.

*

The Phantom Billions

The sun was setting over Munich in June 2020, casting long shadows on the gleaming glass towers of Wirecard's headquarters. Inside, panic was spreading like fire. Reporters were calling, investors were demanding answers.

Auditors at EY had just dropped a bombshell: "We cannot confirm the existence of €1.9 billion in cash."

It was as if the floor had fallen away. For years, Wirecard had been the pride of Germany's tech economy. This payment processor grew from a scrappy startup into a member of the prestigious DAX 30, rubbing shoulders with giants like Siemens and BMW. Politicians hailed it as proof that Europe could produce tech champions to rival Silicon Valley. Investors adored it. Analysts whispered about it being the "future of fintech."

Now, all of it was unravelling.

*

The Boardroom in Denial

Two days before the revelation, CEO Markus Braun had walked into the boardroom with his usual composure. Tall, bespectacled, dressed in a sharp black suit, he carried himself like a man of unshakable certainty.

"The allegations are nonsense," he said firmly, waving away the reports from the Financial Times. "Our growth is real. Our business is solid. We will silence these critics once and for all."

Some nodded—relief flashing across their faces. Others shifted uneasily in their chairs, secretly wondering: how many times could Braun repeat this line before it lost all meaning?

The CFO, Jan Marsalek, leaned back with a faint smile. He had cultivated an aura of mystery—rumoured connections to intelligence services, secret trips to the Philippines, and shadowy dealings in Asia. To his colleagues, he was both indispensable and untouchable.

But beneath the polished boardroom air, cracks were widening. Wirecard's miraculous growth had long been fuelled by opaque subsidiaries, ghost clients, and phantom profits. For years, auditors had raised questions. Regulators had looked the other way. Politicians defended the company, dismissing critics as short-sellers with an agenda.

Now the truth was clawing its way to the surface.

*

The Collapse

June 18, 2020. Wirecard admitted what many had feared: €1.9 billion—nearly a quarter of its balance sheet—did not exist. The supposed funds, said to be held in trustee accounts in the Philippines, were a fabrication.

The revelation sent shockwaves across Europe. Within days, Braun resigned and was arrested on charges of fraud and market manipulation. Marsalek disappeared, vanishing like a character from a spy thriller. Some said he fled to Russia; others claimed he hid in Asia under the protection of intelligence agencies. His whereabouts remain unknown.

Investors were left stunned. Pension funds, banks, and ordinary shareholders lost billions. Germany's financial watchdog, BaFin, faced criticism for defending Wirecard against journalists instead of conducting a thorough investigation. The scandal was not just corporate—it was national.

*

Years Later

Wirecard's name became synonymous with one of the biggest financial frauds in European history. The company collapsed into insolvency, erasing what was once hailed as Germany's fintech crown jewel.

Markus Braun remains entangled in a lengthy trial, facing charges of orchestrating the fraud. Jan Marsalek is still a fugitive, his ghostly presence haunting the narrative—a reminder of how easily billions can vanish into thin air.

For Germany, Wirecard was more than a corporate failure. It was a lesson in hubris, complacency, and the dangers of mistaking growth for truth. A scandal born in boardrooms, shielded by politics, and unmasked by persistence.

***

Chapter 36

The Day Wall Street Stopped Breathing—Lehman Brothers

745 Seventh Avenue, Midtown Manhattan, USA

Reckless Leverage ☑ Mortgage Crisis ☑

Lehman Brothers' collapse on September 15, 2008, marked the darkest day in modern financial history. The once-mighty investment bank, with 158 years of legacy, crumbled under the weight of reckless leverage and the subprime mortgage crisis. Its bankruptcy shattered global confidence, sending shockwaves through markets, wiping out trillions in value, and triggering a chain reaction that spiralled into the Great Recession.

The Road to Ruin

Lehman Brothers was a cathedral of ambition. Its trading floors buzzed like stock-market orchestras—screens flashing green, traders shouting, champagne corks popping after each record-breaking quarter.

At the helm stood Richard "The Gorilla" Fuld, iron-jawed and unyielding. To his employees, he was both a general and a god. He pushed them harder, higher, deeper into risk. "Lehman doesn't follow the market," he'd thunder, "Lehman leads it."

The years leading up to 2008 were gilded with excess. Wall Street had discovered the alchemy of the age: mortgage-backed securities and collateralised debt obligations. To the untrained eye, they were complex bundles of numbers; to bankers, they were gold mines. Every American dream of home ownership became a tradable slice of profit.

Lehman devoured them greedily. Risk officers raised eyebrows, but their voices were drowned by the roar of bonuses. Regulators watched from a distance, dazzled by balance sheets that sparkled under the guise of accounting tricks.

By 2006, Lehman was all-in. It wasn't just playing the mortgage game—it was married to it. The firm gorged on subprime loans, pumping billions into a housing bubble that seemed eternal.

But cracks began to show. Defaults rose. The bubble hissed. Rivals began to hedge; Lehman doubled down. Fuld's mantra—"Don't blink"—was stitched into the culture. Denial became policy.

In the Summer of 2007, Bear Stearns faltered. A year later, markets shivered as Fannie Mae and Freddie Mac collapsed. But inside Lehman's glass tower, denial was wrapped in bravado. Executives clung to their empire of numbers, convinced they were too sophisticated, too seasoned, too big to fail.

And then came the fateful weekend of September 2008. The tide went out. And what was left wasn't gold, but sand.

*

The Day Wall Street Stopped Breathing

The morning of September 15, 2008, was unlike any other in the heart of Manhattan. As dawn broke over the steel canyons of Wall Street, the air itself felt heavy, as if it knew what was about to unfold.

Inside Lehman Brothers' headquarters at 745 Seventh Avenue, sleepless executives walked like spectres. Coffee cups littered the war room; spreadsheets glowed with red numbers that no one could rescue. CEO Richard Fuld, once hailed as

"The Gorilla of Wall Street," stared at the Bloomberg screen, his empire collapsing tick by tick.

On trading floors around the world, silence prevailed. Traders who once barked orders now watched helplessly as the ticker spelt doom. Billions were evaporating in real time. Screens showed not just falling prices, but losing faith.

By mid-morning, the news flashed: Lehman Brothers files for bankruptcy. One hundred and fifty-eight years of legacy erased in a single headline. The fourth-largest investment bank in America—gone.

Outside the headquarters, employees streamed out carrying cardboard boxes. Some clutched family photos, others trophies of deals once celebrated. The sidewalks were littered with disbelief. One trader whispered, "We built castles out of sand, and now the tide has come."

The collapse was not just financial. It was existential. Wall Street, the very symbol of American capitalism, had cracked in full view of the world. The ripple became a tsunami—mortgages foreclosed, jobs lost, economies staggering under the weight of a crisis born in greed and leverage.

*

Years Later

The Lehman building still stands in Midtown Manhattan. But its nameplate is gone, its soul dissolved. Barclays took over parts of its business; Nomura swallowed fragments in Asia. Yet Lehman itself survives only as a cautionary tale.

Years later, the ghost of Lehman still haunts policy rooms. Regulators tightened rules, central banks rehearsed bailouts, and financial textbooks carved an immortal lesson: too big to fail, yet allowed to fail.

Former employees scattered across the globe—some rebuilt careers, others never recovered. Richard Fuld disappeared from the limelight, remembered less as a titan and more as a tragic symbol of hubris.

*

The Ghost on Seventh Avenue

2025

A young banker, just twenty-seven, adjusted his tie as he walked down Seventh Avenue. The city buzzed with the hum of electric cars, digital billboards, and AI-driven trading. He stopped outside the glass tower that once bore the Lehman name.

There was no plaque, no trace of the empire that had ruled from within these walls. But he knew the story. Every finance class, every market lecture, had invoked Lehman like a ghost that refused to rest.

He placed a hand against the cold glass façade, as if trying to feel the echoes of that September morning. Inside, new tenants worked on entirely different businesses, unaware—or perhaps unwilling to remember—the night the world nearly came to a halt.

The young banker whispered to himself, "Never again." And yet, deep inside, he wondered: had the world truly learned? Or was Lehman simply waiting to be reborn in another name, another bubble, another collapse?

As he walked away, the skyline gleamed—bright, beautiful, but fragile. Behind him, the invisible ghost of Lehman Brothers lingered, watching, warning, whispering.

And like a faint crack running through the glass of a skyscraper—barely visible, yet always there—Lehman's legacy remained: a flaw that could never be polished away, a reminder that even the tallest towers can shatter.

***

Chapter 37

The Illusionist—Bernie Madoff's Great Deception

Lipstick Building, 885 Third Avenue, New York City

Fraud ☑ Litigation ☑ Ponzi Scheme ☑

Bernie Madoff's empire collapsed in 2008 when his $65 billion Ponzi scheme—the largest in history—was exposed. For decades, he had lured investors with steady, too-good-to-be-true returns, fabricating trades behind closed doors. When the financial crisis dried up new money, the illusion was shattered. Arrested after confessing to his sons, Madoff was sentenced to 150 years in prison—his name forever etched as the face of financial deceit.

The Art of Illusion

Agra, India, Some Decades Ago

It was a misty morning in Agra. The marble dome of the Taj Mahal glowed faintly under the rising sun. Amidst the crowd, Mithilesh Kumar Shrivastave, alias Natwarlal, arrived—not as a trickster, but as a respectable businessman in a well-tailored suit, carrying a leather briefcase that spoke of authority.

Across from him stood a wealthy industrialist, anxious and eager. Natwarlal unfolded documents bearing the insignia of the Archaeological Survey of India, complete with seals and signatures so convincing that even a seasoned bureaucrat would have paused only to nod.

“This,” Natwarlal said smoothly, tapping the papers with his fountain pen, “is your gateway to immortality.”

The con king of India paused. “Few men in history can claim ownership of a wonder of the world. Today, you can.”

The industrialist’s eyes widened. The thought of possessing the Taj Mahal—even secretly, even just on paper—was irresistible. Money changed hands, papers were signed, and in that moment, illusion triumphed over reality. The marble monument remained untouched, but in the businessman’s mind, it belonged to him.

Years later…

Madoff’s clients would feel a similar thrill. They, too, held documents—account statements promising steady, impossible gains. And just like the Taj Mahal “owner,” they never stopped to ask the most straightforward question: could this really be true?

*

Just as the con king of India sold monuments that never changed hands, Madoff sold returns that never existed. One forged document, and the other forged confidence. Investors believed they were part of an exclusive circle, privileged to receive steady profits in good times and bad. In truth, their money stayed in a bank account and was never invested.

*

Time and again, police caught Natwarlal—and time and again, he slipped through their fingers, escaping custody in ways that became part of urban legend. To many ordinary Indians, he was not just a fraudster but a folk hero, outsmarting the rich and powerful with nothing more than wit and charm.

Bernie Modoff was caught only once and sent to prison for 150 years.

*

The Penthouse Illusion

Duplex Penthouse, 133 East 64th Street

Manhattan, Upper East Side

Bernie Madoff sipped his morning coffee. He lived in a world of quiet opulence. His duplex penthouse gleamed with marble floors, Persian rugs, and floor-to-ceiling windows framing Manhattan's skyline like his personal kingdom. A grand piano stood polished, more ornament than instrument, while rare art adorned the walls with understated extravagance.

There was the Hamptons estate, the Palm Beach mansion, the yacht in the Mediterranean—each a stage where wealth and trust converged. Guests sipped champagne, dazzled by his calm charm, certain they were in the company of a financial genius.

On the surface, he was a genius. In reality, he was a magician, his empire built not on trading brilliance, but on smoke, mirrors, and an ever-hungry flow of new money. Every chandelier, every cocktail, every sunset view was built on borrowed money and broken promises.

The glamour was real, but the foundation was fiction.

*

The Whisper Network

From Palm Beach country clubs to exclusive New York dinner parties, the Madoff name circulated like a secret password. Celebrities, billionaires, and pension funds whispered about his mysterious strategy that always worked. To be "in" with Bernie was to belong to an exclusive club.

But exclusivity was the trick. "He doesn't take just anyone's money," people murmured. That scarcity created desire. Investors begged to be let in, never asking too many questions, blinded by greed and trust.

*

The Black Box

Lipstick Building, Until 2008

Before the Wall Street Crash

On the 17th floor of the Lipstick Building in Midtown Manhattan, Madoff's so-called trading floor hummed with activity. Yet, behind a locked door on the 18th floor, another world existed. Here, a small staff churned out fake statements, printing flawless records of trades that never happened. The "returns" were meticulously fabricated, designed to look just plausible enough.

He lured investors by promising unusually steady profits (often 10–12% annually), regardless of market conditions. Unlike typical investments that fluctuate, Madoff's results looked too smooth and consistent, which gave an illusion of low risk.

The investors believed their money was growing.

Wealthy individuals, banks, hedge funds, and "feeder funds" (investment managers that pooled clients' money and invested it with Madoff) trusted him due to his Wall Street reputation. He was considered the master of "split-strike conversion strategy" (a legitimate options-trading approach).

In reality, he never executed those trades.

He simply deposited the money into a single account at Chase Bank. When investors asked for withdrawals, he paid them using money from new investors. This gave the appearance of real profits being generated. Early investors spread the word about Madoff's "genius," bringing in even more money.

Auditors were either complicit or grossly negligent, as the records had been falsified internally.

*

Wall Street Crash, 2008

Because most investors didn't withdraw their money, the scheme could continue to operate. As long as inflows exceeded outflows, he could maintain the illusion of success.

The 2008 market crash triggered many things.

Massive withdrawal requests started pouring in billions. Investors needed cash. Madoff didn't have enough new money to cover the redemptions. He never invested the funds. He simply moved money around—using new investor money to pay earlier ones, while faking account records to keep the fraud hidden.

Now investors were demanding billions back, and the pipeline of fresh cash dried up.

Madoff knew the game was over. The machine that had fed on trust and greed for decades was starving.

*

The Confession

December 10, 2008

In his penthouse, Bernie sat with his two sons, Mark and Andrew. His voice was flat, almost clinical.

"It's all one big lie," he said. "A giant Ponzi scheme."

The words hung in the air like a death sentence. The illusionist had spoken the truth at last.

The sons, stunned, called their lawyers.

*

The Penthouse

December 11, 2008

Wrapped in a boardroom attire, Madoff was waiting.

He had once chaired NASDAQ. He moved comfortably among senators, billionaires, and celebrities. The wealthy whispered his name as a password to exclusivity: "Madoff is taking clients." For many, gaining access to his fund wasn't just an investment—it was a status symbol.

FBI agents walked into the apartment.

Madoff opened the door. The waiting was over.

The senior agent asked, "Do you know why we're here?"

"Yes," Madoff replied softly. "For me."

Feeling like one of the fractured statues of Bruno Cateliano, he marched ahead—carrying the weight of hollowness.

*

The Fall

News broke like wildfire. "Wall Street Legend Arrested in $65 Billion Ponzi Scheme." Across the globe, victims watched their fortunes vanish overnight. Hollywood moguls, universities, charities, and retirees—none were spared. Fortune 500 companies, banks in Europe and Asia, universities, charities, pension funds—all exposed.

Madoff's name, once synonymous with brilliance, was now etched in history as the architect of the largest financial fraud ever.

*

U.S. District Court for the Southern District of New York

March 2009

In a hushed courtroom, Bernie Madoff stood before the judge. His face, once serene, was now drawn and pale.

He pleaded guilty.

“I am deeply sorry and ashamed,” he said. “I cannot adequately express how sorry I am for my crimes.”

The judge’s reply was merciless. “Here, the message must be loud and clear. This kind of manipulation cannot be tolerated.”

The sentence: 150 years in prison.

*

Epilogue—The Prisoner

But the story didn’t end in the courtroom. The fallout rippled through families and foundations, sparking suicides, bankruptcies, and a reckoning in financial regulation. Madoff became a symbol—not just of greed, but of how trust, once betrayed, leaves scars deeper than numbers can measure.

And yet, the illusion lingered. For decades, the world wanted to believe in the magician who defied markets. They wanted the steady returns, the certainty in uncertainty. Madoff gave them what they craved—until reality caught up.

Behind bars, the man who once controlled billions now wore a prison uniform. The illusionist who fooled the world was stripped of his accolades. His empire reduced to rubble; his victims scarred for life.

He died at the Federal Medical Centre in Butner, North Carolina, at the age of 82. He had previously requested to be released during the coronavirus pandemic. He added that he had end-stage renal disease among other underlying medical conditions, though his request was denied.

The lesson lingered: trust, once betrayed, can never be fully repaired.

Bernie Madoff’s Ponzi scheme wasn’t just financial fraud—it was theatre. A grand illusion performed on the world’s most powerful stage. And like all illusions, it vanished the moment the lights came on.

***

Chapter 38

The Trump Tower Penthouse: The Golden Illusion

Manhattan, USA

Over-Valuation ☑ Alleged Fraud ☑ Litigation ☑
Political Repercussions ☑

The Trump Tower Penthouse controversy became central to investigations into Donald Trump's business practices. For years, the triplex apartment in Manhattan was claimed to span 30,000 square feet, when in reality it was just under 11,000. This inflated size, and the valuations tied to it - sometimes exceeding $300 million—were cited by New York's Attorney General as evidence of financial misrepresentation. The case highlighted how exaggerating real estate valuations can become a tool for securing loans and boosting perceived wealth.

721-725 Fifth Avenue

Manhattan, USA

High above Fifth Avenue, glittering in marble, chandeliers, and 24-karat gilding, the Trump Tower penthouse was once sold to the world as a palace in the clouds. Its sheer opulence—golden ceilings, diamond-encrusted décor, and panoramic views of Manhattan—made it a symbol of the Trump empire itself: bold, brash, and beyond comparison. The tower hosts a handful of high-profile residents, including filmmaker Vincent Gallo, art dealer Hillel "Helly" Nahmad, tequila mogul Juan Beckmann Vidal, and actor Bruce Willis.

But beneath the gold veneer lurked a startling truth.

For years, the penthouse was touted as a 30,000-square-foot masterpiece, a sky palace fit for kings. Its valuation soared accordingly, reaching figures north of $300 million. Investors, banks, and the media lapped up the narrative. After all, if Donald Trump said it was the grandest penthouse in New York, who dared question him?

Only later did cold, hard facts creep in. Public records revealed that the apartment wasn't 30,000 square feet at all—it was just under 11,000. A tripling of space on paper, inflated into hundreds of millions in "value." In one stroke, the penthouse turned from a gilded dream into a case study in valuation deception.

*

Courtroom Drama

The Penthouse on Trial

The marble walls of the New York Supreme Court in Manhattan echoed with the shuffle of papers and the low hum of anticipation. At the front, Justice Arthur Engoron adjusted his glasses, peering over stacks of documents that had already become infamous: the valuation statements of Trump Tower's penthouse.

On one side, the Attorney General's team laid out their evidence—square footage records, architectural blueprints, sworn appraisals. On the other hand, Donald Trump's lawyers stood firm, defending their client's empire of numbers.

"Your Honour," the state's attorney began, raising a finger toward the documents, "this is not a small mistake. The penthouse was claimed to be 30,000 square feet when in truth, it was just under 11,000. This tripling inflated the valuation to over $300 million - a number that exists only in fantasy."

Trump's defence shot back, "It was not fraud. It was branding. Mr Trump is a master of real estate promotion. Every buyer knows his name adds value."

Judge Engoron leaned forward, his voice calm but cutting. "Branding is one thing. Mathematics is another. You can't stretch square footage like taffy. Facts are facts. This valuation was not merely aggressive—it was fraudulent."

The face of the defence attorney turned pale when the Attorney General's team announced, "We want Allen Weisselberg on the witness box." He was the long-serving CFO of the Trump Organisation.

*

The Testimony of Allen Weisselberg

The courtroom fell silent, save for the shuffling of papers and the dull echo of footsteps across the polished wooden floor. At the witness stand sat Allen Weisselberg, the long-serving Chief Financial Officer of the Trump Organisation, a man who had for decades lived in the shadows of Manhattan's gilded towers, quietly moving numbers, balancing sheets, and protecting the empire he had helped build.

But this was no longer the boardroom. This was the reckoning.

The prosecutor's questions cut like scalpels: "Mr Weisselberg, is it not true that you knowingly misrepresented the size of Trump's triplex apartment?" The air thickened. For a moment, Weisselberg adjusted his glasses, his weathered face a mask of calculation. The man who once orchestrated millions with a flick of a pen now struggled under the fluorescent glare of justice.

The courtroom leaned in.

Weisselberg hesitated, then exhaled. The truth could no longer be deferred. He admitted, "Yes, the numbers were wrong, inflated to a grotesque degree, and yes, the deception had been carried on for years."

Whispers rippled across the benches. The illusion of valuation, the empire built on glossy brochures and soaring appraisals, now cracked under his own confession.

When the judge finally spoke—handing down five months in jail—it was not the length of the sentence that carried weight, but the symbolism. A loyal lieutenant had fallen. The arithmetic of power had been exposed as the arithmetic of fraud.

Allen lowered his gaze. The man who once guarded the vaults of Trump's fortune now walked away in chains, leaving behind not just balance sheets but a legacy tainted with betrayal and lies.

The gavel came down. The courtroom went silent. The gold-leaf image of the Trump Tower penthouse, once celebrated as a palace in the sky, had been stripped bare to its foundations of exaggeration and ego.

*

Translation into Political Impact

While the Trump Tower apartment fraud primarily triggered legal and financial consequences, it also had notable political reverberations. Opponents used the rulings to paint Trump as dishonest and ethically compromised, intensifying criticism during his presidential campaigns.

The findings undermined Trump's image as a successful businessman—his political brand heavily depended on projecting financial acumen and wealth. It also amplified calls for stronger ethics rules to prevent conflicts of interest, particularly for wealthy public officials. New York's willingness to strip business licenses and install monitors illustrated how state power can challenge national political figures via financial oversight.

In a counterattack, Trump and his allies labelled these legal proceedings politically motivated, reinforcing his base's narrative of persecution.

*

Years Later

In 2024, the illusion finally carried a price. The New York Supreme Court ordered Donald Trump and his organisation to pay hundreds of millions of dollars in penalties for persistent financial fraud. The penthouse valuation was not just a footnote; it was Exhibit A in proving a pattern of deception.

Trump, defiant as ever, stood before cameras outside the courthouse, railing against "witch hunts" and "political persecution." His words echoed with the bravado of a man unwilling to concede defeat. But inside financial circles, the verdict rang differently: a titan of real estate had been stripped bare, his numbers exposed for what they were—fiction in marble and gold.

Investors whispered, banks grew wary, and the once-proud Trump Tower gleamed less brightly against the Manhattan skyline. The penthouse still stood, its ceilings still painted in gold, but now it carried an invisible stain: the shame of being remembered not as the world's most glamorous apartment, but as one of the world's most notorious valuation misfires.

Donald Trump is now the 47th President of the United States. Since returning to the Oval Office in 2025, his primary residence has been the White House. He still owns and occasionally uses the three-story penthouse at Trump Tower, though it has not been his primary residence. In 2019, he officially changed his primary residence from Trump Tower to Mar-a-Lago in Palm Beach, Florida, mainly for tax reasons and lifestyle preferences.

*

Allen Weisselberg, the CFO, completed his latest prison sentence. In April 2024, he pleaded guilty to two counts of perjury during the civil fraud trial brought by New York's attorney general. He was sentenced to five months in Rikers Island and was released in July 2024, after serving approximately 100 days for good behaviour. Upon release, he embarked upon retirement in February 2024, as the ruling further barred Weisselberg permanently from holding any financial control role in any New York business.

Separately, he previously served a five-month sentence following his guilty plea to 15 felony counts of tax fraud and related charges in 2022, where he agreed to pay nearly $2 million in back taxes, penalties, and interest, and received probation following his release.

***

Chapter 39

Housing.com—When the Dream Home Collapsed

Boston House, Gundavali, Andheri (East)

Startup Failure ☑ Litigation ☑ Internal Clashes ☑ Cash Burn ☑ Valuation Misfire ☑

> Founded in 2012 by a group of IIT graduates, Housing.com sought to disrupt India's real estate market with data-driven property listings and a bold, youthful brand. Flush with venture capital and a valuation soaring over $250 million, it became a poster child of startup ambition. But aggressive spending, internal clashes, and the ouster of its flamboyant CEO, Rahul Yadav, led to a rapid decline. Once a rising star, Housing.com became a stark reminder of how hype can outpace sustainability.

Mumbai, 2012

The city that never sleeps, a maze of real estate dreams and nightmares. Glass towers piercing the smoggy skyline, slums clinging to railway tracks, billboards screaming promises of a "luxury lifestyle." In this city of contradictions, twelve IIT Bombay graduates sat in a cramped flat, plotting to disrupt the opaque market in India—real estate.

Their vision was simple yet revolutionary: to bring transparency to the home-buying process.

Housing.com was born.

The pitch was irresistible: a clean, map-based interface, verified listings, and photographs of actual homes (a rarity in a market plagued by false ads and shady brokers). In a country where buying a house was both an aspiration and a gamble, Housing.com promised clarity, trust, and speed.

*

The Meteoric Rise

The timing couldn't have been better.

The Indian startup ecosystem was exploding with promise. Flipkart had already lit the e-commerce flame. Ola was on the streets. Paytm was knocking on every wallet. Venture capitalists were desperate to catch the "next unicorn."

Housing.com rode that wave.

In just two years, the company raised over $120 million from marquee investors, including Japan's SoftBank, India's Tiger Global, and Helion Ventures. Its valuation soared to nearly $250 million—an astronomical number for a company still trying to figure out a revenue model.

The brand was young, bold, and loud. It plastered billboards across Indian metros with a single cryptic word: "LOOK UP."

The campaign was pure adrenaline: no product details, just a mysterious call to dream. Housing.com became the talk of the town.

At the centre of it all stood its charismatic and unpredictable CEO: Rahul Yadav.

*

Rahul Yadav: The Maverick

Rahul Yadav was unlike any other startup founder in India. Sharp, outspoken, and irreverent, he wore arrogance like a badge of honour. While his peers—Flipkart's Bansals, Paytm's Vijay Shekhar Sharma—chose diplomacy, Rahul chose provocation.

He called out rivals publicly. He sparred with journalists. He taunted competitors with memes and sharp one-liners on social media. Most infamously, he once distributed his personal stake in Housing.com, worth around ₹200 crore, to employees—a move that made him look like a Robin Hood to some and a reckless showman to others.

Investors loved his fire in the early days. He had the swagger of a visionary who could sell a dream. But soon, that fire started burning everything around him.

*

Cracks in the Mansion

By 2015, Housing.com had become a poster child for India's startup boom. Its growth was explosive, but beneath the glossy surface, cracks were widening:

The company spent lavishly on marketing but struggled to monetise. Brokers baulked at paying hefty commissions, and users were unsure about paying for listings.

Housing was a ship with too many captains. With a dozen co-founders and hundreds of new hires, decision-making turned into chaos.

Rahul's defiance turned toxic. In board meetings, he clashed with SoftBank and other investors, dismissing their concerns. His blunt emails to investors became public spectacles, further eroding trust.

The "LOOK UP" campaign had made Housing a household name—but also drained cash at a frightening pace. Offices were expanding. Salaries were ballooning. The burn rate was unsustainable.

And then came the scandals.

*

The Public Meltdown

In early 2015, Rahul penned an infamous resignation letter to the board, laced with sarcasm and contempt. "I don't think you guys are intellectually capable enough to have any sensible discussion," he wrote.

The letter leaked. The media pounced. Investors panicked.

Rahul eventually withdrew his resignation after much drama, but the damage was done. The narrative had shifted: Housing.com was no longer a bold startup—it was a soap opera of egos.

By mid-2015, the board had had enough. Backed by SoftBank, they forced Rahul Yadav to step down as CEO. The once-celebrated maverick walked out of the glass offices he had built, leaving behind stunned employees and an uncertain company.

*

The Slow Demolition

Without Rahul, Housing.com tried to steady the ship. A new leadership team slashed expenses, shut down side projects, and narrowed the focus. But the momentum was gone.

Investors lost faith. Users moved on to rivals like 99acres and MagicBricks, which quietly but steadily expanded.

By 2017, Housing.com was a shadow of its former self. Once valued at $250 million, it merged with PropTiger, effectively ending its independent journey.

*

The Lessons from the Rubble

The Housing.com's collapse wasn't just the story of a failed startup. It was a mirror reflecting the dark side of India's startup boom. A visionary founder can ignite a company, but unchecked arrogance can sink it.

Branding without a solid business model is a ticking time bomb.

Even billions in funding cannot save a company plagued by poor leadership and internal chaos.

In hindsight, Housing.com was both ahead of its time and tragically flawed. It dared to dream big, but its wings were clipped by the very hubris that made it fly.

*

Epilogue

The Ghost of Rahul Yadav

The story of Housing.com's rise and fall is filled with all the drama, hubris, and boardroom intrigue—like a thriller unfolding in a Bollywood movie. Rahul Yadav faded from the startup limelight after Housing, dabbling in a few ventures but never recreating his meteoric rise. Yet his shadow still lingers in conversations about Indian entrepreneurship.

Some call him a misunderstood genius. Others, a cautionary tale. Perhaps he was both.

Because Housing.com wasn't just about real estate. It was about ambition unrestrained, money unchecked, and dreams that collapsed under their own weight.

*

Years Later

Once branded as the poster child of Indian real estate startups, Housing.com was a story of audacity. Founded in 2012 by a group of IIT Bombay graduates, it promised to simplify India's chaotic property market with data-driven listings and bold design. Its pink-and-white billboards screamed ambition across every metro city.

But ambition burns fast. By 2015, its mercurial CEO Rahul Yadav became more famous for controversies than execution—clashes with investors, public spats on social media, and a governance storm that overshadowed the product. Funds that once poured in—nearly $120 million led by SoftBank—began to dry up. By 2016, Housing.com had merged with PropTiger, its identity absorbed into a larger ecosystem.

Years later, what remains? The brand itself has faded into obscurity, remembered mainly as a cautionary tale. Employees scattered into other startups, SoftBank wrote off much of its investment, and India's property-tech dream shifted to rivals like 99acres and MagicBricks.

The promise was real, the product was admired, but the leadership turbulence turned Housing.com into a case study of how ego, immaturity, and unchecked hype can dismantle even the most promising venture.

***

Chapter 40

Uber—The Dream of a Trillion-Dollar Highway

Leadership Shift ☑

> Uber's story is a saga of ambition and turbulence—a meteoric rise fuelled by disruption, an IPO that exposed deep financial wounds, and a leadership shift from Travis Kalanick's aggressive chaos to Dara Khosrowshahi's cautious rebuilding. Once hailed as a revolution, Uber became a parable of modern valuations: bold dreams colliding with the harsh meter of reality.

The Uber Gamble

The boardroom glowed under soft white lights, but the atmosphere was anything but serene. San Francisco's skyline twinkled beyond the glass walls. Inside, the directors sat stiff, papers in hand, their eyes fixed on the glowing screen that painted a brutal picture: billions in cumulative losses.

Dara Khosrowshahi, Uber's CEO, cleared his throat. "We're building the future. But futures are costly. Our investors must keep faith."

A board member leaned forward, fingers tapping impatiently on the table. "Faith doesn't pay dividends, Dara. We've lost China, we're bleeding in India. At what point do we admit this isn't a monopoly, but a money pit?"

The CFO, calm but visibly exhausted, adjusted his glasses. "We still control over 60% of the U.S. ride-hailing market.

Food delivery is expanding rapidly. This isn't collapse—it's investment."

A silence followed, thick enough to hear the hum of the air conditioning.

*

Wall Street

The IPO Day, 2019

The trading floor erupted in cheers as Uber executives rang the opening bell. Cameras flashed, confetti floated. Yet, minutes later, as the stock ticker rolled across screens, jaws tightened. The numbers weren't soaring—they were sinking.

A young analyst whispered to his colleague, eyes glued to the plummeting chart. "Eighty billion valuation, and it's falling like a stone… They sold us the future, but the present can't breathe."

On a private call, an investor's voice was ice-cold. "We were promised dominance, not dependency on subsidies. When will this company make a single cent?"

*

The Quarterly Earnings Call

Shareholders dialled in.

CFO was defensive. "…Operating losses this quarter stand at $1.1 billion. We anticipate narrowing margins over the next fiscal year."

A frustrated voice of the other investor cuts in. "You keep saying next year, next quarter, next phase. At what point does 'later' become 'never'?"

Another investor, calmer but biting, added: "You're not running a company. You're running an experiment—one funded with our money."

Back in the boardroom, Dara leaned forward, his voice low but firm.

Dara tried to explain. "Uber was never meant to be just a ride-hailing app. It's a platform, a global movement. We're building a world where transportation is seamless, where cars drive themselves, where food arrives before you even think of ordering it."

A sceptical director shook his head. "Dreams don't balance sheets. And hope doesn't keep the lights on."

The tension lingered, cinematic, unresolved. Uber's story wasn't over—but the ride was far from smooth.

*

Years Later

The glass towers of San Francisco shimmer in the Californian sun, but for Uber, the shine is different now. Years have passed since the dizzying highs of its aggressive expansion, since boardroom battles made headlines, since Travis Kalanick's ouster had been seen as a corporate morality play.

The company, once the poster child of disruption, has matured—though not without scars. Regulators across continents had clipped its wings. Drivers, once called "partners" but treated as expendable, had won concessions through lawsuits and strikes. Investors, who once believed in an endless fountain of growth, have come to terms with thinner margins and harsh realities.

Uber is no longer just an app—it has morphed into a logistics empire: ride-hailing, food delivery, freight. Yet, the days when it was seen as a revolution have gone. Now it is simply another corporate giant, as cautious as the ones it once mocked.

At tech conferences, people still whisper about its early days—about the brash CEO who had believed rules were for others, about a startup that set entire industries ablaze. But the myth has softened. Uber has survived, but survival has had a price: its wild, rebellious spirit has been traded for compliance and quarterly earnings calls.

Years later, Uber stands tall. Not as a renegade. Not as a fallen angel. But as a sober reminder that even disruptors eventually get disrupted by the passage of time.

***

Tales of IPO Misfire

Chapter 41

Jhunjhunwala: The Oracle in the Classroom

Indian Institute of Management, Ahmedabad, India

Valuation Misfire ☑ Academic Sermons ☑ IPO Hype ☑ Market Euphoria ☑

On a rain-soaked July day in 2022, Rakesh Jhunjhunwala—clearly not an academic—paid a hypothetical visit to IIM Ahmedabad. With blunt wit, he called the Indian IPO market "the most expensive in the world," using the LIC IPO as a cautionary example of overvaluation and Nykaa as a warning about euphoria-driven multiples (EV/Sales, P/E, EBITDA concerns).

Years later, after his death and a legacy of roughly ₹30,000 crore (~US$5.8bn) in listed holdings, the lecture endured as a stark, memorable lesson on market risk.

The Office of The Director

Indian Institute of Management

Ahmedabad, July 2022

It was a rainy day in Ahmedabad. The IIM campus stood drenched, its red-brick walls glistening under a stubborn drizzle that refused to stop. Puddles lined the stone pathways, and students shuffled into the lecture hall, shaking off umbrellas and brushing water from their shoulders. The air inside was damp, heavy with humidity, but charged with anticipation—today was no ordinary class.

Rakesh Jhunjhunwala, the market oracle who rarely played the role of teacher, was scheduled to visit his office before the invited lecture. Outside, thunder rolled faintly over the Sabarmati, as if to underscore the stormy subject he had chosen: the turbulence of India's equity markets and the madness of overpriced IPOs. The restless monsoon mirrored the mood in Dalal Street—unpredictable, forceful, and unforgiving.

The rain drummed softly on the expansive glass windows of the director's office at IIM Ahmedabad. The room, lined with bookshelves and neatly stacked reports, carried the dignified air of an institution that had shaped generations of business leaders.

Rakesh Jhunjhunwala walked in, his gait confident but slightly slowed by the years. Professor Errol D'souza, the director, rose from behind the polished teak desk, extending a warm hand. "Welcome to IIM Ahmedabad, Mr Jhunjhunwala. It's an honour to have you with us."

Jhunjhunwala smiled. "Thank you, Professor D'souza. I have been reading a lot of good things about you. Keep it up."

"Stalking me?" the director flushed, before being polite. "Just trying to maintain the pace. But you outpace me every time."

Jhunjhunwala laughed aloud. "This campus has produced the sharpest minds in the country. I'm no teacher, but I thought it's time I shared a few battle scars from the markets."

They exchanged pleasantries about the city, the monsoon, and the bustle on Dalal Street.

The director gestured toward the lecture hall beyond the office windows. "They've been waiting for you eagerly. IPOs, valuations, market strategy—these aren't just concepts for them, they're questions about their future."

Jhunjhunwala chuckled: "Then let's give them more than theory. Let's talk about how overpriced dreams can sink ships—and sometimes make fortunes."

With that, he adjusted his spectacles, tucked a folder of slides under his arm, and walked toward the lecture hall, the echo of the rain trailing behind.

His voice still lingered in the office: *"Markets are like this weather, my friends—uncomfortable, sticky, and prone to sudden downpours. But if you know how to read the clouds, you'll survive the storm."*

*

The Classroom

IIM, Ahmedabad, Gujarat, India

July, 2022

The IIM lecture theatre was electric. Into the room walked Rakesh Jhunjhunwala—untucked white shirt, casual gait, spectacles sliding down his nose. He waved away the polite applause.

He waved his hands. "Don't clap, don't clap. I'm not a professor. I don't teach DCF models. I live in the market. I've made billions, I've lost crores. My classroom has been Dalal Street, not IIM."

The room chuckled nervously.

Then came the thunderbolt. "Let me tell you straight—the Indian equity market today is the most expensive in the world. You check your P/E ratios, your EV/EBITDA, your price-to-book—there's froth everywhere."

A student raised his hand cautiously. "But sir, India's growth story is real. Doesn't that justify high valuations?"

Jhunjhunwala smiled wryly: "*Beta*, growth story *toh sab likhte hai*. But when you price an IPO at 80 times earnings and 40 times EBITDA, you're selling dreams, not shares. Look at Paytm's IPO—priced at the moon, and then it crashed back to earth. Don't confuse marketing with valuation."

"Look at the IPO mania. LIC was priced as if the Indian middle class would never stop buying insurance."

A slide flashed on screen.

Slide #1 LIC IPO — A Case of Overvaluation

(May 2022)

- IPO priced at ₹ 949, P/E ~ 202× (FY21 EPS ~ ₹ 4.70).
- The share was listed at approximately ₹867 ≈, with an 8–9% discount to the issue price.
- Within a year, the share price dropped ~ 40% from the upper band (₹ 949 to ~₹ 567).
- **~₹ 2 lakh crore of market value wiped off for investors from IPO & listing level.**

"Investors were expecting magic from LIC just because of its name." his voice was sombre. "LIC's embedded value (₹5.39 lakh crore) was not compelling enough to justify the high valuation."

He ran another slide.

Slide #2 Nykaa IPO — Euphoria & Valuation Madness

(October 2021)

Issue Price Band: ₹ 1,085 – ₹ 1,125

Listing: ~₹ 2,001 (≈ 79% premium) | Intraday high ~₹ 2,248

Shares slid to ₹ 1,100 within a year. Investors saw early gains vanish as fundamentals caught up.

Jhunjhunwala was sarcastic. "This is what happens when markets pay 20× sales for lipstick and eyeliner. Fundamentals eventually wipe off the makeup."

A girl student pursed her lips, probably laden with Nykaa product.

He continued. "What happened? Within months, these 'darlings' were trading below the issue price. That's not growth—that's greed in disguise."

Laughter rippled through the hall, though some shifted uneasily.

Another slide glowed on screen.

Slide #3 CarTrade Tech IPO — Valuation Without Traction

(August 2021)

Issue Price Band: ₹ 1,585 – ₹ 1,618

IPO Size: ~₹ 2,999 crore

Listing: Opened at ₹ 1,599 (≈ flat), but slipped 7% on Day 1, closing ~₹ 1,501

By mid-2022, the stock was down ~70% from the IPO price.

"A profitable company," Jhunjhunwala concluded, "is not always a good IPO bet. Without growth, even profits can't justify 30× valuations."

Another hand raised from the back bench: "Should we avoid IPOs altogether?"

Jhunjhunwala chuckled: "Arre, no! I love IPOs. But remember—IPO doesn't mean Initial Public Offering. In India, it often means "It's Probably Overpriced." You must separate marketing from mathematics. Don't buy because the promoter smiles on CNBC; buy only if the EBITDA growth justifies the price you're paying."

The students scribbled furiously.

He paused. “Remember, equity valuation is like gravity. You can defy it for a while, but sooner or later, it pulls you back. Respect it—or pay the fees to the market, and trust me, the market charges interest.”

The sting of truth lingered.

Adjournment.

*

The hush returned after the adjournment.

A student raised his hand nervously and asked, “Sir, how do we select a good IPO? There are so many these days, and it’s confusing.”

Jhunjhunwala smiled mischievously. “*Beta*, remember one thing—an IPO is like a wedding invitation. The family will only show you the good side—the decorations, the sweets, the glamour. But what matters is what happens after the wedding.”

The hall erupted in laughter. He continued, his tone sharp yet fatherly. “Don’t get trapped in oversubscription hype. Look at three things: one, the business model—is it solving a real problem? Two, the valuation—are you paying for future dreams or current profits? And three, the management quality—because in India, more money is lost to bad promoters than bad products.”

He dropped his voice for effect. “And lastly, ask yourself: would you still hold this stock if there was no listing pop on Day One? If the answer is yes, then apply. Otherwise, attend the wedding, eat the sweets, but don’t get married.”

The students scribbled furiously, but one thing was clear—the lesson would stay with them longer than any textbook line.

*

“Is there no control in IPO pricing?” A question was fired from behind.

Jhunjhunwala feigned a gesture as if dodging a bullet.

Students laughed.

"Yes and no…" he said. "The Securities and Exchange Board of India, SEBI, regulates IPOs, but it does not decide the price. Pricing is left to the company and its bankers under the "free pricing regime" since 1992."

Many students sighed.

"So, there is regulation of process, not of price. That's why we see technically compliant cases, but fundamentally overpriced relative to earnings and business risks."

"Have you ever made a mistake in selecting an IPO?" Shooters were scattered all around the classroom.

"Yes. I did."

Many valuation misfires of his career rolled before the eyes of Jhunjhunwala. "I invested heavily in the SpiceJet airline in the mid-2000s, but later realised aviation was a tough sector with limited long-term returns. A2Z Maintenance & Engineering IPO, bought in 2010, collapsed after listing and never recovered. DB Realty IPO, 2010, is another example where my bet soured as the company got mired in controversies."

Students took notes. *Even the Grandmasters falter.*

"I have made more mistakes, he confessed, "than I have made successes, but my successes outweigh my mistakes."

He stared through the windows. Purple and magenta Bougainvillaea flowers were trying to drape over the walls.

His voice dropped. "Markets are the greatest teacher. They don't hand out degrees, but they hand out losses. Respect valuation—because valuation is like gravity. No matter how high you jump, it will always pull you back."

*

And so, Jhunjhunwala continued to share his wealth of wisdom with the students, his words cascading like a free fall in the markets—unpredictable, forceful, yet unforgettable.

With all said, he wanted to, the Big Bull stood up, waved casually, and walked out. The silence in the lecture hall was louder than any applause could have been.

*

Years Later

Rakesh Jhunjhunwala, the legend, died a month later.

But that morning at IIM was still remembered with a sense of awe. He had left behind not only his unmistakable voice on the markets but also an astonishing fortune.

At the time of his death in August 2022, his family's portfolio spanned across 32 listed companies, worth nearly ₹30,000 crore. His single biggest bet—Titan Company—alone accounted for more than half that value, roughly ₹16,000 crore. Other stakes in Star Health, Metro Brands, and Tata Motors added thousands of crores more, cementing his reputation as India's most successful investor.

Even a year later, when his holdings were re-valued, the portfolio still stood tall at around ₹31,800 crore, despite market swings. Analysts said his estate was worth close to US$5.8 billion, a legacy few in India's market history had ever matched.

*

But among the alumni of IIM, it wasn't the numbers that lingered. They remembered the paradox of the Big Bull—a man who believed in India's growth story with unmatched conviction, yet warned them bluntly that the market was "the most expensive in the world." His punchline about IPOs — "It's Probably Overpriced"—was quoted in trading rooms long after.

For those students, his brief lecture had become more than an anecdote. It was a lifelong reminder that markets are the most fantastic teacher, and even the Big Bull himself remained, till the end, their most brilliant student.

***

Chapter 42
Reliance Power IPO—The Day of Blackout

H Block, 1st Floor, Dhirubhai Ambani Knowledge City, Navi Mumbai

IPO Over-Valuation ☑ Brand Value Hype ☑
Brand Inheritance ☑

Launched in January 2008, the Reliance Power IPO was India's biggest at the time, raising a record ₹11,700 crore and attracting millions of investors in a frenzy of hype. But soon after listing, the stock plunged sharply below the issue price, wiping out investor wealth and shattering confidence. Once billed as a symbol of India's booming markets, it became a cautionary tale of overvaluation.

Nariman Point

Mumbai, India, 2008

Clad in designer running gear, a man with an unmistakable air of aristocracy jogged along the Queen's Necklace, the soft morning breeze brushing against his face. Indifferent to the curious glances of onlookers, he seemed lost in the labyrinth of his own thoughts.

His mind wandered to the towering legacy of his father… to his beautiful wife Tina Munim, once celebrated as one of the most enchanting actresses of her time. She had put on weight since then, but he still loved her.

The sea breeze from Marine Drive carried faint traces of salt and melancholy. Oblivious to the world. his mind wandered—not to the rhythm of his steps, but to his father's shadow and brother's empire. His elder brother, Mukesh Ambani, was counted today among the wealthiest men in Asia. They were together until 2005 before the inheritance divide.

But soon, the glitter of memory gave way to the shadows of reality… the crumbling promises of his own making.

Jerking his head, his thoughts drifted back to the present… the upcoming IPO of his company.

Anil Ambani slowed his pace, almost in anticipation. Perhaps it was time to head to the office and tie up a few loose ends.

*

Spark of a Dream

In the mid-2000s, India was basking in economic glory.

The Sensex had soared past 20,000. Malls were rising, call centres were humming, and a new generation of Indians believed prosperity was their birthright. The stock market wasn't just numbers on a screen—it had become a cultural fever, a new religion of wealth.

Amid this euphoria came a promise so dazzling that few could resist.

Reliance Power, the brainchild of Anil Ambani, was announced with thunder and lightning. The younger Ambani was everywhere: on TV screens, in newspapers, on billboards, smiling with folded hands, thanking investors even before they subscribed.

The pitch was irresistible: India needs power. Reliance will deliver it.

It wasn't just an IPO; it was marketed as a nation-building event. For millions, buying shares wasn't just an investment—it was participation in India's energy future.

*

The Frenzy of Subscription

The IPO launched in January 2008, aiming to raise over ₹11,500 crore—the largest in India's history.

The rush was historic. Investors across India queued up like pilgrims. Brokers' offices overflowed with forms.

Housewives pawned jewellery, farmers pledged land, and students borrowed money.

Every retail investor wanted a piece of the Ambani dream.

When the books closed, Reliance Power had been oversubscribed nearly 73 times. That meant if you applied for 73 shares, you were lucky to get just one.

The hype machine had worked. The IPO was hailed as India's Aramco, a once-in-a-lifetime opportunity.

*

The Big Day

11 February 2008

The stock was listed.

It was supposed to be a coronation. The younger Ambani, already ranked among the world's wealthiest men, was ready to prove he could match his brother Mukesh, who had taken over Reliance Industries.

Stock markets opened with tension in the air. CNBC and NDTV Profit broadcast live. Retail investors gathered around trading terminals like cricket fans watching a World Cup final.

The stock opened near ₹530, just above the issue price of ₹450. Cheers erupted. But then—the music stopped.

Within minutes, the price began slipping. ₹500… ₹480… ₹460… and then the unthinkable: it fell below the issue price.

By the end of the day, Reliance Power closed at ₹372, erasing billions in investor wealth.

The dream had lasted just a few hours.

*

The Aftershock

The collapse stunned the nation. People felt betrayed.

For years, the Ambani name had meant unstoppable growth. Dhirubhai Ambani's legacy had built fortunes for small investors in Reliance Industries. But Anil Ambani's Reliance Power did the opposite—it became a furnace that burned money.

Across India, stories emerged of despair:

A retired schoolteacher who invested his pension.

A shopkeeper in Lucknow who mortgaged his house.

Young professionals who borrowed from friends.

All had one thing in common: they lost big, and quickly.

The anger was so intense that Anil Ambani announced a bonus share issue to retail investors to soften the blow. But it was like applying a bandage after a heart attack. The damage was deep.

*

The Unravelling

In hindsight, the signs were always there.

Reliance Power had no operational power plant at the time of listing. It was selling blueprints, not electricity… Only hollow promises.

The IPO was priced at the highest possible band, leaving no cushion for investors.

The timing was wrong. January 2008 was the peak of the market. Within weeks, the global financial crisis struck, dragging all stocks down.

Building massive power plants in India required regulatory approvals, land acquisition, coal linkages, and billions in funding. None of this was easy, but investors ignored the execution risk in the fine print.

Reliance Power was a castle built on projections, not performance.

*

The Fall of a Tycoon

The IPO fiasco was more than just a financial event—it was the turning point in Anil Ambani's empire.

Once celebrated as a visionary, he slowly became a symbol of overreach and debt. Over the next decade, his companies—from telecom to infrastructure—collapsed under loans and litigation. By 2020, the man once worth over $40 billion declared in court that his net worth was "zero."

The Reliance Power IPO was the first crack in his fortune's façade.

*

The Lesson

The Reliance Power saga remains one of India's most dramatic IPO failures. It taught investors three unforgettable lessons:

Brand names don't guarantee returns. Even the Ambani name couldn't shield investors from bad economics.

A story isn't a business. Selling future promises without present performance is like building castles in the air.

Valuations can deceive. The higher the hype, the harder the fall.

For millions, the Reliance Power IPO was their baptism by fire in the stock market. It reminded India of a bitter truth: *In the market, dreams are sold at a premium, but reality always settles at a discount.*

Reliance Power promised to light up India. Instead, it left its investors in the dark—holding shares that became shadows of their dreams.

*

Years Later

Reliance Power—Skeletons in the Grid

The Bangalore office towers of Reliance Power still glow beneath the city lights, a testament to the ambition unquenched. Yet inside the elevators, fervour has given way to quiet tension. The company once projected strength through power plants, solar farms, and expansion plans—now it hums with subpoenas and scrutiny.

*

The Scandal Unfolds

An enormous ₹17,000 crore bank loan fraud has enveloped the house of Reliance. The Enforcement Directorate has interrogated senior executives and even summoned Anil Ambani himself, as probe agencies uncover suspicious loans, forged bank guarantees, and diverging money trails.

Stock prices cratered—the company's shares tumbled nearly 19% over six trading sessions, signalling investor panic and reputational haemorrhage.

*

Echoes in the Corridors

Long gone are the days of sweeping statements about energy dominance. Now, whispers filter through the corridors—about bail conditions, boardroom denials, and pending court summonses.

Power projects still run, but with a lower hum. The solar farms that once promised a green future now stand shadowed by scandal. Where investors saw growth, they now see skeletons in the grid.

In the annals of corporate India, Reliance Power will be remembered less as a utility company and more as a parable of ambition compromised—a testament that, even in energy, the greatest short-circuits may come from within.

***

Chapter 43
Google IPO: The Underpricing Again

Mountain View, 2004. Earlier: Manlo Park; Later: Nasdeq

IPO Under-Valuation ☑ Fraud ✗ Dutch Auction ☑

In August 2004, Google went public with a Dutch auction IPO, aiming to make shares accessible to ordinary investors. Priced at \$85 per share, the offering raised \$1.67 billion, valuing the company at nearly \$23 billion. Critics at the time called it underpriced, but within a year the stock doubled, and in two decades Google's parent company Alphabet soared past \$1 trillion in market value. The IPO became a landmark in tech history, remembered as "the billion-dollar discount."

Transition Scene

Post Google Debacle, 1999

1600 Amphitheatre Parkway, Mountain View, USA

Larry Page slammed the phone shut, his fingers trembling not from fear, but from a kind of silent rage. Excite had walked away. The \$750,000 offer, laughable as it now seemed, had slipped into the dustbin of history. Sergey Brin, pacing the tiny office in Mountain View, muttered, "Maybe it's good they didn't take us seriously. Maybe we're worth more than they think."

The world outside remained oblivious. Google was just another quirky search engine, buried among dozens of startups dotting Silicon Valley's restless soil. Nobody knew then that this rejection, this moment of humiliation, was a blessing in disguise.

But destiny has a wicked sense of humour.

For though Larry and Sergey had escaped one undervaluation, the world would once again place a price tag on their creation. And in 2004, when Wall Street finally opened its doors to Google, the stage was set for another grand act of mispricing—this time not by buyers in a small room, but by the very machinery of global finance.

*

The Billion-Dollar Slip

Google's IPO, 2004

The summer of California shimmered with heat and promise. Golden hills stretched across Palo Alto, jacarandas scattered purple blossoms on quiet streets, and Bougainvillaea flared against white fences. Amid this sunlit calm, Google prepared to make its bold leap into the public markets—a moment that would test whether dreams born in Silicon Valley's garages could conquer Wall Street.

The kind of heat that made the air buzz with the same nervous energy that coursed through Sand Hill Road. Startups were coming of age, the dot-com bust still smouldered in memory, and investors were wary, sceptical, bruised.

And yet, Google was ready.

Larry Page and Sergey Brin stood at the edge of the financial world, preparing to introduce their brainchild to Wall Street. They wanted none of the theatrics of traditional IPOs—the roadshows, the hype, the carefully orchestrated dances with underwriters. No. Google chose a radical method: the Dutch auction.

It was supposed to be democratic, transparent, a rebellion against the cosy deals between banks and favoured clients. Every investor, big or small, would have a fair shot. No hidden backroom negotiations. No Wall Street games.

But rebellions rarely go as planned.

*

The Wall Street Snub

The Boardroom Storm

The glass walls of Google's Mountain View headquarters reflected the blinding California sun that August morning. Inside, the air was colder than the air-conditioning allowed—not from temperature, but from tension.

Larry Page leaned back in his chair, his fingers tapping the edge of a manila folder stuffed with financial charts. Sergey Brin, in his trademark rollerblades, circled the room like a restless hawk. Across the polished table sat the bankers from Morgan Stanley and Credit Suisse, their suits crisp, their smiles strained, their eyes sharp with calculation.

The meeting had one agenda: the IPO.

Everybody in the boardroom was mulling over the Dutch auction. It meant less control, fewer guarantees, and a direct slap at the financial establishment.

"Gentlemen," began the lead banker, sliding a chart across the table, "the Dutch Auction is… unconventional. Investors are nervous. We suggest a traditional approach. Safer. Controlled."

Larry's eyes narrowed. "Controlled? You mean controlled by you. By the same system that underprices companies, hands profits to insiders, and cheats the public. No. We're doing this differently."

The banker's jaw tightened. "With respect, Mr Page, an IPO is not a science experiment. It is about stability. If you insist on this auction, you risk leaving billions on the table."

Sergey stopped circling and leaned in, his palms flat on the table. "Billions on the table? Better billions on the table than billions stolen in backrooms. We built Google to change the world, not to play Wall Street's games."

The room fell silent. For a moment, the only sound was the hum of the projector and the distant chirping of a California jay outside the window.

Another banker cleared his throat. "Investors are jittery. The dot-com crash is still fresh. If you price this too high, if demand falters, this could be seen as arrogance. If you price too low, you will be remembered for the greatest underpricing since… well, ever."

Larry tapped the manila folder once more, then opened it. Inside was a single sheet—bold, uncompromising.

"Eighty-five dollars a share. That's the number. We stand by it."

The bankers exchanged glances. Some smirked, some sighed. In their minds, the two young founders were children walking into fire with matches in their hands.

But the decision was made.

When the meeting ended, the bankers filed out, muttering under their breath about hubris and folly. Larry and Sergey remained behind. Sergey finally sat, unlacing his skates, staring at the sunlight spilling across the carpet.

"Do you think we just made a mistake?" he asked.

Larry didn't look up. "Sometimes the right mistake is better than the wrong compromise."

And so, in that room of glass and tension, history was signed in silence.

Inside the boardrooms of Goldman Sachs and Morgan Stanley, there was unease. The underwriters weren't thrilled with Google's defiance. They smiled in public but whispered in private: "Let's see if these Stanford boys can pull it off."

The 1999 dot-com scars were fresh, and investors still remembered Pets.com, Webvan, and the many fallen angels. Google was different—profitable, growing—but the market had been conditioned to doubt.

The shares were priced at $85 per share. It was meant to be fair. It was meant to reflect value. But Wall Street had other plans.

*

The Opening Bell

4 Times Square, New York City

August 19, 2004

The Nasdaq buzzed with anticipation. Journalists packed the floor, cameras flashing like fireworks. Google was about to step into the light.

The first trade? $100 per share.

The price quickly soared—$110, $120, even brushing against $135.

By the end of the day, Google closed at $100.34 per share.

Investors cheered. Headlines screamed: "Google Soars!"

But inside Google's offices, a quieter realisation dawned.

Had they left money on the table?

On paper, the underpricing was worth about $300 million—the difference between the IPO price and the first-day close, multiplied by the number of shares sold. But suppose one considers the original target range, the number of shares cut from the offering, and the evident demand once trading began. In that case, analysts estimate the company could have raised more.

How much more? Nearly $3 billion.

That gap—the difference between what investors were willing to pay and what Google had priced—wasn't just numbers. It was a narrative of mistrust, of underestimation, of the market's inability to see potential when it stared them in the face.

*

The Echo of 1999

Larry Page sat by the window, reflecting. Just five years ago, Excite had baulked at $750,000. Now, Wall Street was undervaluing them by billions.

Sergey, ever the realist, shrugged. "At least we're public. At least we're free."

But freedom came with irony. Google, in its attempt to outsmart Wall Street, had been outmanoeuvred by sentiment, fear, and the old scars of the dot-com crash. The Dutch auction was noble in spirit, but markets thrive on psychology, not fairness.

The IPO was a triumph. And yet, it was also a failure. A reminder that valuation is less about arithmetic and more about perception—about what people believe, not what numbers say.

*

The Billion-Dollar Irony

By year's end, Google's stock had climbed further, eventually splitting and multiplying, creating one of the most remarkable runs in financial history. Early investors were more affluent than they could have dreamed. And that $3 billion "left behind" became a permanent scar in IPO lore.

Google didn't just miss money—it missed the chance to rewrite how markets worked. The Dutch auction faded, never becoming the norm. Wall Street had won the quiet battle.

And so, history recorded the event not as the triumph of fairness, but as one of the greatest under-pricings in modern finance.

*

Closing Note

In the tale of Google, there are two failures of valuation: In 1999, a failure of vision.

In 2004, a failure of courage.

Both remind us that markets are not calculators—they are stages where drama, fear, and ambition collide.

*

Google: A Corporate of Enigmas

Google is known for several "enigmas" surrounding the company. These range from hidden Easter eggs and obscure origins to more serious concerns about its business practices and influence. These enigmas range from the quirky history of its name to the LEGO computer servers.

Not many are aware that the initially Spartan design of Google's website was not a strategic choice for simplicity. The founders had limited HTML knowledge and wanted a clean, fast-loading user interface. For a time, it even lacked a "submit" button, requiring users to press the "Return" key.

Instead of using lawnmowers that cause pollution, Google has a tradition of renting goats to trim the weeds and brush on its Mountain View campus. The practice is considered a more eco-friendly and enjoyable method of landscape maintenance.

Google has a long history of embedding fun, quirky features known as Easter eggs. Examples include searching "do a barrel roll" to spin the page, or searching "askew" to tilt the results. If you search for "the answer to life, the universe, and everything," Google will return "42," a well-known reference from the book *The Hitchhiker's Guide to the Galaxy*. It is widely believed to be Google's first Easter egg.

Formed in 2015, Alphabet Inc., the parent company of Google, has acquired around 256 companies, with its most recent major acquisition being Wiz in March 2025 for $32. The ultimate fate of some of these acquisitions can be perplexing, with specific products being integrated, others being shut down, and some seemingly disappearing entirely.

God only knows how many more enigmas are buried deep in its LEGO servers.

*

Years Later

At the time of its IPO in 2004, Google was processing approximately 200 million searches per day, already surpassing its competitors. Annual revenue stood at around $3.2 billion, with net income close to $400 million—numbers that looked impressive but hardly suggested the trillion-dollar empire to come.

Two decades later, the scale is staggering. Google now handles over 8.5 billion searches per day and generates more than $300 billion in annual revenue. Its ad engine, once dismissed as a simple text-link marketplace, powers the bulk of that income, making it one of the most profitable business models in corporate history.

For investors, the "underpriced" IPO became a once-in-a-lifetime windfall. The stock, issued at $85 per share, has since split multiple times, effectively turning a $10,000 investment at IPO into well over $1.5 million today. What seemed like cautious pricing back then is now remembered as one of Wall Street's most significant missed opportunities, except for the lucky few who believed in it early.

***

Chapter 44

Paytm IPO—The Fall of a Giant Dream

Noida, Uttar Pradesh, India

Over-Valuation ☑ Fraud ✗

In November 2021, Paytm launched India's largest-ever IPO, raising ₹18,300 crore at a valuation of over $20 billion. Marketed as a watershed moment for Indian fintech, the listing turned into a disaster when the stock plunged 27% on debut, erasing billions in investor wealth. Burdened by mounting losses and questions over its business model, the IPO became a textbook case of overvaluation and broken market euphoria.

India's Biggest IPO

The Biggest Letdown

The story of PayTM is not just about money. It is about ambition, timing, dreams that flew too high, and a sudden fall that rattled India's startup ecosystem. It reads like a Shakespearean tragedy, where the hero is not evil, but undone by the very force that once made him great—unchecked ambition.

*

The Dreamer from Aligarh

In 1997, a young boy from Aligarh arrived in Delhi with little more than a heart full of dreams and a second-hand bicycle. Vijay Shekhar Sharma was not from the world of pedigree entrepreneurs. His English was broken, his background humble.

But he carried an unshakable faith: that the internet would rewrite India's destiny.

By 2010, Sharma's venture—Pay Through Mobile, later shortened to PayTM—was just a small payments service. Few noticed it. But the boy from Aligarh was relentless. He slept on office floors, coded for nights without end, and kept pitching to investors with the zeal of a street fighter.

Then came November 2016—the night India's Prime Minister announced demonetisation. As long queues snaked around ATMs and people scrambled for cash, PayTM's blue-and-white logo became the saviour of daily commerce. From tea stalls to taxi drivers, PayTM's QR codes spread like wildfire.

Overnight, PayTM was no longer just an app—it was a verb. People said, "PayTM karo."

The boy from Aligarh had built India's first digital emperor.

*

The Kingdom Expands

The years that followed were drenched in investor money. Alibaba poured in billions, SoftBank joined the party, and even Warren Buffett's Berkshire Hathaway placed a bet—it's a rare endorsement of an Indian tech company.

PayTM wanted everything… A payments bank… E-commerce… Insurance… Movie tickets… Gold trading. Just everything.

It was no longer just an app. It was a super app, Sharma's attempt at building India's Alibaba.

Every boardroom presentation was filled with big charts, rising user graphs, and Sharma's passionate speeches about financial inclusion and India's digital revolution.

But beneath the glossy decks, a question lingered like an unpaid bill: where are the profits?

*

The Ascent

The winter of 2021 carried a peculiar heat in Dalal Street. Screens glowed in broking houses, retail investors held their breath, and Paytm—the poster child of India's fintech revolution—prepared to step into history.

Vijay Shekhar Sharma, the founder who once carried his dreams on borrowed funds, was now ready to ring the bell for India's largest-ever IPO: $2.5 billion. The numbers were blinding.

Valuation: $20 billion

Offer size: ₹18,300 crore

Issue Price: ₹2,150 per share

The narrative was intoxicating: the Amazon of India, the super app of the future, the fintech juggernaut that would eat banking alive.

Yet, analysts whispering in the corridors of Dalal Street noted the cracks:

Paytm had never posted a profit in over a decade.

Revenue multiples: 26x FY21 revenues, compared to Square (Block) at 12x and PayPal at 8x.

Cash burn was assumed to be over ₹2,000 crore annually, with no visible operating leverage.

DCF projections assumed EBITDA breakeven only by FY2026, with a terminal growth rate of 25%, far higher than the Indian GDP baseline.

It was a valuation priced for perfection. And perfection is a dangerous demand.

*

The Boardroom Scene

Inside the glass-panelled boardroom on Paytm's Noida campus, the air was heavier than the winter fog outside. Laptops clicked open, coffee cups steamed, and the floor-to-ceiling screen displayed the final valuation slides.

The CFO's voice carried a rehearsed confidence: "Ladies and gentlemen, we're going to market at ₹2,150 per share. That gives us a post-money valuation of $20 billion. Our EV/Revenue multiple stands at 26x, which reflects our leadership position."

An investor leaned forward, tapping the table. "Leadership doesn't erase fundamentals. Look at your discounted cash flow—free cash flows are negative for the next five years. Your WACC assumption is 9%, but in India's risk environment, that's not very favourable. At best, this DCF supports a $12–13 billion valuation, not 20."

The founder rose, voice filled with conviction: "DCF is history's tool. The future rewards vision. Look at Amazon—look at Tesla. They were doubted too. We are building India's super app. Market share today, monetisation tomorrow. Valuation is faith, and India has faith in us."

The words hung heavy.

From the corner of the room, a mid-level executive, hesitant but brave, spoke up:

"Sir, with respect, merchant retention is slipping in Tier II towns. Our CAC is climbing. Google Pay and PhonePe are eating into our UPI share. If investors model churn, our lifetime value per customer collapses. Should we temper the projections?"

Silence.

The CFO shuffled his papers. "This is not the forum for second-guessing. The IPO roadshow is built on growth, not caution."

The unease was genuine. But it was buried under billion-dollar slides.

*

The IPO Hype

2021 was India's moment of startup glory. The world was watching. Unicorns were being born every week. Investors were throwing money at tech founders who promised growth, not profits.

For Sharma, the time had come. PayTM would go public with India's biggest IPO ever—₹18,300 crores.

India was ready for history.

The marketing blitz was unlike anything India had seen. Billboards screamed PayTM's promise. Social media echoed with #PayTMIPO. Analysts called it India's Alibaba moment.

November 18, 2021, Mumbai. Cameras flashed at the Bombay Stock Exchange. Sharma walked into the roadshows like a rockstar. Investors crowded to hear his story - the boy from Aligarh who had changed how India paid. His speeches brimmed with emotion, his eyes often moist as he spoke about his journey. Visibly emotional, he quoted poetry and proclaimed a new chapter in India's startup story.

On listing day, the Bombay Stock Exchange building shimmered in excitement. Television anchors were giddy. Cameramen flashed their lenses at Sharma, who walked in, heart pounding, wearing his characteristic half-smile.

India was ready for history.

*

The Debut

Dalal Street, Kala Ghoda, Fort, Mumbai

At 10:00 am, the PayTM stock ticker lit up.

The stock opened weak at ₹1,950.

And then, within minutes, the dream began to unravel.

The stock was listed 27% lower than its issue price. Red numbers flashed across every screen. The company that was supposed to symbolise India's tech pride was now etched in history as India's worst IPO debut.

Silence gripped Dalal Street.

Retail investors who had bet their savings sat frozen. Analysts scrambled to explain the fall: overvaluation, unclear business model, no path to profitability. Global investors quietly shook their heads.

By the close, it had crashed 27% to ₹1,564.

In one brutal day, PayTM's emperor's crown slipped. The man who had been hailed as India's digital visionary now faced whispers of arrogance and recklessness. Paytm's market cap shrank by over ₹45,000 crore.

In the weeks that followed, PayTM's stock continued its downward spiral. Investors lost billions. The media sharpened its knives. "From Pride to Pain," screamed headlines.

Sharma, once the darling of television interviews, now sat across anchors with tears in his eyes. "We are building for the long-term," he said, voice cracking. But the market was unforgiving. Every quarterly result widened the gap between dream and reality.

Behind closed doors, boardroom debates turned tense. Investors questioned the strategy. Employees, once proud to wear the PayTM badge, now wonder about their ESOPs. Competitors like PhonePe and Google Pay surged ahead, quietly taking market share.

The empire was crumbling from within.

*

Aftermath in the Corridors

Back in the boardroom, the celebratory bouquets still lay on the table, their fragrance soured. Phones buzzed with panicked broker calls. Analysts tore into the prospectus:

"The IPO was overpriced compared to global fintech peers."

"DCF assumptions were fantastical."

"Unit economics remain broken."

The CFO whispered numbers to himself: "Down 27%… 75% volume sold by retail… Market cap evaporated."

The founder stared blankly at the floor. The very words he had shouted days before—"Valuation is faith"—now mocked him.

An investor, unsparing, cut in: "We warned you about mispricing. The street has punished you. You cannot sell dreams at 26x revenue when profits are invisible. Faith doesn't protect stock price."

At the far end, the mid-level executive closed his notepad silently. His earlier caution, ignored in the boardroom, had played out in the market.

*

The Lesson

The Paytm IPO became a subject of post-mortem valuation studies. For years, founders had sold the story of growth at all costs. But PayTM's failure forced everyone to pause: What good is growth if it never turns into profits?

A $20 billion tag for a loss-making model was unsustainable. The Fundamentals of valuation were ignored to seek a desired overvaluation. Valuation multiples double those of PayPal and Square, which invited scepticism. DCF fragility was exposed. Terminal growth rates and WACC assumptions were stretched to make numbers fit. The "super app" story collapsed under quarterly earnings.

The IPO was not just about numbers—it was about faith. And when that faith cracked, it sent shockwaves through India's startup ecosystem. Over the next year, the stock plummeted over 75% from its issue price, eroding billions in investor wealth.

It was not a scam. It was not a fraud. It was a dream that lost its grounding in reality.

The fall of PayTM was not the end of Indian startups. But it was a mirror. A reminder that even emperors must balance ambition with accountability.

*

Closing Scene

In the dimly lit boardroom, the executive's words echoed like a haunting refrain: "Should we recalibrate before the market does it for us?"

The board had chosen silence. The market had not. The fall from grace has etched itself in history.

The Paytm IPO was not just a failed listing—it was a public autopsy of India's valuation bubble, dissected live on Dalal Street. The rise and fall of PayTM is a breathtaking story, with boardroom drama and the emotional highs and lows of Vijay Shekhar Sharma. He still walks with that restless energy, still speaks about building for India, still dreams of turning PayTM into a household name once more.

Like all great tragedies, this one was not about evil, but about excess.

The boy from Aligarh had built a digital empire.

The emperor had fallen.

And India watched, silently, as the lessons of ambition were written in red on the ticker boards of Dalal Street.

*

Years Later

Paytm—The Vanishing Unicorn

Once hailed as India's answer to Silicon Valley, Paytm symbolised the digital revolution. Its IPO in 2021 was supposed to crown it as the flagbearer of new-age finance, yet instead it became one of the country's most dramatic market meltdowns. Investors who rushed in at ₹2,150 per share saw billions in value erased almost overnight.

Years later, Paytm's headquarters in Noida Sector 5 still stands—a gleaming glass structure, but without the frenzy that once filled its corridors. Screens that once flashed projections of endless growth now carry muted dashboards. Employees whisper about layoffs, regulatory hurdles, and the fading aura of being India's most celebrated startup.

The dream of a "super app" lies fragmented. Competitors, regulators, and market realities have eroded the vision. For ordinary shareholders, the scar remains—a reminder that even the brightest unicorns can stumble on the sharp edges of valuation hype.

The logo still shines on billboards and payment QR codes across chai stalls and supermarkets, but the myth has dimmed. Paytm survives—but as a shadow of its own promise.

***

Tales of Startups Misfire

Chapter 45
Flashback: The Startup Bubbles

Silicon Valley, 1999

Over-Valuation ☑ Fraud ✗ Cash Burn ☑ Startup Failure ☑ Investors' euphoria ☑

> The late 1990s saw a frenzy of internet startups, with investors pouring billions into companies with little more than a website and a promise. Valuations skyrocketed on hype, IPOs doubled overnight, and the NASDAQ soared. But by 2000, reality caught up—most firms had no profits, no models, only burning cash. When the bubble burst, trillions in market value vanished, leaving behind a graveyard of failed dot-coms and a cautionary tale of unchecked euphoria.

The Euphoria of the Internet

The world was no longer the same.

It was the late 1990s, Silicon Valley. In dimly lit garages, young men and women hunched over glowing computer screens, wires snaking across floors like veins of a living organism. A young twenty-something founder, hoodie on, hunched over a chunky desktop, tells a room full of investors: "This could change everything," and the room erupts in applause. They believed him. Venture capitalists in crisp Armani suits walked into these garages and, with the flourish of a fountain pen, turned scribbled ideas into million-dollar enterprises. Headlines scream of a new economy.

The ".com" at the end of a name was more powerful than decades of business experience. No one asked about profits. No one asked about sustainability. The internet was magic, and magic didn't need explanations. The dot-com boom was not just about technology—it was a revolution wrapped in optimism, arrogance, and caffeine.

"We're going to change the world… all we need is a website."

This was the dot-com bubble, when the internet became the oxygen of dreams. Companies raised billions not because they had customers, but because they had a website. Pets.com spent fortunes on Super Bowl ads, Webvan promised to deliver groceries at the click of a button, and investors nodded along. For a brief, shining moment, it felt as if the old rules of business had been permanently rewritten.

*

The Internet

Hero or Villain?

Unlike old-fashioned brick-and-mortar companies, most of the startups thrived on the power of the internet. Their lifeblood wasn't land or steel; it was bandwidth. And when that failed—either technologically or metaphorically—they crumbled. The internet wasn't just a tool. It was the oxygen, the fire, and the guillotine of startups, taking their ideas overseas with lightning speed.

But oxygen, once again, proved double-edged. The irony of the startup world is that the very thing that gave birth to it—the internet—is also the reason for its most spectacular failures. A bug, a crash, a wave of trolling, a viral tweet, a bad press article—the downfall of a billion-dollar company could begin in a single click. Startups scaled at lightning speed—often faster than they could handle. Apps hit millions of downloads, valuations skyrocketed, and investors pumped in cash as if tomorrow didn't exist. But when growth slowed, when downloads plateaued, when customers stopped clicking "buy," the very oxygen that gave them life became the fire that consumed them.

The internet gave startups scale, speed, and visibility. But it also gave them instant feedback. A one-star rating could destroy months of branding. Global competition was the other thing it gave. The world was no longer far away; Amazon could swoop into India as easily as Flipkart could dream of expanding abroad. But then, millions of downloads didn't always translate to revenue. Vanity metrics masked fragile business models.

It was a stage, vast and bright, but also ruthless. Startups performed daring acts on this digital theatre, hoping to dazzle the audience. Some walked away as legends; many collapsed mid-performance.

But oxygen that fuels growth can also suffocate. By 2000, the bubble burst. Stock tickers bled red, once-darling startups shut their doors overnight, and Silicon Valley turned into a graveyard of broken promises. Still, the internet had already proven itself—it wasn't a fad, it was a revolution. And in the chapters that follow, we will meet many such companies that rose because of it—and fell because they couldn't control it.

*

India's Awakening

India was also catching fire.

It was 2004 in Bangalore, and the air was thick with ambition. The old city, once known for gardens and pensioners, now roared with call centres, internet cafes, and newly minted tech parks. In glass-walled offices off Outer Ring Road, young founders rehearsed their pitches in front of whiteboards smeared with flowcharts. "This isn't just a business," one declared, "it's a disruption." Venture capital firms, freshly imported from California and Singapore, nodded. They loved the word.

Bangalore, 2007. In a cramped apartment with plastic chairs and mismatched tables, two brothers, Sachin and Binny Bansal, dreamed of selling books online. Flipkart was born not in a glittering office but in a one-bedroom flat with slow internet and a big dream. Customers were sceptical—"Who buys books on the internet?"—but trust was built, one delivery at a time.

Fast forward.

Slowly, startups across India realised what Silicon Valley had seen a decade earlier: the internet was a marketplace without borders. Ola offered rides at the tap of a button. Zomato lets you order food while lounging in pyjamas. PayTM promised to make your wallet redundant. Housing.com made house-hunting look like a video game.

And then came 2016, the year India inhaled internet oxygen like never before. With Reliance Jio's cheap data plans, millions of Indians—from tier-1 cities to the smallest villages—came online overnight. Smartphones became the new lifeline. Suddenly, every startup had a market of a billion people, just waiting to be converted into users.

*

The Boardroom Dream

A founder in his mid-twenties, hoodie over jeans, walked into a high-rise conference room in Gurgaon. He carried no business plan, no balance sheet—only a laptop with a bright orange PowerPoint slide that said:

"Changing the Way India Lives."

The investors leaned forward. Coffee steamed on the mahogany table. The founder's voice trembled at first, but soon gathered rhythm: a story about "India's 300 million smartphone users," about "a market larger than Europe," about "growth at lightning speed."

No one asked about profits. The question on every investor's lips was simple: "How fast can you scale?"

A cheque was signed before the coffee cooled.

*

The Timeline of the Dot.com Bubble Burst

March 2000

And suddenly the bubble burst.

The investors watched in awe.

Founders slumped in their workstations.

After a peak in the Nasdaq Composite Index on March 10, 2000, it nosedived for a prolonged period, with the Nasdaq losing over 75% of its value by October 2002.

Many dot-com companies failed, resulting in a significant market correction.

The dot-com crash became a graveyard of dreams—Pets.com, Webvan, ShopOnline.com, and hundreds more. Each is a story of ambition, denial, and collapse.

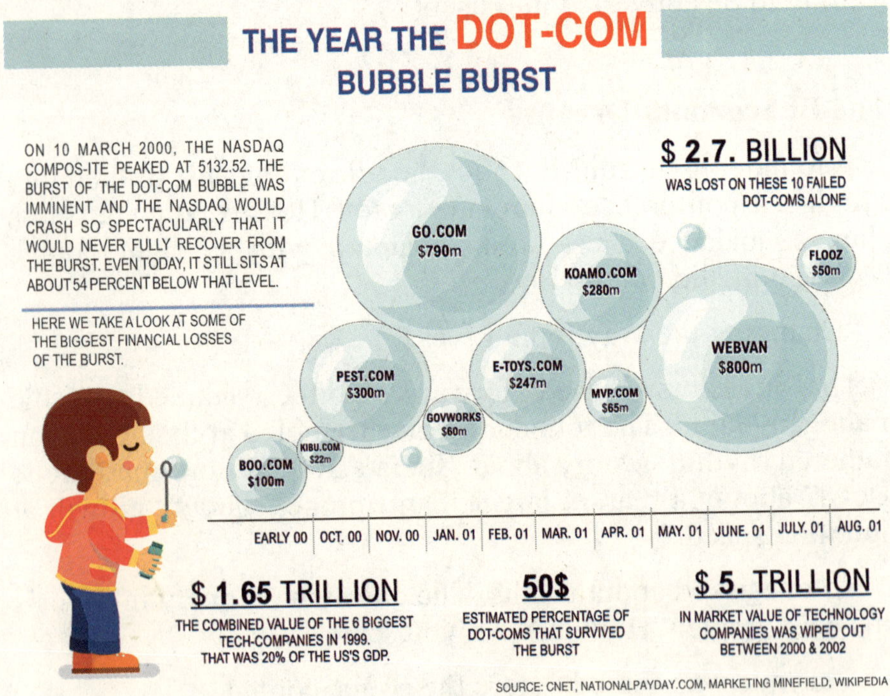

The Carnival of Hype

2010 Onwards

By 2010, the startup world had turned into a carnival—conferences brimmed with neon-lit stages and pounding music. Founders in sneakers and wireless mics strutted across spotlights, announcing funding rounds the way rock stars announced albums.

Television channels ran special prime-time shows: "Unicorns of India." Magazines with glossy covers screamed: "The Billion-Dollar Boys." News anchors spoke of twenty-somethings who drove Lamborghinis before they could drive stability into their balance sheets.

In the buzzing corridors of these events, young employees—fresh out of IITs and IIMs—carried tote bags stamped with motivational slogans. They believed they weren't joining a job; they were joining a revolution.

*

The Backroom Reality

Behind the carnival, however, the math was quietly falling apart.

Late at night, in offices that smelled of stale pizza and burnt-out ambition, accountants stared at spreadsheets. Complex algorithms were churning. Customer acquisition costs were ballooning. Revenues lagged far behind projections. Marketing teams spent millions chasing downloads that were uninstalled the next morning. Yet, every quarter, new funding rounds washed over the problems like a fresh coat of paint.

"Forget the losses," an investor would say over the phone from New York. "Just show me user growth."

And the cycle continued.

*

The Illusion

It was not just about money. It was about belief. A belief that the rules of economics could be rewritten. That valuation was destiny. That "burn rate" was a badge of courage, not a warning siren.

But every illusion, no matter how dazzling, carries within it the seeds of collapse.

The stage was set with actors: charismatic founders in hoodies, cautious CFOs with furrowed brows, hungry investors chasing the next unicorn, and regulators lingering in the shadows. The script was written: ambition, hype, greed, deception, seduction, betrayal. And the audience was vast—employees, customers, shareholders, even governments—all spellbound by the drama unfolding.

This was not just the story of startups.

This was theatre on a global scale.

The curtain is about to rise.

The spotlight will swing.

And one by one, the players will take their place in this drama—some destined to be crowned visionaries, others to be remembered as cautionary tales.

Welcome to the Age of Startups.

Where dreams soared like rockets, and sometimes, crashed like meteors.

*

Years Later

The early 2000s felt like a financial battlefield long after the cannons had stopped firing. Burned-out office parks in Silicon Valley stood as graveyards of forgotten dreams—cubicles gathering dust, whiteboards still covered with half-finished pitches, logos of startups that once promised to "change the world" now peeling off the walls.

Investors who had once tossed money at anything with a ".com" watched their portfolios vanish into thin air. Some never recovered; their paper wealth evaporated like mist at sunrise. Pension funds, college endowments, and small-time dreamers who thought they were surfing the future were left with nothing more than dot-gone memories.

And yet, from the ashes, survivors emerged. Amazon, once dismissed as just an "online bookstore," clawed its way back, brick by brick, quarter by quarter, until it became the giant of giants. Google, which went public just a few years later, became the lighthouse of the new digital era. The crash, though merciless, became a cleansing fire - burning away hype and leaving behind a sturdier, more ruthless Internet age.

In the corridors of Wall Street, the Dot-com Crash is still whispered about—not as a single event, but as a cautionary tale. A reminder that when valuations are built on dreams without foundations, gravity eventually wins.

***

Chapter 46

Pets.com: A Sock Puppet and a Silicon Valley Funeral

San Francisco, California, 1998 Onwards

Startup Failure ☑ Cash Burn ☑ Negative Cash Flow ☑ Dot.com Bubble ☑

Unprofitable Shipping Model ☑

Pets.com (1998–2000) became the poster child of the dot-com bubble. Backed by Amazon and famous for its sock-puppet mascot, it promised to revolutionise pet supplies through online sales. Despite massive marketing spend and early buzz, the company never solved its unprofitable shipping model. By late 2000, just 268 days after its IPO, Pets.com shut down, burning through nearly $300 million and becoming a lasting symbol of dot-com excess.

The Birth of a Dream

The city buzzed with dot-com energy. Coffee shops brimmed with young entrepreneurs whispering about IPOs, VCs, and "changing the world."

In a small office tucked away in South of Market, a group of idealists huddled around a whiteboard. A young executive scribbled in thick marker: "Why carry heavy bags of pet food when we can ship it?"

The room erupted with nods and laughter. It seemed so obvious, so revolutionary. If books could be sold online by

Amazon, why not kibble and cat litter? The internet was the new frontier, and Pets.com would be its pioneer in pet care.

One investor, eyes gleaming, declared: “This is not just a company. This is destiny.”

*

The Puppet That Stole the Show

The marketing team was restless. They needed something bold, something unforgettable.

One night, in a brainstorming session, a copywriter held up a sock, drew two black eyes and a tongue, and made it bark. The room exploded with laughter. A silly idea was born: the Sock Puppet Dog.

Soon, the puppet was everywhere—on TV, in magazines, on talk shows. It became the cheeky face of Silicon Valley’s confidence. In Times Square, a giant puppet billboard grinned down at New Yorkers with the slogan: “Because pets can’t drive.”

Then came January 2000—the Super Bowl.

In front of 90 million viewers, the sock puppet danced across screens, cracking jokes while promoting home-delivered pet food. Families laughed, children pointed, and Wall Street erupted in cheers.

The next morning, the office phones rang nonstop. Customers poured in. Investors called with blank checks. The mascot had turned into a miracle worker.

But in the warehouse, reality told another story: every order shipped was another nail in the coffin.

*

Cracks in the Foundation

Inside the boardroom, tension grew.

The CFO flipped open a folder, his voice strained: "Ladies and gentlemen, for every $10 we sell, we lose nearly $20 in costs. Warehousing, shipping—it's eating us alive."

Silence.

An executive tried to brush it off: "Losses are fine. This is the internet age. We're building market share, not profits."

The board applauded. The CFO looked down at his spreadsheets, knowing the numbers told a different truth.

*

Wall Street's Siren Song

Despite the warnings, Pets.com rushed headlong into an IPO in February 2000. The stock opened at $11 a share, and cameras flashed as the executives rang the Nasdaq bell, smiling for the world.

Investors clapped. Analysts beamed. For a moment, Pets.com was a Wall Street darling.

But beneath the cheers, unease simmered. Competitors like Petopia and Petstore.com lurked, copying strategies and undercutting prices. Customers loved the discounts, but loyalty was shallow. They came for deals, not devotion.

By mid-2000, the dot-com bubble had begun to tremble. Nasdaq stocks nosedived. Pets.com, already fragile, began to crumble.

*

The Fall

November 7, 2000

In a cold San Francisco boardroom, the CEO faced her exhausted team. The sock puppet mascot sat on the table, silent and ironic.

She spoke the words no one wanted to hear: “We’re out of cash. We’re shutting down.”

Some cried. Some cursed. Others stared blankly at the puppet, as if it had betrayed them.

By November 9, the website displayed a farewell message: “Pets.com will cease operations. We thank you for your support.”

The stock, once at $11, was now worth 19 cents.

*

The Funeral of a Mascot

When the company auctioned its assets, the puppet too went under the hammer. A cultural superstar, reduced to a line item on a liquidation list.

One employee, watching the puppet carried away, whispered: “It made millions laugh, but it couldn’t save us.”

The press had a field day. Headlines mocked:

“Sock Puppet Gets Put Down.”

“Pets.com—All Bark, No Bite.”

It was cruel. But it was true.

*

Lessons Etched in Ashes

Pets.com was not a failure of imagination. It was a failure of discipline. A puppet cannot carry 50-pound dog food bags profitably. Super Bowl ads don’t guarantee survival. Investors’ hype silenced hard questions.

Pets.com became the poster child of the dot-com crash, its fall a warning etched in Silicon Valley folklore.

Whenever a new flashy startup emerges, someone inevitably mutters: “Remember Pets.com.”

*

Epilogue

The Ghost Returns

Years later, the sock puppet resurfaced in other campaigns, its stitched grin unchanged. But to those who remembered, it wasn't funny anymore.

It was a ghost—a reminder that startups built on hype, without a foundation of profitability, are destined to end not with a bang, but with an auctioneer's gavel.

*

Years Later

The Mascot Without a Home

The sock puppet still smiles in old commercials, its stitched grin frozen in time. But behind that cheerful mascot lies the rubble of one of the internet's most iconic flameouts. Pets.com—once a Wall Street darling, once a Super Bowl advertiser—burned through nearly $300 million before collapsing in 2000, leaving behind warehouses of unsold dog food and a cautionary tale for the dot-com age.

Today, there is no headquarters, no buzzing office. The URL that once promised a revolution in pet care now redirects elsewhere, stripped of its identity. What remains are echoes - grainy YouTube clips of the sock puppet, nostalgic forums, and MBA case studies dissecting its fall.

For a generation of investors, Pets.com is not just a failed startup; it is a ghost of irrational exuberance, a reminder of how hype devoured substance. The puppet became a pop-culture relic, but its company became a byword for hubris.

The warehouses are gone, the balance sheets buried, but the sock puppet lingers—a mascot without a home, wandering in the archives of internet history.

***

Chapter 47

The ShopOnline.com: Illusions on Silicon Avenue

Underutilization of Brand ☑ Fraud ✗ Startup Failure ☑

> It is not a story of fraud, but a gross example of missed opportunity. In 2014, domain brokers touted it as comparable to billion-dollar brands like Shop.com or Shopping.com. But the founders could not exploit the valuation of a perfect moniker registered on April 25, 1995, making it one of the earlier played titles in the digital space. The invaluable domain existed mostly as an unused asset—its legacy defined more by failed potential than by performance.

Mania (The Rise)

The boardroom buzzed with energy, the kind that only comes from limitless dreams. Ethan Grant, the thirty-two-year-old CEO of ShopOnline.com, strode in like a general marching to victory. The mahogany table gleamed beneath the fluorescent lights, reflecting the shine in his eyes.

"We are not building a company," he declared, his voice booming, "we are building destiny. By 2005, every American home will shop through us. No more grocery aisles, no more malls. Clicks are the new currency."

Slides flashed on the projector:

Users: 100,000 and climbing

Revenue Growth: 400% YoY

Market Size: $800 billion ripe for disruption

Applause filled the room. The venture capitalist, Alan Rhodes, leaned back with a smile. "Ethan, you're not running a company. You're running a revolution. Wall Street eats this up. Forget profits—valuation is about narrative."

At the far end, CFO Richard Lowell shuffled his papers. His voice was steady, but his words were sharp.

"Our valuation is 40x revenues. EBITDA is negative. Burn rate: $5 million a week. At this pace, free cash flows never turn positive—not in five, not in ten years."

Nobody listened. The sound of corks popping drowned him out. IPO day was near.

*

Denial

The Cracks Appear

The year turned. NASDAQ kept soaring, and so did egos. On IPO day, confetti rained from the ceiling. The stock opened at $15, shot to $85 by afternoon.

Ethan climbed onto a desk, arms stretched wide, the messiah of Silicon Avenue. "We did it! Billion-dollar valuation in a single day!"

Kevin Patel, the youngest analyst, scribbled in his diary: "This is history. My first job, my first IPO. The future is unstoppable."

But Maria Chen, head of operations, whispered a different truth.

"Each order costs us $12. We earn $8. Scale doesn't fix broken math."

Richard added fuel to her fears. "The DCF doesn't add up. Terminal value is a fantasy. We're selling losses dressed as growth."

Ethan waved them away. "Valuation is belief. Wall Street believes in us. That's enough."

But outside, belief began to crack. Competitors shuttered. NASDAQ flickered red. Analysts began to mutter: "What if the emperor has no clothes?"

Alan, the VC, still grinned for the cameras, but his voice was sharper in private. "We double down. Hype harder. If we slow down, we're finished."

The boardroom turned into a temple of denial, prayers replacing numbers.

*

Collapse

The Reckoning, 2001

The spring arrived like a storm.

The boardroom was silent except for the hum of the projector. On the screen, a graph flickered—a flat line where growth was supposed to surge.

"Eight hundred visitors a day," the CFO muttered, tapping the numbers with his pen. "That's not traffic. That's a trickle."

Across the table, the marketing chief tried to soften the blow. "The domain name itself is gold. ShopOnline.com—you don't get more direct than that. People will come. They should come."

The CFO's voice sharpened. "And yet, they don't. At this rate, we're generating less than $2,000 a year in ad revenue. Do you realise Amazon makes more than that every second?"

The room shifted uncomfortably. Someone coughed.

An advisor at the far end leaned forward. "The problem isn't the name—it's the execution. A domain registered in 1995 could have been a crown jewel. Instead, it's a ghost town, ranked in the millions globally. Even scam detectors can't decide if we're real."

The chairman stared at the glowing numbers as if they were courtroom evidence. He had bought the name believing it was destiny. Now it felt like an accusation, a reminder that the internet rewarded builders, not dreamers.

"Our global ranking," he sighed, "is languishing around 3.6 millionth, a far cry from any thriving e-commerce site."

"Web reputation ratings vary wildly," someone muttered. "One platform flagged it as high-risk and potentially phishing-related, while others considered it average or safe but lacking in traffic."

The silence grew heavy until he finally spoke: "A perfect address with no house built upon it. That's what we've become."

Richard's voice trembled as he presented the final numbers. "EBITDA is negative $200 million. Cash reserves drained. Covenants breached. The DCF model doesn't just show low value - it shows zero. We are insolvent."

Maria slammed her binder shut. "I told you. You can't build castles on losses. Scale multiplied the problem. The model never worked."

Alan's grin was gone. "Wall Street won't back another round. IPO money is burned. Ethan, you're not a unicorn—you're roadkill."

Ethan stared at the table, hands shaking. His dream had grown too big, too fast, too hollow.

"We… we just need more time. The market will turn. It has to…"

But silence answered him. The boardroom, once a theatre of applause, now echoed like a courtroom delivering its verdict.

By April, ShopOnline.com was gone.

Linda Hayes, the schoolteacher who had poured $20,000 into shares, sat in her kitchen staring at the screen. Her investment, once worth a down payment on her children's college, was now worth $500. She wept.

Kevin walked out with a cardboard box in his arms, balloons deflated, dreams punctured.

Richard returned to academia, teaching students the cold discipline of cash flow.

Maria joined Amazon.

Alan found the next "hot" startup.

And Ethan? He vanished from headlines, another fallen prophet of the dot-com gospel.

*

Epilogue

The crash was not just about numbers. It was about hubris disguised as valuation, about humans chasing illusions and mistaking them for inevitability.

It left behind one eternal lesson for markets: *Valuation is not prophecy. It is discipline. Without cash flows, every empire of clicks will someday vanish into silence.*

*

Years Later: The Shoponline.com

In the late 1990s and early 2000s, the internet was alive with domain goldmines—names that promised instant recognition and traffic. Among them was ShopOnline.com, a clear, compelling branding opportunity that could've been e-commerce royalty. In fact, in 2014, domain brokers touted it as comparable to billion-dollar brands like Shop.com or Shopping.com, suggesting that with exemplary leadership, it could have become a global retail giant.

Yet despite its perfect moniker, the actual platform never achieved prominence. Instead, the domain mainly existed as an unused asset—its legacy defined more by failed potential than by performance. In the booming chaos of early e-commerce, a memorable domain wasn't enough. Execution, timing, funding, and trust mattered just as much—if not more. ShopOnline.com reminds us that even the brightest digital brands need real-world momentum to make their mark.

In the end, ShopOnline.com stands not as a tale of success, but as a cautionary emblem of the dot-com era: a potent label with no substance behind it, ultimately dormant, overshadowed by competitors with actual traction.

***

Chapter 48

Webvan: The Billion-Dollar Grocery That Never Arrived

Startup Failure ☑ Cash Burn ☑ Fraud ✗

Webvan, launched in 1999, promised to revolutionise grocery shopping with online orders and doorstep delivery, soaring to a peak valuation of $8.5 billion. However, reckless expansion, billion-dollar infrastructure spending, and razor-thin margins resulted in massive losses of $830 million in under two years. By 2001, the dot-com darling collapsed into bankruptcy, becoming one of the most infamous failures of the internet bubble.

The Intoxication of Dot.Com

The year was 1999, and Silicon Valley was drunk on the intoxicating fumes of the dot-com bubble. In a sprawling office in Foster City, California, Webvan's executives huddled around a glossy pitch deck, their voices brimming with conviction.

"Grocery shopping," declared CEO George Shaheen, a former Andersen Consulting executive poached for millions, "is about to be revolutionised. No more lines. No more parking lots. The supermarket is dead. The future is here—delivered to your doorstep."

Investors erupted in applause. Goldman Sachs, Sequoia Capital, SoftBank—all lined up to pour money into the dream. Webvan went public in late 1999, and its stock skyrocketed. At its peak, the company was valued at $8.5 billion, despite never turning a profit.

The advertisements captured the spirit of the age: smiling families clicking a mouse to have fresh produce, meat, and milk arrive at their doors. Grocery delivery was no longer a mundane chore—it was a lifestyle.

*

The Dream of Perfection

Webvan wasn't just a startup; it was an empire under construction. Instead of testing the waters with a single city, the company tried to conquer America in one grand sweep.

They built massive state-of-the-art warehouses—each costing $30–$40 million—equipped with robotic systems that hummed like futuristic factories. Delivery vans painted in bold blue and green logos roamed suburban streets like soldiers of a new economy.

In boardrooms, the PowerPoints glowed with staggering projections: $1 billion in revenue by 2001, 30 cities in five years, and domination of a trillion-dollar grocery market.

But in their hunger for scale, Webvan forgot the basics. Grocery delivery had razor-thin margins, high spoilage risks, and required dense, consistent demand. Instead of solving those first, Webvan poured billions into infrastructure for a future that never came.

*

The First Signs of Rot

By mid-2000, cracks began to show. Warehouses stood half empty. Trucks returned with undelivered orders. Customers complained of missing items, late deliveries, and prices higher than those at supermarkets.

Inside boardrooms, voices of caution rose. "We are expanding too fast," warned a director. "Let us prove the model in one city before rolling it out nationwide."

But George Shaheen, buoyed by investor pressure and media hype, brushed aside doubts. “We are building an empire. We cannot slow down.”

Burning nearly $1 billion in capital, Webvan charged forward.

*

Collapse

Mid-2001

The dot-com bubble burst. Investors who once showered money now demanded profitability. But Webvan’s numbers were brutal.

Losses of $830 million in less than two years.

Warehouses in 10 cities were bleeding money.

Revenue was far below projections.

The once-bustling offices grew quiet as layoffs began. Delivery vans were grounded, warehouses shuttered, and employees walked out carrying cardboard boxes of personal belongings.

In July 2001, Webvan filed for bankruptcy, one of the largest dot-com busts of its era. Over 2,000 employees lost their jobs, and billions in investor money evaporated overnight.

*

Years Later

By 2025, Webvan existed only as a case study—a parable of excess ambition and poor execution. Ironically, the very concept it championed—grocery delivery—would later flourish, with Amazon Fresh, Instacart, and Walmart thriving in the space.

In business schools, Webvan became a cautionary tale of scaling too fast, building infrastructure for demand that did not yet exist.

George Shaheen faded from the limelight, remembered not for his consulting legacy but for presiding over one of Silicon Valley's most infamous failures.

The Webvan warehouses, once futuristic marvels, were sold for scrap or repurposed as distribution centres by other companies.

For the dot-com generation, Webvan became a symbol of hubris—proof that even billion-dollar dreams can crash when built on fragile foundations.

The groceries never arrived. What did come was a lesson etched into corporate memory: vision without discipline can turn promise into ruin.

***

Chapter 49

Stayzilla—The Homestay Dream That Checked Out Too Early

2005-2007; Earlier; Chennai (2005); Later: Bengaluru, India

Startup Failure ☑ Litigation ☑ Cash Burn ☑
Negative Cash Flow ☑

> Founded in 2005 as an online hotel aggregator, Stayzilla pivoted to homestays to take on Airbnb in India. Backed by nearly $33 million in funding, it scaled rapidly but struggled with high burn rates, fierce competition, and limited demand in smaller towns. By 2017, mounting losses forced it to shut down, and its co-founder's brief arrest over unpaid dues turned its fall into a cautionary tale of India's fragile startup ecosystem.

The Arrest That Shook Indian Startups

March 2017

What began as an ordinary evening ended in shock when plainclothes policemen walked into the home of Yogendra Vasupal—Yogi, as Chennai's startup circles knew him. By nightfall, the founder of Stayzilla was behind bars.

The charge? Fraud and intimidation.

Stayzilla, once India's largest homestay marketplace, had shuttered operations just weeks earlier. Now, its founder was accused of cheating a Chennai advertising vendor out of ₹1.7 crore. Civil dues had suddenly become a criminal case.

It wasn't just Yogi's arrest—it was the arrest of an idea: that startups could fail without fear of handcuffs.

From Entrepreneur to "Accused No. 1"

For Yogi, the transition was brutal.

Yesterday's media darling became today's Accused No. 1. The charges were serious. He was charged with cheating (IPC Section 420) and criminal intimidation (IPC Section 506).

In the courtroom, his lawyers argued this was a business failure, not fraud. But the police insisted he had defrauded the vendor, and even threatened him when pressed.

Suddenly, an entrepreneur who had raised millions from Sequoia and Nexus Venture Partners was trading pitch decks for court summons.

*

The Hashtag Revolution

The startup ecosystem reacted with fury, and the #ReleaseYogi movement galvanised India's startup ecosystem.

Twitter exploded with #ReleaseYogi.

Founders whispered: "If this can happen to Yogi, it can happen to any of us."

Nasscom and iSPIRT warned that criminalising startup failure would drive away global investors.

Yogi's blog post, smuggled from jail through his wife, became a manifesto: don't treat unpaid debts as crimes.

The community no longer defended Stayzilla. They were defending the right to fail.

*

Letters From Prison

In his blog, Yogi confessed that Stayzilla had made mistakes, but not crimes. He described sleepless nights, the humiliation of handcuffs, and his fear for the future of Indian entrepreneurship.

It read less like a defence, more like a plea for reform.

*

The Turning Point

After a month in jail, Yogi was granted bail. The relief was palpable. Yet Stayzilla was gone—its investors silent, its employees scattered, its dream dissolved.

Yogi's legacy was no longer a startup, but a cautionary tale.

*

The OYO Parallel

Same Dream, Different Destinies

While Yogi languished in courtrooms, a young 23-year-old in Gurgaon was racing ahead. Ritesh Agarwal's OYO Rooms was becoming India's biggest budget hotel aggregator.

Both started with a dream: to democratise travel stays.

Both raised venture capital: OYO from SoftBank, Stayzilla from Sequoia.

Both aimed to scale: one with hotels, the other with homestays.

But while Stayzilla collapsed under debt and legal fire, OYO grew into a $10 billion unicorn (at its peak), attracting global investors and expanding abroad.

*

What made the difference?

Stayzilla spent aggressively on expansion and marketing, but failed to maintain viable unit economics. OYO, despite its controversies, has mastered investor storytelling and has been relentless in capital raising. It failed in execution & capital discipline.

Ecosystem timing was not correct. In 2017, India's ecosystem lacked strong bankruptcy protections for failed startups. Stayzilla became the victim of systemic gaps. By contrast, OYO's rise coincided with India's startup darling era, when failure was tolerated and even celebrated.

Many times, luck and perception make all the difference. Stayzilla's founder was thrown into a police van. OYO's founder was invited to Davos.

*

Two Roads Diverged

Imagine this: If Stayzilla had survived its cash burn and navigated vendor disputes differently, it could have been India's Airbnb.

Instead, its offices were shut, its founder jailed, its name forgotten.

Meanwhile, OYO's red-and-white branding still lights up highways and airports across India.

Both companies played the same game. One ended in courtrooms. The other in boardrooms.

*

Legacy of the #ReleaseYogi Movement

Stayzilla's collapse ignited a critical debate in India.

Should unpaid dues be settled through bankruptcy courts or police stations?

Should founders risk handcuffs when their startups fail?

Can India really become a startup hub if failure is criminalised?

The case sparked conversations that eventually fed into India's Insolvency and Bankruptcy Code (IBC) reforms, though progress remains uneven.

*

Epilogue

The Room That Stayed Empty

Stayzilla's story is not just about a failed homestay startup—it's about the fragility of the ecosystem itself.

OYO continues to face its own battles—lawsuits, customer complaints, and governance issues. Yet it lives on, while Stayzilla has faded into memory.

The difference? Sometimes, it isn't the idea or the execution—it's the ecosystem's readiness to forgive failure.

Stayzilla checked out early. OYO stayed on.

*

Years Later

The office that once buzzed with dreams of becoming India's Airbnb is now a co-working space, filled with startups chasing their own fragile futures. The Stayzilla logo has long been peeled off the walls, but some locals in Chennai still whisper the name—half with nostalgia, half with regret.

Founders scattered into quieter lives, far from the limelight of venture capital. Investors moved on, writing it off as just another entry in their portfolio's graveyard.

And yet, the story lingers in India's startup corridors. Over cups of chai, when someone speaks of scaling too fast, burning cash too freely, or trusting valuation over vision - someone always murmurs: "Remember Stayzilla."

Not as fraud, but as innocence undone.

***

Chapter 50

TinyOwl: The Startup That Ate More Than It Could Chew

Powai, Mumbai, India, 2004-2006

Startup Failure ☑ Fraud ✗ Cash Burn ☑

> TinyOwl (founded 2014) was one of India's early food delivery startups, quickly expanding across major cities with heavy investor backing. But reckless scaling, cash burn, and operational chaos soon caught up. By 2016, the company shut most operations after mass layoffs and mounting losses. Once valued as a rising unicorn-in-the-making, TinyOwl became a cautionary tale of how overexpansion without sustainability can kill a startup dream.

Platter With Wings

It began, like so many startup dreams in India, with the food. Young founders fresh out of IIT Mumbai wanted to transform the way India ordered meals. In 2014, they launched TinyOwl, an app that promised to bring your favourite biryani, pizza, or paratha to your doorstep with just a few taps.

The timing was perfect. Smartphones were exploding in popularity. Venture capitalists were hungry for the "next Zomato." TinyOwl raised $20 million from Sequoia, Matrix Partners, Nexus Venture Partners, and Tiger Global. The money rained down, and with it came confidence, swagger, and the belief that nothing could go wrong.

Expansion was furious. From Mumbai to Delhi, Bengaluru to Hyderabad, TinyOwl spread its wings in a matter of months. Billboards screamed its name, college students became brand ambassadors, and India's food-tech revolution looked unstoppable.

But growth without a foundation is a castle built on sand.

*

The Cracks Appear

Customers complained of delayed deliveries, missing orders, and unresponsive support. Restaurants grumbled about late payments. Internally, the company burned cash like a raging bonfire - offering discounts so steep they were unsustainable.

By 2015, the investors grew nervous. The pressure mounted: cut costs, survive, or perish. Layoffs followed. In one dramatic incident in Pune, employees facing sudden termination locked up a company official inside the office, demanding answers. The dream had soured into a nightmare.

*

The Boardroom Reckoning

The walls of TinyOwl's glass-walled conference room in Powai stood witness to dreams and despair. The founders sat across the table, their faces drawn, the glow of youthful ambition replaced by the pale shadow of reality. Outside, the hum of Mumbai traffic roared on, but inside, silence screamed louder.

The CFO read the figures once again—cash burn rate unsustainable, investor funds nearly exhausted, revenues a trickle against a raging tide of expenses. The air felt heavy, as if the fluorescent lights themselves were bearing down on the room.

One founder broke the silence, his voice trembling, "We built an app to feed millions. Now we can't even feed ourselves."

Tears welled in the eyes of an employee sitting near the corner, a silent observer. She had seen colleagues pour their nights into code, branding, logistics—everything that should have made TinyOwl a unicorn. Yet, the numbers on the screen betrayed them.

And then came the most dreaded words from an investor dialled in on the speakerphone: "You must shut down operations immediately. Scale down. Cut jobs. Preserve what's left."

It wasn't just a company closing—it was a dream collapsing in real time. The same boardroom that once echoed with laughter, pizza boxes, and slogans of "disruption" now reverberated with the death knell of ambition.

*

The Fall

By 2016, TinyOwl's operations had shrunk dramatically. Offices closed. The workforce was reduced to a skeleton team. The once-hyped app that promised convenience and disruption was now little more than a cautionary tale. Eventually, it merged into Roadrunnr (later rebranded as Runnr) and then disappeared completely when Zomato acquired Runnr. TinyOwl itself ceased to exist.

*

Who Paid the Price?

Every corporate collapse leaves behind not just empty offices, but shattered lives and burnt money. TinyOwl was no different. Behind its glittering promises of food-at-your-fingertips, the downfall carved deep wounds.

The titans of venture capital—Sequoia, Matrix, Nexus, Tiger Global—all believed they had found the next Zomato. Their millions were poured in like gasoline on a fire, fueling TinyOwl's reckless expansion. But when the smoke cleared, all that was left was ash. Their spreadsheets told the story of vanished fortunes: entire funds written off, valuations reduced to zero, and partners forced to explain to their backers how a sure bet became a cautionary tale. They had tasted limelight and lived the dream of wealth. But when the bubble burst, their equity turned worthless. They were left with scars and lessons, often cited in business schools as a textbook example of startup hubris.

For these giants, TinyOwl was not just a loss; it was an embarrassment.

On paper, the founders were once worth crores. They had tasted the heady cocktail of media spotlight, investor applause, and youthful arrogance. But when the bubble burst, their equity turned to confetti—colourful, but worthless. The same founders who once declared they'd disrupt India's food economy were now left with nothing more than scars, lessons, and an infamous case study in business schools.

The small eateries and cafes that partnered with TinyOwl believed in the promise of more orders and quicker visibility. But as the app began to sink, so did their payments. Many never saw the money they were owed. For them, TinyOwl was not just a failed startup; it was betrayal dressed as innovation.

The cruellest cut of all… hundreds of young men and women, who had pinned their futures on the startup dream, found themselves jobless overnight. Some waited months for unpaid salaries. Others carried the trauma of a hostage incident in Pune, where desperation turned to chaos. Their faith in startups—in the myth of "join us, grow with us"—was forever shaken.

TinyOwl's collapse was not just about vanished investor millions. It was about trust broken at every level—from boardrooms to dining tables.

*

Years Later: TinyOwl

The name TinyOwl has all but vanished from the food-tech skies, replaced by giants like Swiggy and Zomato, who rule the ecosystem TinyOwl once dreamt of dominating. The app is gone, the company dissolved, and its brand erased from consumer memory.

But the ghost of TinyOwl still lingers in boardrooms and business schools. Whenever a startup pitches hypergrowth fuelled by discounts, investors whisper: "Remember TinyOwl." It has become a cautionary proverb.

Some founders retreated into quieter entrepreneurial ventures, their names no longer front-page headlines. For them, TinyOwl was both a badge of honour and a scar: proof they dared, but also a reminder of how quickly dreams can burn out.

The Investors wrote off their millions and moved on to the subsequent bets. But every term sheet they now sign carries an invisible footnote: no more Owls.

The Employees found new jobs, but they carry a story to tell: the story of a startup that soared too quickly and then crashed. In meetups and coffee shops, they laugh about the Pune hostage incident, but deep down, they remember the fear, the uncertainty, the betrayal.

And for the ordinary Indian customer, who once tapped TinyOwl to order a thali, the memory is faint, almost gone. The food arrived late, the app disappeared, and another one took its place.

TinyOwl's flight lasted barely two years, but its fall left a shadow much longer than its wingspan… A story more than a tale of numbers gone wrong.

It is a reminder that valuation without value is an illusion, and growth without grounding is nothing more than a mirage.

Big or tiny, an owl is still an owl!

***

Chapter 51

Quibi—The Billion-Dollar Show That Nobody Watched

Los Angeles, California, USA (April 2020 - October 2020)

Poor Timing ☑ Confusing Vision ☑ Fraud ✗
Startup Failure ☑

Launched by Hollywood mogul Jeffrey Katzenberg and CEO Meg Whitman, Quibi promised to revolutionise streaming with "quick bites" of mobile-only content. Backed by nearly $1.75 billion, it debuted with fanfare in April 2020—but audiences never came. Poor timing, confusing vision, and fierce competition led to a shutdown within just six months, making Quibi one of the fastest, most expensive failures in media history.

Beverly Hills

California, 2018

Hollywood mogul Jeffrey Katzenberg, the man behind Disney's renaissance of the '90s and co-founder of DreamWorks, had a new dream. Partnering with tech executive Meg Whitman, former CEO of eBay and Hewlett-Packard, he wanted to revolutionise entertainment for the smartphone era.

The idea was bold, even seductive: A platform delivering "quick bites" of video content—episodes 7 to 10 minutes long, designed exclusively for mobile viewing. Big budgets, top-tier

Hollywood talent, innovative tech like Turnstyle, which lets you seamlessly switch between portrait and landscape mode.

*

They Called it Quibi

The temptation was too high and investors couldn't resist it. Before even launching, Quibi raised nearly $1.8 billion from an A-list roster of backers—Disney, WarnerMedia, NBCUniversal, Viacom, Sony, Alibaba, and more. It wasn't just a startup; it was Hollywood royalty meeting Silicon Valley money.

*

Lights, Camera… Silence

In April 2020, Quibi finally launched. The timing couldn't have been worse. The world was in lockdown. People were stuck at home, bingeing long-form Netflix shows on big screens. Nobody wanted "quick bites" on their phones while commuting—because nobody was commuting.

Yet, Quibi insisted it was different. It had star power: Steven Spielberg, Chrissy Teigen, Idris Elba, Reese Witherspoon, Liam Hemsworth, Sophie Turner. The content appeared to be a mix of Hollywood gloss and TikTok-length convenience.

*

But Something Felt Off

Users who downloaded Quibi (a few did) complained that they couldn't share screenshots or clips on social media, killing organic buzz. The app itself felt clunky. Worse, the "exclusive" shows lacked the magic of storytelling. They were neither addictive like YouTube nor immersive like Netflix.

Quibi assumed people would pay $4.99 per month for content they hadn't asked for. They didn't.

*

The Fall

Faster Than a Skip Button

By July 2020, just three months after launch, reports showed Quibi had lost 90% of its early subscribers. Downloads plummeted. Viewership was negligible. The platform burned through cash while failing to build even a loyal niche audience.

Katzenberg tried to save face, at one point blaming the pandemic for Quibi's flop. But the truth was harsher:

Quibi misunderstood consumer behaviour.

It overestimated the appeal of star-driven "short-form" shows.

It ignored the virality and interactivity that fuelled TikTok and YouTube.

In October 2020—barely six months after launch—Quibi announced it was shutting down. A $1.8 billion empire had evaporated almost overnight.

*

The Hollywood Autopsy

When Quibi died, it left more questions than answers. How could two industry titans, with such vast wealth and talent, fail so spectacularly?

The postmortem revealed deeper flaws.

Katzenberg believed Hollywood magic could override market reality. He misread the times. He targeted a pre-pandemic commuting class that no longer existed. In an era of sharing, memes, and virality, Quibi locked content behind walls, refusing to let audiences participate.

Ultimately, Quibi was a solution in search of a problem. Nobody had asked for "quick bites," and certainly not at premium prices.

*

Curtain Call

Quibi is a Hollywood-meets-Silicon Valley tragedy—a billion-dollar idea that collapsed in less than a year. Its failure is often mocked as one of the costliest blunders in startup history. But beyond the memes, it serves as a cautionary tale:

Money and fame cannot manufacture demand.

A billion dollars can buy stars, studios, and technology—but it cannot buy attention in an economy where the scarcest resource is time.

Quibi wasn't just a startup that failed. It was a spectacular reminder that in the digital age, audience loyalty is earned, not engineered.

*

Years Later

The name has already faded from the app stores, erased as though it never existed. No buzzing notifications, no vertical dramas, no celebrities pitching "the future of streaming." Quibi—once launched with a war chest of nearly two billion dollars—has become a footnote in Silicon Valley's Museum of hubris.

The headquarters was vacated quietly, its screens turned dark, its promise dissolved into bankruptcy filings. Investors wrote off the loss; Hollywood veterans returned to safer contracts. What remained was a cautionary whisper in venture circles: money cannot manufacture attention.

Today, when startups boast of "changing the way we consume content," an old venture capitalist might chuckle and say softly, "Quibi tried that." The room falls silent. Everyone knows what comes next: attention is not bought, it is earned, and no fortune can compensate for ten wasted minutes.

***

Chapter 52

Solyndra: The Shattered Promise of a Solar Revolution

47700 Kato Road, Fremont, California, USA

Startup Failure ☑ Poor Financial Management ☑ Competitive China Market ☑

Solyndra, a U.S. solar startup founded in 2005, became a symbol of clean-tech ambition after receiving a $535 million federal loan guarantee from the Obama administration. Its innovative but costly cylindrical panels couldn't compete with cheaper Chinese alternatives, leading to $172 million losses in 2010 alone. By 2011, Solyndra filed for bankruptcy, laying off 1,100 workers and leaving taxpayers with heavy losses—turning the company into a lasting cautionary tale of hype, politics, and failed economics.

The Power of the Sun

The morning sun cast its first rays over Fremont, California, where a futuristic factory with gleaming glass walls stood like a monument to innovation. Inside, engineers in crisp white coats moved with almost religious devotion, assembling cylindrical solar panels that looked like something out of a science fiction novel.

This was Solyndra, the company that promised to change the world.

Founded in 2005, Solyndra captured Silicon Valley's imagination by developing thin-film cylindrical solar modules that could harness sunlight from all directions. Investors were dazzled. Policymakers swooned. At a time when climate change was rising to the top of global agendas, Solyndra was hailed as America's clean-energy saviour.

In 2009, the U.S. Department of Energy granted Solyndra a staggering $535 million federal loan guarantee, personally endorsed by the Obama administration. Vice President Joe Biden appeared via satellite at a ribbon-cutting ceremony, proclaiming Solyndra "a shining example of how America will win the future."

*

The Dream Turns Sour

But beneath the shine, shadows were gathering.

Solyndra's innovative design was costly to manufacture. While its cylindrical tubes were technologically elegant, they struggled to compete on price. In China, government-backed manufacturers like Suntech and Yingli were flooding the market with cheaper, flat solar panels.

Executives at Solyndra remained defiant. In boardrooms, PowerPoints glowed with projections of $2 billion in revenue and global market domination. Investors nodded, enchanted by the charts, while sceptics outside whispered that the math didn't add up.

By 2010, losses were mounting—$172 million in one year alone—but the company insisted profitability was just around the corner.

*

The Boardroom Reckoning

The boardroom in Fremont grew tense. Stacks of financial statements told the grim truth: spiralling costs, declining margins, shrinking demand.

"China is undercutting us at every turn," one executive admitted, his voice breaking the uneasy silence.

CEO Brian Harrison tried to keep the room from collapsing into panic. "We have government support. We have innovation no one else can match. This is temporary."

But as the months wore on, even the most loyal directors knew the truth. Solyndra was running out of time—and out of cash.

*

Collapse

In August 2011, Solyndra shocked the world by filing for bankruptcy. Over 1,100 employees were laid off overnight. The pristine Fremont factory, once a symbol of America's clean-tech future, stood deserted, its shiny equipment gathering dust.

The scandal was immediate and brutal. Critics accused the Obama administration of favouritism and poor oversight in granting half a billion taxpayer dollars to a failing company. Congressional hearings devolved into a political circus, with executives grilled under harsh lights about forged financial statements, unrealistic projections, and misused funds.

The very name Solyndra became shorthand for the dangers of mixing politics with venture capital.

*

Years Later

By 2025, the Fremont factory had been repurposed by Tesla, a cruel twist of fate for a company that once dreamed of being the Tesla of solar energy. Solyndra itself existed only in case studies, footnotes, and political debates.

The bankruptcy left taxpayers on the hook for hundreds of millions, while China emerged as the undisputed global leader in solar panel manufacturing.

In business schools, Solyndra became a parable of misplaced ambition: a dazzling idea that crumbled under the weight of poor economics, overconfidence, and political theatre.

For the laid-off employees, Solyndra was a wound that never fully healed—a reminder that the promise of innovation, when inflated by hype and hubris, can shatter overnight.

Ultimately, Solyndra was not just a failed company. It was a mirror reflecting America's uneasy struggle between vision and viability, between politics and markets, and between dreams and reality.

***

Epilogue
The Curtain Falls, The Stage Awaits

An Unknown & Lonely Place

The silence in the office was deafening. Once, this space had been a battlefield of ideas, ringing with the hum of laptops, hurried footsteps, and the nervous laughter of interns balancing too much coffee and too many dreams. The walls had absorbed a thousand stories—of late-night breakthroughs, of desperate pitches, of arguments that ended with slammed doors and broken friendships. Now, those same walls echoed nothing but absence.

The founder stood alone, his shadow stretching long in the cold, white glow of the overhead light. The city outside pulsed with neon life, yet he felt detached from it, as though he were watching a stage from behind the curtains after the play had ended.

He thought of the journey. The pitch decks that had dazzled investors. The headlines that once crowned him the messiah of disruption. The flood of venture money seemed infinite. And then—the unravelling. Lawsuits. Crumbling trust. Customers fleeing. Employees whispering resignation. The once-mighty fortress had collapsed into rubble faster than he could comprehend.

But failure, he realised, wasn't silent. It screamed through unanswered emails, the knock on the door from creditors, and the relentless churn of the news cycle, hungry for a fallen hero. Failure had a sound, and it wasn't very merciful.

On his desk lay a notebook. It was worn at the edges, its pages filled with hurried sketches of products that never shipped, diagrams of growth plans that never saw the light of day, and slogans that once promised immortality. He flipped through the pages, and for the first time, instead of regret, he felt something else. A strange kind of peace.

Because the truth was this: he had not been the first to fail, and he would not be the last. Startups were born of the same fevered dream, and most would die the same slow, painful death. Yet, for every failure, there would always be another beginning.

His eyes wandered to the cover illustration of a draft manuscript on his shelf. A chick breaking out of its shell, fragile and alive, unaware of the noose that dangled before it. That image was more than a metaphor; it was prophecy. Startups were born into the world with hope and fragility, with promise and peril. For every shell broken, there was a trap waiting. For every heartbeat of innovation, there was the quiet tightening of risk.

And yet—the chick still emerged. Again, and again.

The founder closed the notebook and leaned back. He could almost hear the whispers of other stories—Pets.com, Quibi, Housing.com, Enron, Satyam, Lehman Brothers — each of them a chapter in the same never-ending play. Their boardrooms had been stages, their IPOs opening acts, their collapses the tragic finales. Some were comedies of errors, others were pure tragedies, but all were unforgettable performances.

Failure was not the end. It was simply the pause before the next act.

Somewhere, right now, in a cramped garage, a college dorm, or a noisy co-working space, another founder was scribbling dreams on a napkin. Another investor was rolling the dice on ambition. Another chick was breaking through its shell, blind to the dangers ahead, alive with the thrill of possibility.

The curtain falls on this story, but the stage will not remain empty for long.

For the theatre of startups is eternal.

And perhaps, that is the most incredible truth of all:

In the world of startups, there are no endings—only endless beginnings, forever fragile, forever at risk, forever alive.

Startups are not just businesses; they are human dramas—of dreams and doubts, courage and cowardice, triumph and betrayal. They mirror the eternal human quest: to defy the odds, to rewrite the rules, to craft meaning in numbers, technology, and markets.

However, the truth this book reveals is sobering—many dreams do not survive the test of time. Valuations rise on fragile scaffolding. Ambitions clash with reality. Greed often overtakes prudence. And when the curtain falls, what remains is rarely just money lost. It is trust broken, lives scarred, promises shattered.

And yet… There is resilience. For every fallen empire, a new generation of dreamers rises. For every headline of collapse, somewhere, a small team is sketching a new idea on the back of a napkin. The cycle does not end; it only resets.

The stories in these pages were not written to mock failure, but to illuminate it. To show that behind every number, there is a heartbeat; behind every collapse, there is a choice that could have gone differently. Failure is not just destruction. It is an instruction. It has happened before and will happen again because the world of startups is collapsing and re-emerging, almost like a cyclical tragedy.

*

Final Spotlight

The lights dim.

The noise of the boardroom fades.

The courtroom battles, the IPO celebrations, the investor pitches—all dissolve into silence.

And then, from the shadows, a lone figure steps forward. Not a founder. Not an investor. Not a journalist. But the voice of the stage itself is the narrator of this endless theatre.

He looks out, straight at you.

"You have walked with us through ambition and betrayal, through greed and collapse. You have seen how dreams can dazzle, how numbers can deceive, how valuations can rise like fire and fall like ash. These stories were not just about companies—they were about people. People who gambled everything on the idea that they could bend the future to their will."

The narrator pauses. A faint spotlight lingers, casting a long shadow across the empty stage.

"And yet… do not mistake these failures for endings. For every empire that crumbles, a new dreamer rises. For every ledger that turns red, a new hand sketches another vision on a napkin. This theatre does not close. Its curtains fall, only to rise again. Its tragedies end, only to give way to new comedies, new dramas, new beginnings."

A hush grips the stage.

"So, reader, as you close this book, know this: the next act is already being written. Perhaps in a garage down the street. Perhaps in a dorm room tonight. Perhaps even in your own hands."

The spotlight narrows to a single beam.

"The stage is set. The actors are ready. The question is not whether another story will unfold. The question is—will you be a spectator… or will you dare to step on stage?"

The lights cut out.

The curtain falls.

And the theatre of startups waits, eternal, for the dreamers who dare to fail.

The show will go on.

***

References

1. Boatsman, James R., and Joong-Won Dong. "Market Valuation with DCF: An Empirical Analysis." The Accounting Review 66.4 (1991): pp. 627–643.

2. Brown, Eliot & Farrell, Maureen, "The Cult of We: WeWork, Adam Neumann, and the Great Start-Up Delusion," HarperCollins, July 2021.

3. Brueggeman, W. and Fisher, J.; "Real Estate Finance and Investments," McGraw-Hill LLC, 2024.

4. Carreyrou, John, "Bad Blood: Secrets and Lies in a Silicon Valley Startup," ISBN-13: 9781524731656, Alfred A. Knopf (2018).

5. Cassidy, John; "Dot.Con: The Greatest Story Ever Sold," HarperCollins (U.S.), Allen Lane/Penguin Press (UK), 2002.

6. Cassidy, John; "How Markets Fail: The Logic of Economic Calamities," Farrar, Straus and Giroux (U.S.), Allen Lane (UK), 2009.

7. Cooper Cynthia, "Extraordinary Circumstances: The Journey of a Corporate Whistleblower," John Wiley & Sons, Inc., ISBN-10:0470124296, (2008).

8. Copeland, Tom, Tim Koller, and Jack Murrin. Valuation: Measuring and Managing the Value of Companies. Wiley, 2020 (7th ed.).

9. Damodaran, A.; "Damodaran on Valuation," Wiley, 2nd Edition, ISBN-13: 978-0198736479, ISBN-10: 0198736479, 2006.

10. Damodaran, Aswath. "Tesla: Valuation Story or Valuation History?" Musings on Markets Blog, multiple entries, 2020–2022.

11. Damodaran, Aswath; "Investment Valuation: Tools and Techniques for Determining the Value of an Asset," ISBN-13: 978 1118206584, Wiley, 3rd Edition, March 2012.

12. Damodaran, Aswath: "Narrative and Numbers: The Value of Stories in Business," Columbia University Press, 2017.

13. Damodaran, A. "The Little Book of Valuation: How to Value a Company, Pick a Stock, and Profit," John Wiley & Sons Inc., Updated Edition, March 2024.

14. Damodaran, A.; "The Dark Side of Valuation: Valuing Young, Distressed, and Complex Businesses," 3rd Edition, Pearson Education (US), 2018.

15. Damodaran A.; "Applied Corporate Finance," Wiley, 5th Edition, 2018.

16. Feldman, Stanley J.; "Principals of Private Firm Valuation," Wiley, 2005.

17. Fernandez, Pablo. "Valuation Using Discounted Cash Flows: A Practical Guide," IESE Business School Working Paper, 2013.

18. Ghosh, Shona. "WeWork's $47 Billion Valuation Was Always a Fiction." Business Insider, 2019.

19. Gilpin, Dawn R. & Murphy, Priscilla J.; "Crisis Management in a Complex World," Oxford University Press, 2008. (It includes Starbucks as a case study).

20. Gorton, Gary B. "The Subprime Panic," European Financial Management 15.1 (2009): 10–46.

21. Gupta, Rajat, "Mind Without Fear," Juggernaut Books, March 2019.

22. Healy, Paul M., and Krishna G. Palepu. "The Fall of Enron." Journal of Economic Perspectives 17.2 (2003): 3–26.

23. Henriques, Diana B., "The Wizard of Lies: Bernie Madoff and the Death of Trust," Times Books (an imprint of Henry Holt and Company), 2011.

24. Kahneman, Daniel. Thinking, Fast and Slow. Farrar, Straus and Giroux, 2011.

25. Kritzman, Mark; "Applied Corporate Finance," Wiley, 2006.

26. Levy, Steven, "In the Plex: How Google Thinks, Works, and Shapes Our Lives," Simon & Schuster, ISBN-13: 978-1-4165-3904-3; ISBN-10: 1416539045, 2011.

27. Makwana, Vaishaliben K.; "Subprime Mortgage Crisis: An Introduction," Createspace Independent Publishing Platform, June 2015.

28. McKinsey & Company Inc.; "Valuation: Measuring and Managing the Value of Companies," Wiley, 2020 (7th Edition).

29. McLean, Bethany et. al.; "The Smartest Guys in the Room: The Amazing Rise and Scandalous Fall of Enron," Portfolio Trade, October 2003.

30. Nag, Kingshuk, "Kingfisher: The Rise and Fall of Vijay Mallya," HarperCollins, June 2017.

31. Ofek, Eli, and Matthew Richardson. "Dot.Com Mania: The Rise and Fall of Internet Stock Prices." The Journal of Finance, 58 (3), 2003, pp. 1113–1137.

32. 32. Parab, Varsha et.al.; "The 'Diesel Gate: A Case Study on Volkswagen Scandal of Inserting a Cheat Device for Manipulating Emission Norms," https://doi.org/10.1093/oso/9780192869432.003.0018, PP. 143–148, August 2022.

33. Penman, Stephen H. Financial Statement Analysis and Security Valuation. McGraw-Hill, 2022.

34. Pratt, S.J.; "Valuing a Business: The Analysis & Appraisal of Closely Held Companies," McGraw-Hill, 2007 (Fifth Edition).

35. Rathore, S. S.; "Can Reliable Value-Projections be Made by the Use of Scientific Methods?" Editorial Published in the (J.) Indian Valuer, IOV (India), Vol. XXX, No. 8, August 1998, pp. 675-678.

36. Rathore, S. S.; "A Brief Commentary on Capitalisation Factor," (J.) Indian Valuer, Vol. XXVII, July 1995.

37. Rathore, S.S.; "Philosophy & Practice of Valuation," ISBN 81-7764-162-X, Allied Publishers Limited, New Delhi, India, 2001.

38. Rathore, S. S.; "Rathore on Valuation of Assets," ISBN: 979-8-89673-490-1 (Paperback), 979-8-89699-6 (Hardcover), Notion Press, January 2025.

39. Rathore, S.S.; "Rathore on Real Estate Valuation," ISBN-13 979-8899843365, Notion Press, June 2025.

40. Rathore, S.S.; "Diving Deep in DCF Valuation," ISBN 979-8-89879-881-9 (Paperback), 979-8-90023-312-3 (Hardcover), Notion Press, September 2025.

41. Rathore, S. S.; "Caveats, Limitations, and Disclosures in Valuation Reports," (J.) Indian Valuer, ISSN 2583-3553, Vol. 57, February 2025.

42. Rathore, S. S.; "The Scope of AI in Real Estate Valuation in India," Submitted for Publication, (J.) Indian Valuer, ISSN 2583-3553, August 2024.

43. Rathore, S. S.; "Can Economic Theories Explain the Trends in Real Estate Market?" (J.) Indian Valuer, ISSN 2583-3553, Vol. 57, No. 7, July 2025.

44. Rathore, S. S.; "How to Determine Distress Discount Factor in the DCF Method of Valuation?" (J.) Indian Valuer, ISSN 2583-3553, Vol. 57, No. 8, August 2025.

45. Rathore, S. S.; "RISK & DISTRESS: Are they Two Different Things?" (J.) Indian Valuer, ISSN 2583-3553, Vol. 57, No. 9, September 2025.

46. Regester, Michael & Larkin, Judy, "Risk Issues and Crisis Management: A Casebook for Best Practice," 4th Edition, Kogan Press, 2008.

47. Reserve Bank of India, "PMC Bank - Fraud Detection Report," 2019.

48. Russell, Atwater; "Google: The Story of Larry Page, Sergey Brin and the Birth of a Tech Giant," Independently Published, 2024.

49. Saleh, Yunus D., "Crisis Management: The Art of Success & Failure - 30 Case Studies in Business & Politics," Mill City Press, Inc., 2016.

50. Sebe, George. "Corporate Governance Failure: The Case of Satyam." International Journal of Business and Management, Vol. 6, No. 3 (2011).

51. Sharma, Jay Prakash, "Corporate Governance Failure: The Case Study of Satyam," Indian Journal of Corporate Governance, Vol. 3, Issue 2, pp. 136-175, July 2010.

52. Schultz, Howard, "Onward: How Starbucks Fought for Its Life Without Losing Its Soul," Wiley, 1st edition, May 9, 2011.

53. Shiller, Robert J. Irrational Exuberance. Princeton University Press, 2015 (3rd ed.).

54. Shree, "Anil Ambani: The Bankruptcy Myth or Reality?" Notion Press, 2024.

55. Swain, Samrak, "The Great Indian Fraud: Serious Frauds That Shook the Economy," Bloomsbury, India, 2020.

56. Swartz. Mimi & Watkins, Sharon; "POWER FAILURE: The Inside Story of The Collapse of ENRON," A Currency Book Publication, March 2003.

57. Titman, S. & Martin, J.D.; "Investment Valuation," Pearson, 2011 (2nd Edition).

58. Toffler, Alvin; "The Third Wave," Penguin Random House, 1980.

59. Tversky, Amos, and Daniel Kahneman. "Judgment under Uncertainty: Heuristics and Biases." Science 185.4157 (1974): 1124–1131.

60. Wiedeman, Reeves, "Billion Dollar Loser: The Epic Rise and Spectacular Fall of Adam Neumann and WeWork," Hodder & Stoughton, 2020.

***

Annexure
Innocent Misfire of Startup Valuations

Stage: Across the Globe

Innocence has a Price Tag

There are failures born of greed. And then there are failures born of innocence—ventures that stumbled not because of lies, but because of dreams too large, too early, or too poorly executed. Imagine, for a moment, a dimly lit stage. Each startup walks out, delivers its line, and then fades into the shadows of history.

These are not scandals of greed. They are tales of overreach, of timing missed, of markets that refused to cooperate. Innocent failures. Each one, a play performed briefly on the grand stage of venture capital.

Startups, being inherently volatile in nature, make survival inherently challenging. These companies often lack stable revenues, may not be profitable, and face considerable uncertainty.

*

Global Startup Failures & Survival Odds

Many stories remind us that startup success isn't just about big ideas or funding—it's grounded in execution, honesty, adaptability, and strong fundamentals. Here are some of the most notable recent startup failures:

Merit Street Media (founded in early 2024 by Dr Phil McGraw) filed for bankruptcy in July 2025 after technical failures, unmet distribution commitments from TBN, over $96 million in damages alleged, and listing 200+ creditors.

Plenty Unlimited (ag-tech and vertical farming, backed by Jeff Bezos & SoftBank) filed for Chapter 11 in March 2025. The company failed to secure new funding, paused facility operations, and sought restructuring while continuing limited farming efforts.

Canoo Inc. (EV startup) filed for bankruptcy in January 2025 and ceased operations entirely. Once valued in the billions, it collapsed under heavy losses with fewer than $50,000 in assets.

Nikola (electric/hydrogen trucks) filed for Chapter 11 in February 2025. The company struggled after facing accusations from investors and an inability to commercialise its technology.

Builder.ai (formerly Engineer.ai) entered insolvency in mid-2025 after revelations that its AI capabilities were greatly overstated and its financials inflated. Laid off ~80% of staff and began bankruptcy proceedings.

Edukoya (Nigeria, ed-tech) shut down in February 2025 despite reaching ~80,000 students and struggling with monetisation, connectivity issues, and low disposable incomes.

Bento Africa (Nigeria, payroll/HR tech) temporarily ceased operations in February 2025 amid alleged financial misconduct and internal turmoil.

Lipa Later (Kenya, BNPL fintech) entered administration in March 2025 due to rising debts and the inability to raise further funding.

CaaStle (fashion rental tech) faced a board-led fraud investigation after dramatically inflated revenue claims in 2025. The CEO resigned, employees furloughed, and operations halted.

Pandion (US delivery startup) raised $125 million but shut down in early 2025—couldn't compete in a crowded logistics market.

EasyKnock (prop-tech) closed in December 2024 due to interest rates and a cooling housing market, which impacted its home-sell/rent-back model.

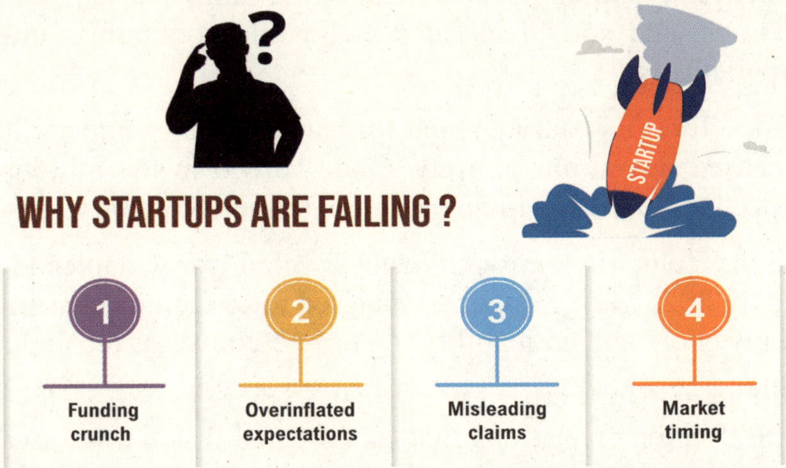

Innovating is one thing; building a scalable, sustainable business is another. Exaggerations (financial or technical) can lead to swift collapse and legal consequences. Broad macroeconomic shifts (like interest rate hikes) can sink even well-funded startups.

Here are some startling statistics on startup failure rates and common pitfalls:

Timeframe	Failure Rate
1st year	~20–21%
2nd year	~30–32%

5 years	~45–51%
10 years	~65–66%
Long-term (15 yrs+)	~75–90%

Reasons Behind the Failures

The CB Insights and aggregated industry studies suggest that:

- 38% of startups fail due to running out of cash
- 35–42% fail because of no market need or poor product–market fit
- 20–23% due to competition or misaligned teams
- 18–19% fail due to flawed business models or pricing strategy
- Legal or regulatory issues contribute to about 15–18% of failures
- Additional factors include ineffective marketing (22%), funding stage drop-offs (60% fail pre-Series A), and solo stewardship (higher risk).

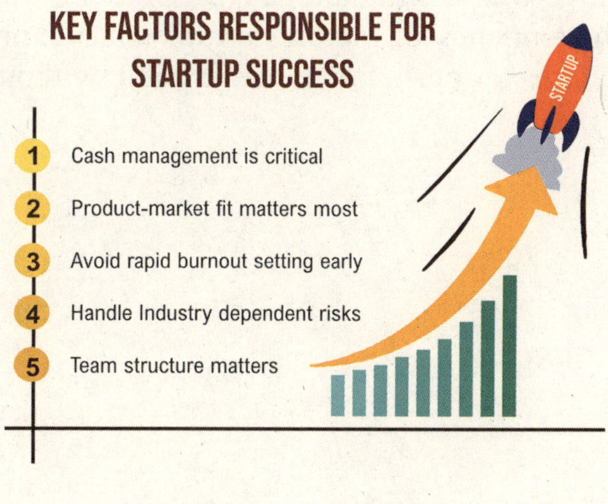

Industry & Stage Variations (Global Scenario)

- **Tech/IT startups:** ~63% failure within 5 years
- **Fintech:** 75% VC-backed startups fail; 37–75% overall failure rates
- **E-commerce/retail:** 45–53% fail within five years
- **Hardware startups:** ~70% fail
- **Healthcare/EduTech:** 55–60% fail.

If you are valuing startups, focus primarily on the evidence of strong financial planning, rapid market validation, and the competency of the founding team—these remain the most effective levers to tilt the odds of success.

*

Startup Failure Statistics in India

90% of Indian startups fail within the first 5 years of their launch. (Source: IBM Institute for Business Value in collaboration with Oxford Economics, 2016). It was reaffirmed by various industry reports in later years.

The year 2023–24 saw over 2,000 startups shut down, according to Tracxn and Inc42 reports. Layoffs affected over 30,000 employees across Indian startups in the same period. This highlights the tendency of Indian startups to scale prematurely, expand too fast, or burn too much capital without product-market fit.

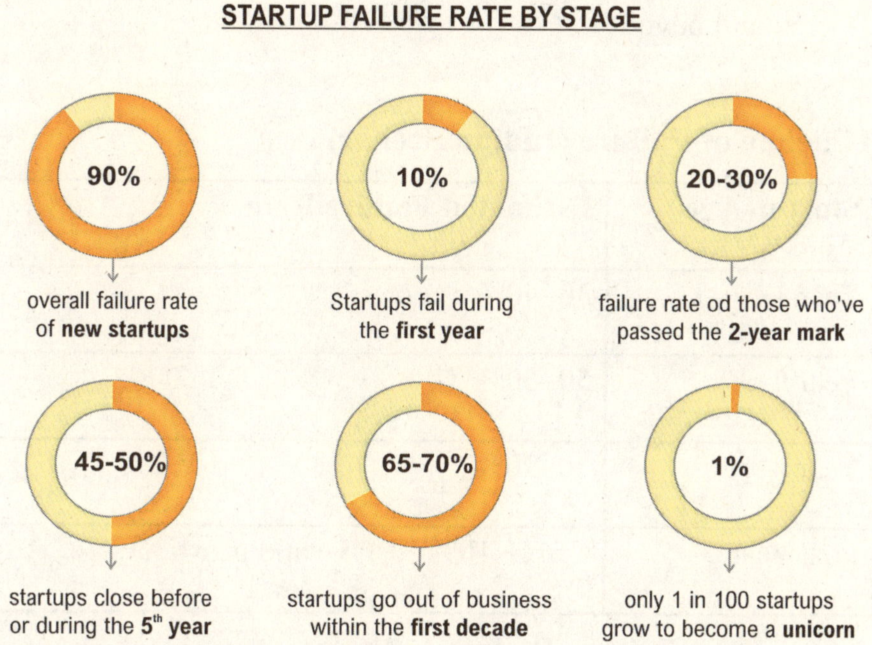

Startup Ecosystem in India

- There are over 1,00,000 recognised startups (as of 2024) in India under the *Startup India Initiative*.
- India is the third largest ecosystem globally (after the USA and China).
- Edtech, fintech, agritech, healthtech, and e-commerce see high churn rates.
- 110 unicorns (valued over $1Billion, but many struggle with profitability.
- In 2023, startup funding in India dropped 70% YoY, creating a *funding winter*.
- Over 60% of Indian startups are bootstrapped or rely on early-stage angel funding.

- Only 10% manage to raise follow-up rounds (Series A and beyond).

*

Timeline of Failure (Indian Scenario)

Startup Age	Estimated Failure Rate
Year 1	30–40%
Year 2–3	50–60%
Year 4–5	70–90%
Post Year 5	Only ~10% survive and grow

Sector-Wise Failure Risk in India

Sector	Failure Risk
E-commerce	Very High
Food Delivery	High
Edtech	High (esp. post-COVID)
Software as a service (SaaS)	Medium
Finte	Medium
Healthtech	Medium

Deeptech/AI	Low (but capital-intensive)

Characteristics of Surviving Startups

Despite all odds and dismal pictures painted by the statisticians, many startups survive. The following are the characteristics of surviving startups:

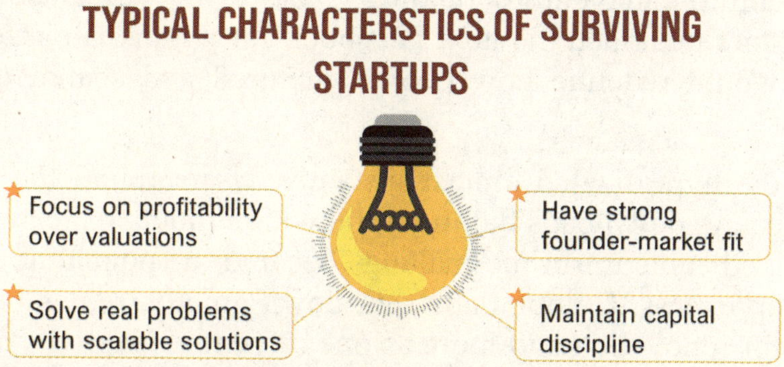

How are Startups Valued?

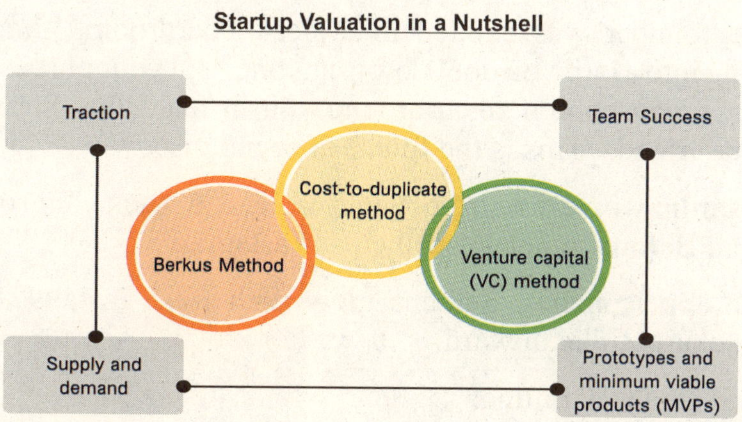

Here are some innocent startup failures:

Colour Labs (2011-2012)

201 Hamilton Avenue, Palo Alto, California, USA

Silicon Valley buzzed with anticipation as Colour Labs unveiled its photo-sharing app. With no proven product and only a bold pitch, the startup stunned the tech world by raising $41 million in venture funding—before it even launched. Investors imagined the next Facebook for photos, a platform that would redefine how people captured and shared their lives.

But the hype fizzled almost instantly. Users found the app confusing, downloads flatlined, and within months, the much-heralded unicorn-in-the-making became a punchline for startup excess. Colour Labs shut down quietly, remembered less for innovation and more as one of venture capital's most infamous misfires.

Palo Alto…

The founder was excited in a sleek boardroom. "Imagine walking into a bar. You don't know anyone. But your phone does. It shows you photos taken around you in real time. Strangers become friends. This is the future of social discovery."

A smiling investor from Sequoia leaned back. "Forty-one million. Before launch. You'll crush Instagram."

The app launches. Screens glow with fresh installs. For a week, charts spike upward.

User feedback online:

"I don't get this. Why would I use it?"

"Feels creepy."

*

A Year Later…

Chairs were empty in the same boardroom. The whiteboard marker scrawl is faintly visible: “Social = Proximity.” Silence hangs. The dream had too many millions and too few users.

*

GameStop Mania

The Rebellion of the Screens

GameStop’s short squeeze in 2021 was not just about a stock. It was a cultural uprising: retail investors versus hedge funds, Reddit memes versus Wall Street suits. Billions were made and lost, but the greater story was the exposure of how fragile—and theatrical—the world of modern finance had become.

A dimly lit basement in suburban Ohio. A young man hunched over his computer, hoodie pulled tight, eyes bloodshot from nights of scrolling through Reddit threads. On the screen: GameStop, ticker symbol GME, trading at $19.84. He hovers the mouse over the green button.

“Buy.”

The click is quiet, almost insignificant—like the flick of a match in a storm. Yet it sparks a chain reaction destined to rattle the world’s wealthiest men.

*

Somewhere in Manhattan…

High above the city skyline, in Melvin Capital’s sleek boardroom, executives in tailored suits glare at the red streaks pouring down their screens. Billions are at stake. A man slams his palm on the table, his voice sharp and cracking under pressure.

“This is madness. Who the hell is buying GameStop?”

Back in the basement, the young man smiles. His phone buzzes with notifications from Reddit:

“Hold the line.”

“Diamond hands, boys.”

The two worlds—the gamer’s basement and the billionaire’s boardroom—had never seemed further apart. Yet on that cold January night, they were colliding, stock by stock, share by share.

The revolution had begun.

*

The winter of 2021 was supposed to be bleak. The pandemic had shuttered malls, emptied streets, and forced millions into their homes. But in dimly lit basements, cramped apartments, and cluttered bedrooms across America, a new kind of revolution was brewing - not with muskets or barricades, but with screens, memes, and a trading app called Robinhood.

GameStop—the dusty video game retailer long written off as a relic of the past—was the unlikely spark. Its stores, filled with second-hand discs and posters from another era, seemed destined for bankruptcy. Hedge funds like Melvin Capital had already placed their bets, shorting the stock into oblivion. To them, GameStop was a corpse, and they were circling vultures ready to pick it clean.

But the corpse twitched.

*

On Reddit’s r/WallStreetBets, a ragtag band of traders rallied under usernames like DeepF*ingValue. They weren’t just buying shares—they were waging war. To them, Wall Street’s shorts weren’t bets, but arrogance: billionaires profiting from destruction. And GameStop? That was their banner, their flag.

“Hold the line!” one post screamed. Another declared, “This is not just a trade. This is payback.”

Screens lit up across the country. A cashier in Ohio poured his paycheck into GameStop shares. A college kid in Florida mortgaged his future tuition. A father in Texas told his children he was "saving their inheritance" through stonks.

The stock, which had been languishing at $20, began to rise. Then it exploded—$50, $100, $200, soaring past every analyst's model. Traders screamed in delight, watching Robinhood apps glow green with life-changing gains.

*

Meanwhile, in glass towers of New York, hedge fund managers were not cheering. They were sweating.

At Melvin Capital, phones rang like fire alarms. Billions in short positions bled red across their screens. "This isn't trading," one executive barked, "this is an assault!"

Ken Griffin of Citadel was called. Billions were pumped into rescuing Melvin, but the tide didn't stop. The swarm of retail traders was relentless, an army too chaotic to predict, too passionate to silence.

One hedge fund manager slammed his fist on the boardroom table: "They're not trading rationally. They're trading to hurt us."

*

Then came the twist. Robinhood, the very app that promised to "democratise finance," suddenly froze. On January 28, 2021, traders woke up to find they couldn't buy GameStop anymore—only sell.

Panic set in. The stock tumbled. Conspiracy theories flew. Was Robinhood protecting Wall Street? Was the game rigged all along?

On Reddit, fury erupted: "They're stealing from us to save their billionaire friends!"

What began as euphoria turned into a courtroom drama waiting to happen. Politicians weighed in, hearings were called, and the Robinhood CEO was grilled on national television.

*

Years Later…

The frenzy cooled. GameStop's stock, once brushing $500, drifted down. Many small traders were left with losses they could not afford, clutching screenshots of their accounts as bittersweet souvenirs of a digital revolution.

But something had changed forever. Wall Street had felt the sting of the mob. Retail traders had tasted power—the idea that ordinary people with memes, willpower, and a trading app could shake billion-dollar hedge funds.

And somewhere, perhaps in a messy apartment, DeepF*ingValue sat back, staring at his screen, his smirk half triumph, half exhaustion. He had become the accidental general of the strangest rebellion in financial history.

*

Boo.com: The Fashion Fantasy That Burned Out

Carnaby Street, London, UK

Boo.com (1999–2000) was a high-profile online fashion retailer that raised $135 million and tried to reinvent shopping with flashy 3D graphics and global branding. But the site was too slow for the dial-up era, customers abandoned it, and within 18 months it collapsed, becoming one of the most infamous failures of the dot-com bubble.

The year was 1999…

Europe had found its dot-com darling. Boo.com promised to revolutionise fashion retail—a global online boutique where the young and stylish could order the latest designer brands with a click.

The founders, Kajsa Leander and Ernst Malmsten, spoke of it as if it were more than a business. "It's a lifestyle," they declared, "the future of shopping." Venture capital poured in. Offices opened in London, New York, Paris, and Munich—staff dressed in Armani and Prada. Parties were legendary. Boo.com wasn't just selling clothes — it was living the brand.

But behind the glossy façade lay a fatal flaw. Their website, designed with 3D models and flashy graphics, was so slow that most users gave up. Broadband was still rare; dial-up connections struggled to cope with Boo.com's heavy interface. Orders failed. Customers fled.

Investors grew nervous as burn rates spiralled. Within just 18 months of its glamorous launch, Boo.com had consumed $135 million of investor money. In May 2000, the dream collapsed. Boo.com filed for bankruptcy, becoming one of the most spectacular symbols of the dot-com crash.

*

Years later…

The name Boo.com lives on as a cautionary tale. Its lavish spending, glossy branding, and technical missteps epitomise the excesses of the dot-com bubble. What was once hailed as the future of fashion retail is remembered instead as a lesson: technology without substance, like fashion without fit, never lasts.

*

Better Place (2007–2013)

2470 Embarcadero Way, Palo Alto, California, USA

In 2007, the world seemed ready for a revolution on wheels. Better Place, founded by the charismatic Shai Agassi, promised nothing less than the end of gasoline. Its vision was bold: an electric car ecosystem powered by swappable batteries and a vast network of charging stations.

Governments lined up, billions in funding poured in, and headlines hailed it as the future of clean mobility.

Yet by 2013, the dream had sputtered. After burning through nearly $1 billion, Better Place filed for bankruptcy, leaving behind a handful of charging stations, a fleet of unused cars, and a cautionary tale of ambition outpacing reality.

Jerusalem…

Shai Agassi, tall and charismatic, addresses a packed room of investors and ministers.

He proclaimed. "We don't need oil. We don't even need to wait for charging. We'll swap batteries faster than refuelling a car. Imagine: an entire nation powered by electrons!"

Thunderous applause. $850 million pledged. Headlines scream: "The Future of Cars."

Years pass—a deserted battery-swap station. Dust gathers. No cars arrive.

Engineer to Shai, in a hushed voice: "Sir… the infrastructure costs are killing us. Tesla's charging solution is winning. Nobody wants to build our cars."

*

Boardroom, 2013...

CFO closes a thick binder.

"We're bankrupt. The dream was right—but the world wasn't ready."

Shai stares at the map of highways behind him. The lights dim.

*

Jawbone (1999–2017)

200 Kansas Street, San Fransico, USA

> Jawbone began as a pioneer in sleek Bluetooth headsets before reinventing itself as a maker of stylish wireless speakers and fitness trackers. Backed by Silicon Valley's elite investors, it was once valued at over $3 billion, hailed as the company that blended design with cutting-edge wearable technology.
>
> But the shine didn't last. Beset by product flaws, mounting lawsuits, and a brutal war with Fitbit and Apple, Jawbone bled cash. In 2017, after nearly two decades of hype and billions in funding, the company quietly shut its doors—leaving behind another cautionary tale of a unicorn undone.

San Francisco loft office…

Music thumps, champagne pops. Employees dance around boxes of brand-new fitness trackers.

The manager was ecstatic. "Three billion valuation! Apple has to buy us now!"

Flash-forward. Apple launches the Watch. Fitbit rises. Xiaomi floods the market.

Lawyer in the boardroom, dropping a file: "Another lawsuit. Patent infringement. Cash is burning."

Employee whispered, "We're losing staff every week. No one's fixing the core tech."

By 2017, desks were empty. A single Jawbone headset lies forgotten. Once Silicon Valley's darling, Jawbone exits not with scandal, but with silence.

*

Katerra (2015–2021)

E Via De Ventura, Scottsdale, Arizona, USA

In 2015, Katerra burst onto the scene with a promise to revolutionise construction. Backed by billions from SoftBank's Vision Fund, the Silicon Valley startup envisioned sleek, tech-driven factories mass-producing building components the way Tesla built cars. Efficiency, speed, and cost savings—Katerra vowed to transform one of the world's most stubbornly traditional industries. But by 2021, the dream had collapsed. With debts mounting, projects unfinished, and its grand vision of "construction as manufacturing" unravelling, Katerra filed for bankruptcy. More than $2 billion in funding had vanished into what became one of the most spectacular startup implosions of the decade

Menlo Park…

A massive presentation. Digital renderings of skyscrapers flash on giant screens.

The executive said in a confident tone: "Construction is broken. We will fix it. Modular parts, built in factories, shipped worldwide. Two billion dollars. SoftBank will back us all the way."

SoftBank partner claps slowly, then faster. Applause fills the room.

*

Years later…

A construction site. Half-finished walls, idle cranes.

The engineer was frustrated. "Shipments delayed again. Costs triple what we forecasted. We're scaling too fast."

Year 2021. In the boardroom, the tone of the director was sombre. “SoftBank is pulling the plug.”

Silence.

The dream of disrupting construction collapses under the weight of its own concrete.

*

The Fall of Archegos Capital Management, LP

1211 Avenue of the Americas, 24th Floor, New York

Archegos Capital (2021), led by Bill Hwang, used extreme leverage hidden in derivatives to build massive stock positions. When the bets soured, margin calls triggered one of Wall Street’s fastest collapses, wiping out over $20 billion and exposing the fragility of unchecked financial engineering.

In a glass tower overlooking Manhattan, Bill Hwang sat in silence as screens around him bled red. Archegos Capital, once an obscure but mighty family office, had quietly amassed billions in leverage through swaps and hidden bets. For months, it was Wall Street’s invisible whale—moving stocks like ViacomCBS and Discovery with the flick of a finger.

But leverage is a merciless master. When stock prices dipped, margin calls came thundering in. Credit Suisse, Nomura, Goldman Sachs—names that once courted Hwang’s business—now scrambled to dump billions in shares. In just days, $20 billion in value evaporated, dragging global markets into chaos. The empire had no foundation, only borrowed chips stacked too high.

*

Years later…

The Archegos collapse left deep scars on Wall Street. Credit Suisse alone lost $5.5 billion, leading to mass resignations and a permanent dent in its reputation. Regulators tightened scrutiny around family offices, demanding transparency where shadows once thrived. Bill Hwang, once a quiet billionaire, found himself facing criminal charges for fraud and racketeering.

The Archegos is now remembered not just as a financial implosion, but as a cautionary tale—proof that even in the heart of global finance, one man's hidden bets could topple giants.

*

Luckin Coffee Inc.: Brewing Scandal in a Cup

Siming District, Xiamen, Fujian, Beijing, China

Luckin Coffee (2017–present) rose with dizzying speed as China's homegrown rival to Starbucks, but collapsed in scandal after admitting to $310 million in fabricated sales. Though its stock was delisted from NASDAQ, the company restructured and rebounded, eventually surpassing Starbucks in China.

Beijing, 2019…

The neon glow of Luckin Coffee stores lit up every corner of the city. Students, young professionals, and businessmen sipped cappuccinos with QR-code discounts, their phones buzzing with loyalty rewards. To many, Luckin wasn't just coffee—it was a statement: China's answer to Starbucks.

Inside the boardroom, however, another brew was boiling. Numbers were being stretched, receipts fabricated, and sales inflated. Executives knew the truth: much of Luckin's "unstoppable growth" was a mirage. But the pressure to outpace Starbucks in China pushed them deeper into deceit.

By early 2020, the truth spilt out—$310 million in fake sales, a fraud as frothy as the cappuccinos they sold. Shares on NASDAQ collapsed, wiping out billions, and investors who once believed in the "Starbucks killer" were left holding empty cups.

*

Years later… Luckin did not vanish. After restructuring, ousting corrupt executives, and rebuilding trust, it staged an unlikely comeback. By 2023, Luckin surpassed Starbucks in China by number of stores, proving that even a scandal-burned brand could reinvent itself in a market thirsty for caffeine.

*

Zirtual (2011–2015)

A Virtual Address

Founded by Maren Kate Donovan, Zirtual promised to transform the way busy professionals worked—offering on-demand virtual assistants at the click of a button. Backed by Silicon Valley optimism, it grew to more than 400 employees and thousands of clients, hailed as a revolution in outsourcing.

But in August 2015, the dream imploded overnight. With no warning, Zirtual froze operations, employees were locked out of their accounts, and clients were left stranded. What began as the "future of work" ended in one of Silicon Valley's most abrupt and shocking shutdowns.

Las Vegas startup office. Energy buzzes. Dozens of virtual assistants type furiously.

The founder beamed before her team: "Look at the growth! Clients everywhere—Silicon Valley's finally taking us seriously."

One weekend. CFO barges into the boardroom, face pale. "We can't pay salaries on Monday. Revenues aren't catching up. We're done."

The founder's voice was broken. "But… we didn't cheat. We just miscalculated."

On Monday morning, employees find themselves locked out of accounts, and their emails are cut off. Dreams vanish with a single payroll.

*

Within days, Zirtual's assets were acquired by Startups.com, which resurrected the service on a smaller scale. But the magic was gone. For many, Zirtual became a symbol of how quickly a hyped startup could rise—and how brutally it could fall when cash flow dried up.

*

Curtain Call

One by one, they walked onto the stage. Bold, ambitious, sure that the future was theirs. One by one, they stumbled, not from fraud, not from deception—but from the innocence of overreach.

Color Labs drowned in confusion.

Better Place was too early for its time.

Giants overtook Jawbone.

Katerra fell under its own ambition.

Zirtual died from simple arithmetic.

Not all failures are crimes. Some are just tragedies of misplaced faith.

"Fraud makes headlines," an investor once said, "but innocence makes history."

***

Acknowledgments

Though a dramatised narrative, this book draws its plot from my previous four books on valuation, as well as my 150+ scholarly articles and editorials published in the *Indian Valuer Journal* since 1991, and the articles I have published in the Proceedings of many National Conventions of the Institution of Valuers, India. This is my sixth book, the fifth in a row on the background of valuation, which also revolves around valuation, but this time on corporate valuations' misfires. My lectures across India and the UK on this subject add flavour to it.

I am grateful to all those who, knowingly or unknowingly, contributed to the writing of this book. To authenticate the geographical locations and timelines in the backdrop, I have taken many online and offline references from outside sources. They are as accurate as my sources are.

I can be contacted via my email—s_s_rathore@rediffmail.com. Follow me on LinkedIn: https://www.linkedin.com/in/dr-shailendra-singh-rathore-76ba35258/.

***

About the Author

Referred to as the Dean of Valuation in India, Dr. Rathore has held distinguished academic and administrative positions, including serving as Principal of two renowned engineering colleges and as Vice Chancellor of a university.

With a career spanning over four decades, he has authored five books, four of which are on valuation. His pioneering work began with the publication of his first valuation book in 2001. He has also contributed more than 150 scholarly research papers, earning numerous awards and accolades, including the prestigious *Silver Medal* from the Institution of Valuers (IOV), India, in 1993. In recognition of his expertise, he served on the Editorial Board of the *Indian Valuer Journal* and held editorial responsibilities with several international journals.

Even after retirement, he continues to enrich the field of valuation through books, research articles, and lectures in both India and the United Kingdom. He also serves as a panel valuer for the leading nationalised banks and several other financial institutions. Additionally, he is a regular columnist for leading newspapers.

A proud father of two accomplished daughters, he combines professional excellence with personal fulfilment, leaving a legacy of scholarship and leadership in the world of valuation.

***